Effective marketing management

The authors

Martin Christopher, BA, MSc, PhD, is Professor of Marketing and Logistics Systems at Cranfield School of Management. The author of numerous books and research papers on marketing topics, he has held a variety of acadamic posts, including a period as co-director of the European Logistics Management Programme in Holland and later as Visiting Research Professor at the University of British Columbia, Canada.

Sherril H. Kennedy, BSc, MSc, PhD, is Director of the Marketing Communications Research Centre at Cranfield, a consortium of major industrialists set up in 1968 to explore and improve the management of advertising and other communications. She is also Associate Director of the Cranfield Management Resource. A social psychologist by training, Dr Kennedy was responsible for developing and implementing the marketing strategy for Cranfield School of Management. She is currently a director of a publishing company and chairman of an electronics company.

Malcolm McDonald, MA, MSc, pursued a successful career as Marketing Director of Canada Dry and as a senior management consultant before taking up a Senior Teaching Fellowship at Cranfield, a post he now combines with varied consultancy work and a company directorship.

Gordon Wills, BA, DMS, FInsM, MBIM, is Professor of Customer Policy at Cranfield where he has been since 1972 and is currently also Director of Cranfield Management Resource. He has held professorial posts at Bradford, Alberta, Prince Edward Island and Tulsa Universities, and has also lectured throughout Europe, Australasia and Central America. The author of a score of books and editor or co-editor of several scholarly journals, he is a director of two companies and one of Europe's leading authorities on marketing.

Effective marketing management

Martin Christopher
Sherril H. Kennedy
Malcolm McDonald
Gordon Wills

Published by
Gower Publishing Company Limited,
Westmead, Farnborough,
Hants. England.

© Martin Christopher, Sherril H. Kennedy, Malcolm McDonald and Gordon Wills 1980.

All rights reserved. No part of this publication may be reproduced, stored in a retrieval system, or transmitted in any form or by any means, electronic, mechanical, photocopying, recording, or otherwise without the prior permission of Gower Publishing Company Limited.

Cranfield edition ISBN 0 566 02238 9

Gower edition ISBN 0 566 02237 0

Printed in Great Britain by:
Biddles Ltd, Guildford, Surrey

Preface

Our aim in developing *Effective marketing management* was to provide a practical textbook on marketing - a book which would be of primary interest and value to those managers who have an interest but no formal training in marketing and who have neither the time nor the inclination to decipher jargon-ridden specialist volumes where theory seems to have totally usurped practice. A concern to see marketing in its total business context does not, of course, apply solely to non-marketers and we anticipate that both marketing practitioners and marketing students will find the book useful for their different purposes.

There is nothing remarkable in a group of authors finding their book unusual and exciting. When we claim these qualities for *Effective marketing management*, however, we are drawing on an experience of authorship which is rather out of the ordinary. The book appears in its present form as a result of a lengthy and rigorous process of collective work, involving not only the present authors but also several other contributors.

The process by which the book was produced is an unusual one and one which has profoundly affected both content and form. *Effective marketing management* is the main textbook for a distance-teaching resource prepared by a team at Cranfield School of Management and available for the use of in-company training personnel. The Cranfield Management Resource includes, amongst other elements, a comprehensive tutor's guide, overhead transparencies, a collection of case studies and a series of films which expand on the concepts given in the texts. The present book, however, has been designed to be self-sufficient in introducing, explaining and illustrating the key areas of decision making in marketing management. The individual reader of the text will benefit from the work which has been undertaken in the other areas of the resource but will find no unexplained gaps or cross-references.

We believe that the book has benefited from our team-work on a number of counts. First, constant close collaboration between marketing specialists has ensured the development of an integrated and cohesive approach to marketing issues. Second, the inclusion in the team of an educational technologist, Alan Fields, and an editor, Marsaili Cameron, has resulted in an increased clarity of language and structure. Third, the wide business experience of the different members of the team has led to inclusion throughout the text of practical examples of different marketing situations from organisations working in industrial, consumer and service markets.

In earlier editions, with the titles *Introduction to marketing* and *Introducing marketing*, the book has proved successful both as a background text for training programmes and as an aid to individual learning. The text has its origins in our experience of teaching marketing to students of management at Cranfield, all of whom are post-graduate. This is an audience which has no formal training in marketing but has considerable business experience and knows well which areas present particular problems to management. It was a challenging audience for us and one which forced us to concentrate on providing a text which clearly explained the marketing concept but also described in some detail how that concept could be successfully implemented in practice. The first edition of the text had as a co-author Dr David Walters who is now at the Oxford Centre for Management.

One of the features which readers found particularly useful in the earlier editions was the structuring of the text round a series of questions which are commonly asked about marketing. This feature we have retained but in a revised form which allows for a greater ease of reference. By posing application questions at the end on the discussion of different issues, the book also continues to encourage readers to relate what they have learned to the activities of their organisations.

It is likely that some readers will wish to explore the various aspects of marketing in more depth. To help those readers sift through the wealth of literature on marketing and identify books and papers which will be helpful to them, we have prepared a booklet which provides a selected and annotated list of further reading. This booklet, which will be constantly up-dated, is available on request from any of the four authors at Cranfield.

The text in its final form owes a great deal to the criticisms and contributions made by Dr David Corkindale, Senior Lecturer in Marketing Communications at Cranfield, Dr Malcolm Harper, Professor of Enterprise Development at Cranfield and Dr Robert Sweitzer, Associate Professor of Marketing at the Graduate School of Management at the University of California at Los Angeles.

We are also extremely grateful to Norene Layton, David Seekings and Derry Young for their hard work, skill and patience during the production of the book.

M.G.C.
S.H.K.
M.McD.
G.S.C.W.

July 1980

Cranfield School of Management,
Bedfordshire, England.

Contents

		page
Unit I	The role of marketing	1
Question 1	What is marketing?	3
Question 2	What is the difference between marketing and selling?	10
Question 3	What is our marketing plan?	14
Question 4	Are industrial and consumer marketing different?	18
Question 5	Does the marketing of services differ from the marketing of products?	23
Question 6	Is international marketing different?	28
Unit II	The behaviour of customers	33
Question 7	Who are our customers?	35
Question 8	Are all our customers the same?	40
Question 9	Why do customers behave the way they do?	45
Question 10	How can consumerism affect marketing?	50
Question 11	Is marketing unethical?	55
Unit III	Product decisions	61
Question 12	What products should we market?	63
Question 13	How do products make profits?	68
Question 14	How can we select and develop new products?	74
Question 15	Can we test new products before they reach the market?	79
Question 16	How can we estimate how much product we will sell?	84
Unit IV	Place decisions	89
Question 17	What routes could lead to the customer?	91
Question 18	How can we get our products to the customer?	96
Question 19	What level of availability does our customer want?	101
Unit V	Price decisions	105
Question 20	What price should we charge our customer?	107
Question 21	What margins should we allow to our distributors?	113
Unit VI	Promotion decisions	119
Question 22	How can we communicate with our customers?	121
Question 23	How can we persuade our customers to buy our products?	130
Question 24	How can we measure the effectiveness of our advertising?	136
Question 25	Do we need a sales force?	143
Question 26	How should our sales force be organised and managed?	148

page

Unit VII   Planning and control   153

Question 27   What is marketing research?   155
Question 28   What role does marketing research play in effective marketing? 161
Question 29   How can we audit our environment and operations?   166
Question 30   How can we prepare our marketing plan?   170
Question 31   How can we organise a marketing department?   177
Question 32   How can we set the marketing budget?   184

List of tables

Table 1   Some national differences in the ownership of household appliances   37
Table 2   Product-market strategies   66
Table 3   The role of margin management in the determination of profitability 116
Table 4   The operation of two companies at different levels of margin   117
Table 5   Various types of sales promotion   128
Table 6   Breakdown of a salesman's total daily activity   149
Table 7   Marketing planning and its place in the corporate planning cycle   171
Table 8   Sales promotion – product 1 (extract)   187
Table 9   Consolidated promotional budget – product 1   188
Table 10   Examples of marketing budgets   191

List of figures

		page
Figure 1	Marketing environment	4
Figure 2	Marketing mix	8
Figure 3	Different levels of selling	12
Figure 4	The marketing planning process	16
Figure 5	The service product	23
Figure 6	The product service package	25
Figure 7	The key questions in international marketing	32
Figure 8	The 80/20 rule or Pareto effect	38
Figure 9	Which market segment?	43
Figure 10	Consumerism's way to better marketing	51
Figure 11	The product links customer and company	65
Figure 12	The product life cycle	68
Figure 13	Product-market strategies and the product life cycle	70
Figure 14	Boston matrix – product categories	71
Figure 15(a)	Boston matrix – ideal product development sequence	72
Figure 15(b)	Boston matrix – internal flow of funds	72
Figure 16	Boston matrix – product portfolio movement	72
Figure 17	Planning gap	75
Figure 18	The time cost relationship in testing a new product	80
Figure 19	Stages of new product development	81
Figure 20	Market potential curve	85
Figure 21	What routes could lead to the customer?	92
Figure 22	The total system	100
Figure 23	Influences on pricing policy	109
Figure 24	Breakeven analysis	110
Figure 25	The framework for the pricing decision	112
Figure 26	The main factors involved in margin management	116
Figure 27	The customer's decision to buy	130
Figure 28	Choice of paint – the decision process	133
Figure 29	Forms of marketing research 1. Reactive	158
Figure 30	Forms of marketing research 2. Non reactive	159
Figure 31	The role of marketing research	161
Figure 32	The marketing audit	167
Figure 33	Sequence of marketing planning	173
Figure 34	Co-ordinating marketing functions	177
Figure 35	One marketing department's operational structure	179
Figure 36	The matrix structure	181
Figure 37	Allocating a marketing budget	185

Unit I The role of marketing

Question 1   What is marketing?

Question 2   What is the difference between marketing and selling?

Question 3   What is our marketing plan?

Question 4   Are industrial and consumer marketing different?

Question 5   Does the marketing of services differ from the marketing of products?

Question 6   Is international marketing different?

Question 1

What is marketing?

Overview

The focal point of an organisation's activities should be the wants of its customers. Marketing provides the match between the organisation's human, financial and physical resources and these wants. It must do this against a background of the dynamic characteristics of the environment in which the matching takes place. This includes direct and indirect competition, economic uncertainties, legal and political constraints, cultural and social trends, technological change and institutional patterns.

The matching is typically undertaken for an organisation by a formalised department headed by a senior executive at board level. He plans, coordinates, and controls the PRODUCT or service offered, the PRICE that is charged, the style of PROMOTION and the PLACE where it is to be made available. In doing so, he is concerned with not only the separate effects of these four 'P's, but also their interactive effects. This blend of the four 'P's is known as the marketing mix.

Meeting customers' wants

Marketing is the way in which an organisation matches its own human, financial and physical resources with the wants of its customers. Since many organisations continue in business over relatively long periods of time, it is necessary for them to plan both the particular human, financial and physical resources they offer and the particular customer wants they wish to serve. The need to look ahead and to develop products, services and groups of customers normally requires all medium or large organisations to formalise marketing as a specific activity if the matching process is to be successfully accomplished. Whether or not a formalised activity is present, the matching inevitably proceeds. Unless its causes are speedily detected, any mis-match leads to failure because customers will simply refrain from acquiring the product or service offered. The customer is also undertaking a continuous process of matching his or her wants with the offerings of the competing organisations.

In the simplest market place the customer and the marketer meet personally. The customer can respond directly to the product or service offered and, if any mis-match is present, inform the marketer in order that the offering can be adjusted to conform accurately to what the customer wants. Regrettably, few organisations work today in such a simple situation. A successful UK manufacturer of industrial metal bearings has some 6,000 customers throughout Europe and a further 4,000 in North America and Australasia. He offers a full range of products together with maintenance servicing, as well as financial support for the purchase of specific items. He deploys technical sales representatives travelling to meet his major customers once or twice a year, but in many countries he deals through agents rather than directly. His marketing activity is complex but its success is also dependent on matching his organisation's resources with the wants of its customers. And he will continue to succeed only if he gleans regular information about what customers want in the future as well as how they are reacting to his present range of products or services.

Lest any metal bearing manufacturer should be daunted in his task, however, let him count his blessings when he compares his marketing challenge with that faced by a food manufacturer who sells his produce throughout the EEC. Whilst the preferences for metal bearing technology the world over have some striking similarities, the diets of fellow Europeans in Denmark, Holland and the UK, to cite but three, differ distinctly. Just observe the Dutch preference for cheese at breakfast time in contrast to the tastes of the UK population; or consider that while the Danes like to eat crispbread for breakfast, the British have an observable preference for toast. Then recall that there are just short of 300 million customers in the EEC for breakfast most days and some 85 million housewives doing their shopping from something in excess of one million retail stores. As one can well imagine, it takes a great deal of planning to meet the varied needs of so many folk successfully. Yet in the pan-European food manufacturing companies like Unilever, that's exactly the measure of the marketing task they face. The principle that guides this task is the basic marketing concept that the focal point of the organisation's activities is the wants of its customers.

Fortunately, the task is not as daunting as it can sound. Even large organisations have neither the ability nor the desire to enter such vast markets in one step. They add to their resources and knowledge of customer wants as they go. The organisation itself and its employees become a bank of information and knowledge about what customers want. This bank of information means that most established organisations know in rough and ready terms what customers will want in the immediate future. All too frequently, however, much of that information is lost, either by inadequate analysis or codification, and lessons have to be learned again at the expense both of customers and organisations.

The marketing environment

There is a variety of environmental factors beyond the control of any one organisation that affect the attainment of marketing objectives. Domestic and international competition are continually becoming more vigorous. The state of the economy in terms of inflation, changes in income levels, recession, and foreign exchange fluctuations affect the level of consumption and the standard of living. The legal environment is becoming more complicated and restrictive while governments play a more and more prominent role in the economy as participants, regulators and manipulators. Changes in birth rates and marriage patterns and increases in the number of women entering the workforce indicate social trends to which marketing activities must respond. Rapid changes in technology make today's product innovation tomorrow's antique. The evolution of retail, wholesale, and other distributive institutions takes place over a time span that often limits the marketer's ability to change in the short term. As Figure 1 illustrates, all these environmental variables need to be considered in planning marketing activities.

Figure 1

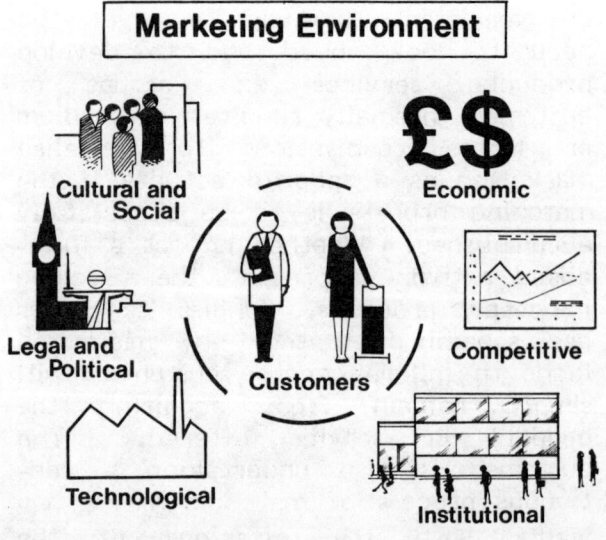

Direct and indirect competition

Few organisations are left alone in our world to match their human, financial and physical resources with their customers' wants. The matching process goes on in an open environment with varying degrees of competition either from similar or identical products or from quite different opportunities for customers to spend their limited financial resources. In the short-term savings market the banks compete not only with building societies but also with alternative uses of the available funds, such as a long holiday, redecorating the outside of the home, or a pony tethered in a paddock for the children. There is a great deal of competition for these short-term savings, and the building societies have done particularly well, increasing their share of this segment of the savings market from 24% to 41% in less than a decade. The building societies have more than tripled the number of branches in the last decade and therefore can offer convenience as an important service to customers. In addition, societies are open on Saturday mornings while banks are not. More importantly, a share account in a building society earns a high rate of interest while a current account in a bank does not. The ease of withdrawal and attractive interest rates provide competitive advantages for the building societies which serve to intensify the competition in the short-term savings market place.

Economic uncertainties

In times of economic uncertainty, folk may postpone purchasing certain products or services which do not seem immediately essential, while at the same time they may maintain or increase expenditures in other areas. With the rapid rise in oil prices in recent years, for example, the demand for motor cars fell along with the level of economic activity, but the demand for holidays held up. The status of the economy has affected the growth of the do-it-yourself market which tends to expand when the economy turns down. Consumer expenditure in the UK on repairs and maintenance has quadrupled in the last decade. Black and Decker reorganised their industrial orientation to take advantage of this consumer opportunity whilst continuing to serve their traditional industrial markets.

Economic uncertainty reduced capital investment in new equipment and plant during periods of very rapid European inflation, often accompanied by high interest rates. When the cost of labour is increasing relatively much more rapidly, substitution of capital goods for labour should logically occur. The movement towards more capital-intensive activities occasioned by these changes in the respective productivity of labour and of capital does occur, but with a lagged time effect.

Legal and political constraints

The environment in which the organisation's marketer operates also includes legal and political facets. Within the EEC there are Community Laws and Regulations, made as a consequence of the terms of the Treaty of Rome, which govern numerous aspects of trade, from transport and distribution to the description and packaging of products.

Each nation within the EEC has its own laws in addition, such as the UK's Fair Trading Act or Supply of Goods Act. Outside the EEC, each and every country will have further laws and regulations governing export/import activities and trading terms. Many countries, for instance, require that products sold within their borders must be partly or wholly manufactured or assembled there, regardless of whether this is in the best economic interests of either an organisation or its specific customers in any particular transaction.

Legal issues of this kind merge into political issues very easily. Sanctions against Rhodesia for more than a decade, the long-term boycott of South African or Israeli goods by individuals or countries, oil sanctions against Holland and the USA by the OPEC countries - all are outstanding instances of international political environmental factors. Less obvious examples, but nonetheless just as effective in distorting a simple organisation to customer matching process, are quota schemes between countries, or barter deals such as have been widely concluded between Comecon countries and Western nations for the past two decades.

UK government controls on the economy have had serious repercussions for marketing activities. As a response to double digit inflation, the Price Commission required financial justification for price increases. In the opinion of some businessmen this resulted in greater price increases than would have been the case had the government allowed only market forces to apply.

An example of UK legislation affecting marketing activities is the Order laid before Parliament by the Department of Prices and Consumer Protection which banned bargain offers. In an attempt to ban misleading offers based on 'worth and value', 'price elsewhere' and 'savings up to x%', the Order sweeps away legitimate pence-off claims, free goods, and coupon offers. In an attempt to stop misleading practices this legislation may also decrease price competition and result in fewer actual bargains for customers.

Similar regulatory examples can also be found in the EEC. There is already an EEC Directive to prohibit cosmetics advertisements which 'suggest a characteristic which the products in question do not possess'. Unfortunately, this type of proper regulation has been improperly extended. Another Directive will regulate the advertising of foodstuffs, covering misleading characteristics as above, but also forbidding claims regarding properties which similar foods possess or any medicinal claims even though the claims may be true. For example, under the latter Directive tea could not be advertised as 'picking you up' because this is a a characteristic possessed by other teas and coffee, assuming that tea and coffee are judged as similar. It would appear that advertising the nutritional benefits of any foodstuff as a means of preventing disease or of easing the symptoms of disease is likewise prohibited.

Cultural and social trends

Across the EEC the different cultures reflect the different behaviour patterns of each nation's society. A variety of ethnic groups comprise the market place within each nation as well. Britain today is a multi-racial society; the coloured segment of the UK market is of sufficient size, over $1\frac{1}{2}$ million, to present a marketing opportunity. For example, the Asian religious aversion to animal fat provided Blue Band, a vegetable oil margarine, with a marketing opportunity to promote the product to the Asian market as a valuable source of vitamin D. Regional tastes in food suggest different marketing efforts in certain parts of the country. The people of the West Midlands and Wales consume 40% more bacon and ham than do the Scots. And the Welsh have just taken over from the East Midlanders as the nation's biggest butter eaters with a 40% greater consumption than the people of Yorkshire and Humberside.

Trends in population growth, such as births, deaths and migrations, exert great pressure on the future plans of marketers and influence how they approach a market. The advent of the Pill, women's lib, working wives and the fashion for smaller families have turned the baby boom into a slump. Between 1971 and 1977 the baby food market dropped by 50%. The startling decline of the baby market means that manufacturers have had to adapt their marketing strategies. In the mid 1960's, when the birth rate started to fall, Johnson and Johnson began to promote the use of its baby-care items, like baby powder, shampoo and lotion, to adults. Now a mere 30% of its volume is used on babies and the company's turnover has increased four times in the last decade. The toy industry is faced not only with the steady decline in the number of children but also with the fact that children are maturing faster. At the age of twelve a child is no longer interested in toys, but in cassette players, jeans and cosmetics.

The number of housewives working in full or part-time employment has increased by over 33% in the last five years. This has brought about a number of changes in family lifestyles: for instance, the amount of family income has increased, the housewife has less time to spend on family chores, and the housewife's expectations about the quality of life are different. For a growing number of working wives, time really means money. Thus, convenience products have shown considerable growth. But the growth of convenience foods has been moderated by the belief that convenience foods contain too many artificial ingredients. One manifestation of this is the increasing ownership of home freezers. The desire to return to more natural ways of living juxtaposed with the time constraints of working women has produced a boom in home freezing which is believed to offer a nutritional or health advantage over convenience foods.

Technological change

Rapid product obsolescence due to changing technology is the rule rather than the exception in modern industry. Today the advent of microelectronics is the second version of the industrial revolution. On a broad scale it has accelerated the pattern of transfer of jobs from the manufacturing to the service sector. Specifically, the microprocessor has changed the fabric of many industries. Microprocessors have allowed the introduction of small, low-cost, micro-computers that have household applications for monitoring weather conditions and adjusting room temperatures as well as home record keeping and budgeting. Motor car manufacturers are using microprocessors to control the operation of the car engine by matching speed, petrol, air flow and ignition timing.

In many markets consumers have rapidly accepted microelectronics. Traditional companies have suffered because they were tied to their existing technologies. Consider this quote from a Swiss watch manufacturer: "The major slice of the market will remain with the traditional watch manufacturers because we have the distribution, the style and the brand name. Our policy on watch design for the next five years is to concentrate on the production of the mechanical watch for the middle and upper end of the market." But the market didn't remain loyal to traditional, mechanical watches. Today electronic watches are distributed not only through jewellers but also through chemists, camera dealers and electronics shops and are manufactured by large, reputable electronics companies, new to the watch business but not new to the arena of a competitive marketplace.

Institutional patterns

Another aspect of the marketing environment is the pattern of institutions bequeathed to contemporary marketers by years of trading activity. Until the late 1960's, the major pattern of food distribution throughout Europe was relatively small grocers or multiple chain stores operating through local retail outlets. The advent of mass car ownership has transformed this pattern in two decades to one of hypermarkets, supermarkets, and shopping centres in almost every EEC country. Along with this development, several other traditional retail institutions have decreased in numbers - the pharmacist, the butcher, the greengrocer, the fishmonger, the dairy, and even the baker.

The roots of modern franchising stem from the eighteenth century British brewers. This early form of franchising tied economically beleaguered public houses to a particular brewer, requiring pubs to serve only that particular brewer's beer, in return for a capital investment from the brewer. The agreement precluded the distribution of any other brewer's products through a tied public house. This form of exclusive agreement is common to all forms of franchising. The current generation of franchises includes Budget Rent-A-Car, Dyno-Rod, Prontaprint, ServiceMaster, Wimpy and Ziebart, to name a few. In effect, wholesaler-retailer agreements, such as Spar and VG in food distribution, are forms of franchising. Franchising seems likely to grow in Britain in the next decade and maufacturers who fail to take note may find their distribution options quite limited. These instances of change demonstrate the need for the marketer to identify the pace at which customers are willing and able to respond to new institutional patterns.

Because of increasing difficulties in world money markets, bartering has partially replaced the traditional exchange of goods for money as a method of payment for goods amongst companies involved in world trade. This calls for change in the attitudes, skills and organisation structure within companies.

The organisation must respond to the changes in the marketing environment as they happen in the short and medium term. The long-term changes in the environment are beyond the planning horizon for most organisations. Besides, in the words of the well known economist, John Maynard Keynes, "In the long run, we are all dead." This is the dynamic backcloth against which, and the milieu within which, the matching of organisational resources and customer wants must take place.

The marketing activity

Formalised marketing activity in an organisation is concerned with analysis, planning and control of the process of matching human, financial and physical resources with customer wants. It has already been demonstrated how vital it is to have a flow of evaluative and behavioural information back from the customer in the market place. This, plus accumulated learning about the markets served, provides the effective basis on which marketing plans can be prepared, put into effect and subsequent performance assessed and controlled.

Successful matching depends on customers being aware of the products or services on offer, finding them conveniently available and judging the products' or services' attributes, in terms of both price and performance, to be capable of satisfying the customers' needs and wants. This satisfactory state of affairs is best accomplished by attention to what are often termed the four 'P's - product, price, promotion and place. As will be demonstrated in some detail in the answers to the questions in Units III to VI of this book, each 'P' is a continuing problem to the marketer. It must be both attended to separately and as it interacts with the other elements in what is termed the *marketing mix* (see Figure 2). A satisfactory solution one year may well expect to be challenged in the next. Products or services will be introduced, improved upon, and made obsolete.

Figure 2

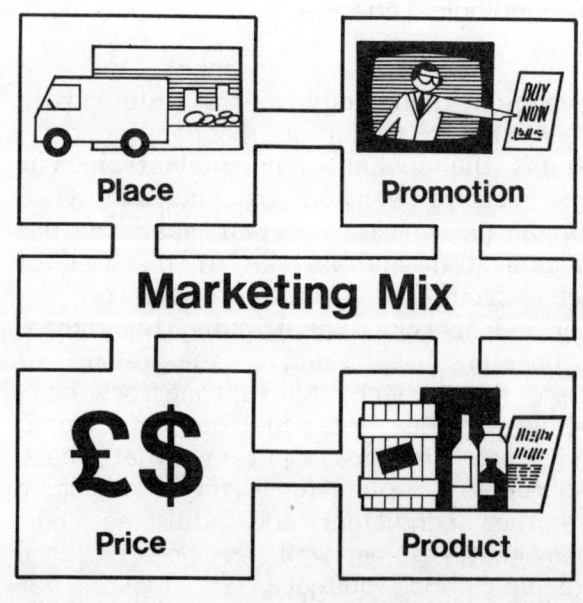

Prices may be undercut. Promotions can be upstaged by competitive campaigns. The place where customers buy can change at any time as alternative retail shopping opportunities emerge or distribution develops.

And these comments all assume that a sufficiently robust solution has been identified in the first place, which will take account not only of the separate importance of each of the four 'P's to the customer, but of their interactive impact as well. For example, to what extent can a higher price with more effective promotion improve the overall profitability of a branded herbal soap, rather than some other combination of strategies? To what extent can more rapid availability of metal bearings, involving as it must a more expensive total distribution system, more than recoup those new costs in terms of extra sales and go on to add even more profit contribution? These are marketing mix problems.

To wrestle with such mixing problems, and to plan for and to implement solutions, most medium and large organisations establish a marketing department and charge one of their senior executives to co-ordinate all such activities at director or boardroom level. This, along with the activities discussed above, comprises the marketing function. Its aim is to produce the *marketing plan* for the organisation. This plan will be discussed in Questions 3 and 30.

Application questions

1.1 What major types of external factors, beyond your control, influence your organisation and its marketing effort? What important changes have taken place in these factors in the last ten years? Is the marketing effort of your organisation co-ordinated so that it can:

(a) maximise opportunities presented by a changing environment,

(b) minimise potential losses due to changes in the environment?

What precautions is the organisation taking to manage future changes in the environment?

1.2 Compare a selection of your own recent purchases, such as a house, a tube of toothpaste, a newspaper, an insurance policy and an electric appliance. In each decision, what was the relative importance of the product itself, its price, the place where you could get it and the way it was promoted?

1.3 Think of some recent purchases made by your organisation. In each decision, what was the relative importance of the product itself, its price, the place where it was available and the way in which it was promoted? Identify any ways in which your purchasing behaviour as a private individual differs from your behaviour at work. Can you explain any of these differences?

Question 2

What is the difference between marketing and selling?

Overview

Selling is simply that part of marketing concerned with persuading customers to acquire the product or service which best matches an organisation's human, financial and physical resources with its customers' wants. If the marketing job has been well done, such selling may still be tough, but it will be effective. If not, salesmen all too often find themselves trying to sell what the producing organisation wants the customer to want.

Selling frequently takes place through intermediate organisations, engaged either in undertaking manufacture or in assisting distribution, as well as direct to the customer. It can also be undertaken at a personal level with face-to-face contact, or impersonally, as via the telephone.

Market or product oriented?

Marketing has been described in reply to Question 1 as the matching of an organisation's human, financial and physical resources with the wants of its customers. It has also been indicated that the matching is achieved by an organisation's careful integration of the four 'P's - product, price, promotion and place - into the marketing mix. *Selling* is one aspect of promotion. It is quite specifically intended to clinch a transaction, to persuade a customer to agree to acquire the product or service offered at the prevailing price. As such, it should represent the consummation of marketing's efforts to match what the organisation is offering with what the customer wants. If the marketing process has been well done, then selling may be difficult, but it will not be impossible. If little or no planning of the marketing mix has been undertaken, all but the lucky must expect to fail. Unless the item just happens to be one which the customer really needs and for which there is no viable alternative, only good marketing can sell a product or service twice to a customer.

Selling any product or service to a customer for the first time round is a somewhat different matter. Half truths or exaggerated claims for efficacy can often persuade folk to acquire a product or make use of a service that is subsequently found wanting. No further sales follow and few organisations face a situation where they can make an adequate profit from single purchases by subsequently dissatisfied customers. Naturally, in any circumstances, some who buy once will fall by the wayside later, but the selling effort of the well planned marketing mix gives rise to only a small proportion of dissatisfied customers. Furthermore, information feedback from the market place alerts the organisation to the main reasons why customers fail to buy again. If necessary, this then becomes the basis for improving or modifying the product, service, or any element of the marketing mix.

Selling is not about half truths or exaggerated claims for what is on offer. These practices are folly because they reflect a poor image of the organisation and, as a result, they are counter-productive. Their occurrence is overestimated because the news media report them with a frequency disproportionate to the number of actual incidents.

When it is part of a carefully thought out marketing activity, a well planned sales effort is about persuasion. The sales representative or the direct mail leaflet or the industrial/technical advisory service, depending on the organisation's chosen mode of selling, seeks to persuade the customer to take the leap from *wanting* to *acquiring* the product or service. The more the organisation knows about the customer's wants before the salesmen make the effort, the greater is the probability of success. The salesman should not discover that he has a product or service in search of a customer. This cannot happen in a market oriented organisation. Where it does occur, the phenomenon is normally described as product orientation. In other words, the organisation has developed a product or service that the organisation wants the customer to want. The organisation relies on its salesmen to persuade customers to buy, come hell or high water. If the salesmen fail, they tend to get the blame, rather than the organisation's overall stance towards its customers. Question 23 describes persuasion in the context of a marketing approach.

Fifteen years ago a modest sized European engineering firm developed a splendid idea into a viable technology. It harnessed the heat from factory chimneys, diesel exhausts and other industrial processes, thereby recycling energy. The inventors believed in their process, but fifteen years ago, well before the first oil crisis, potential customers, even when assailed by salesmen, did not want it and they did not buy it. Only today, with the massive escalation in world energy costs, has a viable market emerged for the long viable technology. Its savings are now sufficiently attractive to command attention. The inventors have been one of the few organisations lucky enough to benefit from the OPEC cartel's activities. But their product development, no matter how clever, could have been their downfall. The premature timing of the introduction wasted the cost of introducing this product fifteen years ago. The firm incurred the additional cost of reintroducing the product once the market was more inclined to buy. Few organisations have the cash reserves to survive too many poorly timed introductions.

In contrast is the marketing orientation of a large French printing engineering company which was established by an electronic engineer and a salesman from one of the more traditional industries. The salesman's frequent visits to printers had given him a clear understanding of the bottle-necks in production, especially the problem of maintaining a correct "register" for long print runs. An automatic electronic process was perfected, specifically for printing, which, although primitive in the sophisticated world of space electronics, exactly met a readily perceived need with printers across the world. Furthermore, it was engineered to give value in the context in which it was expected to operate. Its price was seen as realistic in terms of the savings it afforded on the more traditional processes of human adjustment. Technical selling of the electronic registration device was still needed, but it was undertaken on fertile, marketing prepared soil in some 84 countries throughout the world by the mid-seventies.

Different levels of selling

There are two levels of selling, *direct to the customer* and *indirect through intermediaries*. The latter can be divided into two types. Figure 3 illustrates the pattern of the relationships:

Indirect selling

There are two types of indirect selling. One is to intermediate manufacturers who use materials or semi-finished components in producing end products or services. This type of indirect selling is often coordinated with direct selling to stimulate end-user demand. The second type is where the agent or broker offers service availability or stocks on a localised and more convenient basis for the customer. Any particular organisation can have either of the two types, both, or neither. It depends on the resources of the organisation and the wants of customers, and how the organisation chooses to meet them.

Figure 3

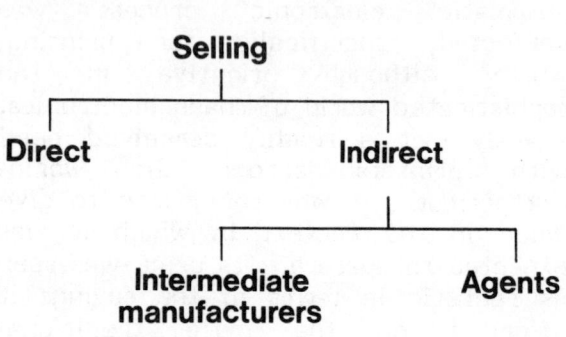

The different levels of selling

Examples of markets which use the first type of indirect selling, through intermediate manufacturers, are those where customers are purchasing low value items on a frequent basis, such as consumable household items, or where customers for industrial items are geographically widely spread. In such situations, the organisation making the product or service needs first to sell to the intermediary, and then to assist the intermediary to sell to the eventual customer on his behalf. This is the way in which Svenska Cellulosa sell their pulp, paper fibres and newsprint to European industry and Courtaulds sell their synthetic fibres to cloth manufacturers or carpet producers throughout Comecon, EEC countries, and the rest of the world. In circumstances such as these, both the producer and the intermediary must of necessity sell to their eventual customer, the newspaper readers or the consumers of clothing, furnishing fabrics, carpets and the like. Their sales activities must be based on a careful analysis and understanding of the role which the newsprint or the fibre used plays in the satisfaction the customer wants. This is the way most retailing has worked since the start of the twentieth century, although in recent years the growth throughout Europe of 'own label products' has somewhat reduced its role in food distribution.

Different forms of selling

All the levels of selling mentioned above can be accomplished in a variety of ways by an organisation, but they can all be characterised as either *personal* or *impersonal* selling. A clear example of personal selling is the use of representatives to visit the customer's premises. Impersonal selling can be illustrated by the use of advertising designed to elicit a direct response.

Personal selling

The most obvious example of personal selling is the call of a representative at a customer's premises. Knowing whether this is the most fruitful form of selling and, if so, how frequently to visit and how long to spend on each visit, are problems which call for careful analysis. Quite obviously, the nature of the product or service will influence the requirements. Selling a complex technical product or service may well only be achieved after the most complex series of discussions and negotiations between teams of individuals. In industrial markets a myriad of individuals may influence the sales outcome within a customer organisation, and some will play a more significant role at certain stages in the process.

However, once a customer has become familiar with an organisation's offering, a representative's call can often become almost a matter of courtesy or public relations, provided always that such a pattern does not indicate complacency in an ever-changing marketing environment.

Question 2   What is the difference between marketing and selling?

It will be supplemented on occasion by telephone selling or follow-up calls; this pattern is common, for example, amongst routine, frequently ordered industrial components.

Exhibitions, where customers come to meet salesmen and technical advisers, are an interesting variant of direct calling by a representative on a customer. In certain industries, and especially in Eastern Europe, exhibitions are a widespread selling technique. The method is most widely used at the introductory stages of new products where sufficient curiosity exists to persuade potential customers to travel at their own expense. The data processing industries and camping and caravan manufacturers have, for instance, used this method regularly. It has the disadvantage for any sales organisation that many of the competitors' products are arranged alongside one's own, but this can rebound to one's advantage when there is a clear product or service superiority.

Impersonal selling

Impersonal selling has grown massively in popularity throughout Europe in the past half century. Most typically, it takes the form of orders placed as a direct result of promotion either in the mass media or on the telephone. By offering a "no questions asked" refund service, organisations have been able to persuade customers to acquire products or services simply on the basis of descriptions and/or pictures. In European retailing alone, mail order is estimated at somewhere in the region of six to ten per cent of all selling activity today, although there are distinct differences in levels between EEC member states. Question 22 will consider the levels and the forms of selling as part of the communications mix.

Selling and buying

If a producer has sold something, then a customer must have bought it. Throughout this text, the terms "acquire", "buy", "lease", and "hire" will be used interchangeably to mean any method by which monies pass from the customer to the producer or intermediary in return for goods and services.

Application questions

2.1 Who "sells" and who "markets" in your organisation? How do their jobs and objectives differ? In what ways are they co-ordinated?

2.2 Compare the roles of the sales representatives employed by the manufacturer of the steel used in your car, the manufacturer of the car itself and the dealer from whom you bought the car. To whom were they actually selling in each case?

2.3 What type of product or service would you be prepared to buy (a) by mail as a result of reading a catalogue or other advertisement, or (b) after discussion with a sales representative? What are the common characteristics of products or services which are sold in these two different ways? Which of your organisation's products and services could be sold by indirect means and which need a personal selling approach? Are both means of selling employed by your organisation?

Question 3
What is our marketing plan?

Overview

Marketing planning is the systematic application of marketing resources to achieve marketing objectives. It is the means by which an organisation seeks to monitor and control the hundreds of external and internal influences on its ability to achieve profitable sales. Marketing planning also provides an understanding throughout the organisation of the particular competitive stance that an organisation intends to take to achieve its objectives. This helps managers of different functions to work together rather than to pursue their own functional objectives in isolation.

A marketing plan will contain a review of the marketing environment, assumptions, overall objectives and strategies, and more detailed programmes concerning responsibilities, timing, and costs. The degree of formalisation of the planning process will depend on the size and diversity of the organisation, although the planning process itself is universally applicable. This Question describes the general issues considered in a marketing plan. Question 30 explains the detailed development of the marketing plan.

Is marketing planning essential?

There can be little doubt that marketing planning is essential when we consider the increasingly competitive and dynamic environment in which organisations operate. Most managers accept that some kind of formalised procedure for marketing planning helps to reduce the complexity of business operations and adds a dimension of realism to the organisation's hopes for the future. Without some planning procedures there is a danger that the organisation will exhaust much of its energies in internecine disputes, whilst its marketing may become little more than an uncoordinated mixture of interesting bits and pieces.

Consider for a moment the four typical objectives which organisations set, of maximising revenue, maximising profits, maximising return on investment, and minimising costs. Each one of these has its own special appeal to different managers within the organisation, depending on the nature of their particular function. In reality, the best that can ever be achieved is a kind of "optimum compromise", because the different objectives often seem to demand conflicting courses of action. Managers must understand how all the variables interact. They also need to *plan* their business decisions, no matter how important the contribution of intuition, feel and experience are in this process.

A recent Cranfield study of the marketing planning practices of leading European industrial goods companies has shown that:

- most companies understand the importance of, and the need for, formalised marketing planning procedures;

- only 15% of the companies have any such procedures other than forecasting and budgeting;

- this results in grave operational difficulties;

- in spite of this, companies do not institutionalise marketing planning

Unit I   The role of marketing   15

procedures because they do not know how to design and introduce planning systems which will help them to reduce their operational problems.

The challenge of marketing planning

The organisation needs an institutionalised planning process, one designed to work out and write down the plan of the organisation's particular competitive stance. The marketing function must find a systematic way of identifying a range of options, choose one or more of them, and then schedule and cost out what needs to be done in order to achieve the objectives. This plan should be communicated throughout the organisation so that everyone knows what is necessary to take the organisation towards its objectives. This whole process can be defined as *marketing planning*, which is the systematic application of marketing resources to achieve marketing objectives. Whilst it is easy to understand the marketing planning process in principle, in practice it is the most difficult of all marketing tasks to accomplish successfully. There are several reasons for this.

One reason is that it involves bringing together into one coherent plan the four 'P's discussed in Question 1. In order to do this, institutional procedures must be introduced, and it is this formalisation which seems to be so difficult for organisations. One difficulty arises from the fact that there is little guidance available to management on how the planning process itself might be managed. It proceeds from reviews to objectives, strategies, programmes, budgets and back again, until some kind of acceptable compromise is reached between what is desirable and what is practicable, within the organisation's operating constraints.

Another reason is that, although a planning system itself is little more than a structured approach to the process just described, the varying size, complexity, character, and diversity of commercial operations means that there can be no such thing as an "off the peg" system that can be implemented without some fundamental amendments to suit the particular requirements of each organisation. Also, the elements of the marketing environment -- competitive, economic, legal, political, cultural, social, technological and institutional -- differ sufficiently from organisation to organisation to require an individual marketing planning process.

A further reason for the difficulty which organisations experience in drawing up a marketing plan is that the degree to which any organisation can develop an integrated, consistent plan depends on a deep understanding of the marketing planning process as a means of clarifying the objectives of all levels of marketing management within an organisation.

The marketing planning process

The Cranfield study also showed that a marketing plan should contain:

- a summary of all the principal internal and external factors which affected the company's marketing performance during the previous year, together with a statement of the company's internal strengths and weaknesses vis-a-vis the competition;

- some assumptions about the key determinants of marketing success and failure;

- overall marketing objectives and strategies;

- programmes containing details of timing, responsibilities and costs.

These elements are the substance of the marketing plan. At the very heart of successful marketing management is a conceptually simple marketing planning process which consists of the following steps:

1. gathering relevant information about the external environment and about the organisation's internal resources (that is, carrying out a marketing audit);

2. identifying the organisation's internal Strengths and Weaknesses vis-a-vis the external market Opportunities and competitive Threats facing the organisation (this is generally done by means of a SWOT analysis, discussed further in Questions 14 and 29);

3. formulating some basic assumptions about the future;

4. laying down the marketing objectives of the organisation, based on the results of the first three steps;

5. laying down strategies for achieving the objectives;

6. laying down programmes for implementing the strategies to include timing, responsibilities and costs;

7. measuring the progress towards achievement of the objectives, reviewing and amending the plan as necessary.

These steps are summarised in Figure 4.

Figure 4

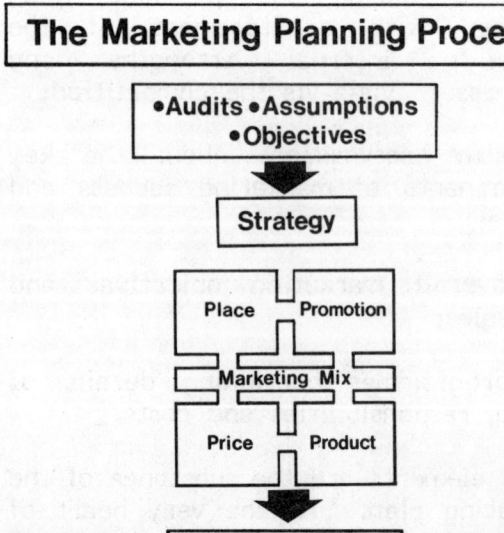

In principle, the marketing concept, which states that the focus of the organisation's activities is the wants of its customers, is very easy to understand. But, in practice, the marketing concept is sometimes difficult to implement because marketing management does not know how to focus on its customers' wants. Likewise, the marketing planning process is also very easy to understand in principle. In practice, the problem is also implementation. Institutionalised procedures are necessary in order to implement the marketing planning process. It is these procedures which cause so much practical difficulty.

Formalised planning procedures

Although research has shown that these marketing planning steps are universally applicable, the degree to which each of the separate steps in the diagram needs to be formalised depends to a large extent on the size and nature of the organisation. For example an *undiversified* organisation, one with only one product line, generally uses less formalised procedures, since top management tends to have greater functional knowledge and expertise than subordinates, and because the lack of diversity of operations enables direct control to be exercised over most of the key determinants of success. Thus, situation reviews, the setting of marketing objectives, and so on, are not always made explicit in writing, although these steps still have to be carried out.

In contrast, in a *diversified* organisation with many different product lines, it is usually not possible for top management to have greater functional knowledge and expertise than subordinate management. Thus the whole planning process tends to be formalised in order to provide a consistent discipline for those who have to make the decisions throughout the organisation. There is a substantial body of evidence to show that formalised marketing planning procedures generally result in greater profitability and stability in the long term and also help to reduce friction and operational difficulties within organisations.

Common planning failures

Where marketing planning has failed, it has generally done so because organisations have placed too much emphasis on the procedures themselves and the resulting paperwork, rather than on generating useful and comprehensible information for management. Also, where organisations relegate marketing planning to someone called a 'Planner', the planning invariably fails for the simple reason that planning for line management cannot be delegated to a third party. The real role of the 'Planner' should be to help those responsible for implementation to draft the plan. Failure to recognise this simple fact can be disastrous.

Planning failures often result from organisations trying to do too much too quickly, using staff untrained in the new procedures. One UK metal bearings company tried three times without success to introduce a marketing planning system. It failed each time because managers throughout the organisation were confused by what was being asked of them. Also, not only did they fail to understand the need for the new systems, but they were not provided with the necessary resources to make the system work effectively. Management training and careful thought about resource requirements finally overcame this company's planning problems.

In contrast, a UK soap company lost profits and ran into grave operational difficulties through not having an effective marketing planning system. Over a three-year period they introduced a system that provided adequate resources and a training programme about the use of the new procedures, thus making them work effectively. This company is now firmly in control of its diverse activities and has recovered its confidence and its profitability.

We shall consider the marketing planning process in more detail in Unit VII, 'Planning and Control'. The role of marketing research will be discussed in Question 28, the marketing audit in Question 29, followed by the detailed preparation of the marketing plan in Question 30 and the marketing budget in Question 32. All these activities relate to the method of organising the marketing department, which is discussed in Question 31.

Application questions

3.1 Does your organisation develop an annual marketing plan? If so, what are seen as the advanatages of having such a plan? Do you consider that your organisation does in fact gain these advantages. If your organisation does not develop an annual marketing plan, what reasons are given for the decision? Are they really justified?

3.2 Who is or should be responsible for producing a marketing plan in your organisation? How do, or should, they produce it? To whom is the plan made available? Is it used in the most effective way possible?

3.3 During the last five years what problems have been avoided by your organisation's use of a marketing plan? Were there instances where the plan should have forewarned you of problems but did not? Why was this? Where no plan existed, were problems encountered which could have been avoided by the use of a plan?

Question 4

Are industrial and consumer marketing different?

Overview

On the face of it, there are many differences between marketing to industrial customers and to household consumer markets. However, upon closer examination many of these differences are more apparent than real.

An analysis of all marketing situations will reveal that the PRINCIPLES are constant but that it is in the APPLICATION of these principles that the true differences between industrial and consumer marketing emerge. In practice, the observable distinction lies in the particular blend given to the marketing mix. In other words, the consumer mix may place the emphasis, say, on media advertising, whilst the industrial mix may shift the emphasis to direct selling. Despite the difference in EMPHASIS, the same principles are common to both.

Marketing principles

Any company wishing to achieve a profitable and durable penetration of a market must base its marketing strategy upon a thorough understanding of customer needs and wants. It must also make itself thoroughly familiar with the buying process utilised by the customer and the factors that influence the customer in his or her choice. This requirement holds for all companies, no matter what their products or the market to which they direct them.

The demand for industrial products is ultimately derived from that for consumer products. For example, a silicon chip may be bought and sold across several intermediate levels between the sale of the product by the manufacturer and its consumption in the end market embodied in a consumer product. Thus, the silicon chip might be sold as a component to a company specialising in the use of micro-processors for control instrumentation. The producers of control instrumentation may be many and various, all of them manufacturing products - some for end markets and some for still other manufacturers. The control instrument could become part of a washing machine or some other household appliance. Accordingly, the nature of the demand for that basic silicon chip can be seen to be derived from the demand for consumer products.

Thus, the immediate answer to our Question might well be, "No, industrial and consumer marketing are not different". However, this is too simplistic a conclusion and it is necessary to take a deeper look into the Question.

What are industrial products?

A useful working definition might be that industrial products are those products that are sold to industrial, institutional or government buyers to be incorporated into their own products, resold or used by them within their own organisations.

But does this really make such products distinctive? Clearly, it does not because in many instances the same physical product can be classified as either an industrial or a consumer good. An example of this is the electronic calculator. If it were sold to a business firm, it would be classified as an industrial good; if it were sold to a student, it would be considered to be a consumer good. There are many other examples. The same model of motor car is sold both as a representative's car to a business firm and as a family saloon.

If the product type cannot be used to differentiate marketing types, can the method of production be used to make a distinction? A power station, aircraft or ocean liner is usually custom built, on a one-off basis. The marketer is involved in developing the product with his customer for a period which could extend over a few months or over a number of years. But much the same could be said for a bespoke tailored suit. Again we find no clear-cut differences.

Perhaps the institution or outlets used to sell products could give a lead. Here, again, we find problems. Both the family and the business firm can buy a calculator or a car from the same dealer. Builders' suppliers sell to do-it-yourself consumers as well as to professionals who use the goods in their own businesses.

Thus, developing a clear dichotomy between industrial and consumer goods is not easy. What can be shown is that, while we can identify some principal types of industrial goods, the approach to their marketing follows common basic principles. The principal types of industrial goods are basic raw materials, components, capital goods/equipment, and maintenance, repair and operating equipment.

Industrial terms of sale

Basic raw materials are usually sold on a contractual basis often involving tight specifications. Sales are usually determined by competitive pricing, credit terms and delivery reliability. For semi-manufactured items, such as steel, a standard industry specification can be set. However, some firms have highly individual technical requirements. In these circumstances, an associated technical service is vitally important.

Components differ from basic materials because of their wider variation. Product quality and reliability become extremely important. In such markets (for example, plastic mouldings) a supplier can capitalise on a reputation for reliability.

Capital goods are usually dominated by high technical ability on the part of both buyer and seller. Because a total package is sold, the marketer's sales team must be able to discuss all the aspects of the equipment from installation through to maintenance scheduling.

Maintenance, repair and operating goods are consumable items, usually of low unit value, and are often sold through distributors rather than directly. Industrial firms will often purchase these items from many different distributors to ensure constant supply from one source or another.

Buyer behaviour

It is sometimes suggested that a major difference between industrial and consumer marketing lies in the behaviour of buyers. Industrial buyers, it is often presumed, tend to be 'rational' in their decision making whilst consumer buyers are open to influence from a whole range of sources such as media, merchandising, packaging, word-of-mouth and even impulse. Yet, if we look more carefully at industrial buyers, we find that they are influenced by much the same factors. The many studies which have been conducted of the industrial buyer all suggest that the buying process is highly complex and that non-price factors tend to predominate in the purchase decision. Thus, the marketer of industrial goods needs to pay careful attention to the nature of the buying process and to adapt the marketing mix accordingly.

Difference in emphasis

The concept of the marketing mix has already been introduced in Question 1 in the context of the four 'P's. We have found that it is difficult to make clear-cut distinctions between industrial and consumer marketing; indeed, we might conclude that the principles for both are the same and that the significant differences lie in emphasis in the use of marketing mix elements.

Selling

Selling industrial goods usually requires a quite different emphasis by the salesman from that required to sell consumer goods. The salesman makes far fewer calls than for consumer goods, say two or three per day as opposed to ten or more. His sales call is predominantly one of liaison and problem solving. He spends a lot of time with each customer.

Sales literature is a distinctive feature of industrial marketing. The technical data and product specifications contained in leaflets are in many instances kept on file for reference purposes as well as being used for initial appraisal of competitive products. This is not usually the case for consumer goods, although for consumer durables, such as cars, hi-fi equipment and other technically oriented purchases, comparisons can be made.

Advertising

Advertising in industrial marketing also works with a different emphasis. Because of the need to build a reputation, it often takes some time before advertising can be seen to make an impact on sales. Apart from the need to build a reputation, there is always the problem that, unlike consumer goods, where many sales are made on a daily or weekly basis, the sales of many capital goods can occur only once in the life of a firm. This suggests that, for many industrial goods, advertising is often viewed as a source of information for industrial buyers, information on which they may not act for some considerable time. Clearly, most consumer advertising is aimed at generating more immediate sales.

A number of differences of emphasis also exist in promotional media selection. For example, the industrial advertising campaign is often aimed at eliciting a response from a comparatively small number of people across Europe rather than a mass market in France or Italy. The wide range of the technical press makes the task of media selection a difficult one.

Research techniques

While some areas of marketing research may not be particularly appropriate to the industrial field, in general all the research disciplines are relevant. Again it is a question of emphasis. For example, product testing in industrial marketing often involves developing a product in association with a customer to meet his specific needs and to solve his particular problems. A consumer product may be tested on a very much broader scale with quite different parameters determining its success or failure. Industrial attitude surveys can also be extremely useful when used to probe customer reaction to such things as technical service - often a particularly important aspect of industrial goods marketing.

Promotion

Because industrial markets are usually well defined, the industrial goods manufacturer can make very good use of direct mail advertising, such as personal postal advertising consisting of a letter and often sales literature directly aimed at specific prospective purchasers. Accurate and current mailing lists are vital to the success of a direct mail campaign. Although the sophistication of the computer enables direct mail techniques to be applied to consumer markets, success rates are generally lower than in industrial marketing. This is partly because of the difficulty in consumer markets of identifying the prime target audience and partly because costs continue to escalate,

Question 4 Are industrial and consumer marketing different?

making direct mail techniques non-viable for low value items.

Exhibitions are very important to industrial marketing. They provide an excellent opportunity both for meeting prospective customers and for demonstrating products. Similarly, public relations form a significant part of industrial marketing. Many prospective customers can be convinced of a product's performance and value to their business by reading about successful applications in competitor organisations. Public relations in this case is defined as the management function which evaluates public attitudes, identifies the policies and objectives of an organisation and plans and initiates a programme aimed at earning public understanding and acceptance.

In all our discussion so far, we have been at pains to emphasise that there is no change in *principle* when marketing industrial products compared with consumer products. The major differences are in the *emphasis* that is placed upon each element of the mix. This emphasis is determined as a result of a careful examination and analysis of the industrial buyer's decision process just as the consumer goods marketer would attempt to build a strategy based upon an understanding of the buyer's behaviour.

Successful industrial marketing

A UK manufacturer of commercial motor vehicle seating was faced with increasing competition by low cost firms. For some time it met the competition's low prices but eventually reached a point where further price reductions were impossible. The company had mistakenly hoped that its reputation for quality and service would be sufficient to fight off the competition's low price levels. In addition to its commercial motor vehicle seating, it made and sold a range of institutional furniture such as stacking chairs for churches and tubular steel canteen furniture. When it became clear that the company's strategy in the face of aggressive price competition was not the right one, management chose to develop a new product range.

The new product range, office chairs, had only its steel tube construction in common with existing products. In almost all other respects there was no compatibility. Marketing seemed a problem. The new General Sales and Marketing Manager had recently joined from a consumer goods company. After an initial appraisal of the situation, he made plans to make the new range known both to end users and to office equipment dealers in what was at the time a very conservative market throughout the EEC. In addition, the trade structure differed in each member country.

To deal with the problem of the dealers, in-store displays were designed and stocking incentives were offered in the form of a bakers' dozen: that is, an extra chair was delivered free with each order for twelve typist chairs. For a period of two months a dealer lottery was run in each country in which an order above a certain minimum value entitled the dealer to enter his name into a lottery, with "Weekends in Paris for Two" as the prizes. (For the French traders it was Rome).

The approach to users was also unusual. Large companies were selected and offered substantial introductory discounts. Competitions were also used. The promotion featured the fact that the new range was ergonomically designed but, rather than stress the technical aspects of the design, it majored on the benefits. The creative approach taken featured an attractive secretary enjoying after-work activities as well as working efficiently on her new typist chair.

This new approach took the trade by surprise. The results of this untypical industrial, but thoroughly professional, marketing approach were outstanding.

Today the company has a profitable and established range of office furniture.

Application questions

4.1 What do you see as the difference between marketing industrial and consumer products? Relate your answers to the four 'P's'. Are there fundamental differences or are they differences of degree?

4.2 If you are selling into both industrial and consumer markets, how are these differences reflected in the marketing approaches adopted by your organisation?

4.3 What scope is there for your organisation to make greater use of the approaches adopted in consumer marketing when developing its strategy for its industrial markets?

Question 5

Does the marketing of services differ from the marketing of products?

Overview

The principles of marketing apply in the marketing of services just as they do in the marketing of consumer and industrial goods, although, again, differences of emphasis are present.

We can distinguish between two basic types of service. The "service product" offers the customer an intangible series of benefits which in most instances cannot be stored for future use; the "product service" is vital to the functioning of the product and therefore an intrinsic part of it.

Service products can be usefully classified as either commercial or non-profit making, but, in each case, the marketing approach and the management of the marketing mix can be seen as appropriate. Product services are essential for the marketing of many products and the service element should be taken into account in the marketing mix.

Marketing principles

Marketing seeks to establish what customers want, both explicitly and implicitly, and to provide for their needs. This process of matching customer wants with organisational resources is applicable to service products in the same way as it is to consumer and industrial products, even though, on occasion the criteria for success are less obvious. Take, for example, the range of government services. In the absence of profitability as a measure, how can customers' needs be established and appropriate efficiency criteria developed? In this Question we shall consider how the principles of marketing can be used successfully in the marketing of services.

Because of the confusion commonly found between "service products" and "product services", we should examine the differences between the two. The *service product* is marketed purely as a service (as, for example, banking, insurance and hotels). *Product services*, on the other hand, are offered along with industrial or consumer goods and are often an inseparable part of a package (as, for example, computer installation and maintenance).

Service products

Service products (see Figure 5) are those products which produce a series

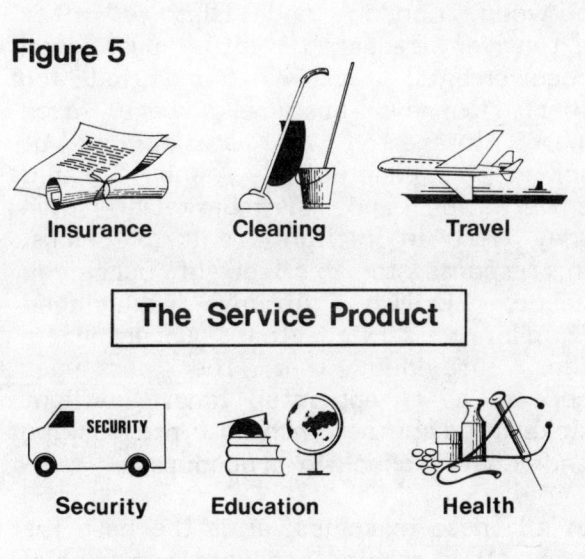

Figure 5

Insurance   Cleaning   Travel

The Service Product

Security   Education   Health

23

of benefits which cannot be stored. They must be consumed at the moment of manufacture. If we consider this aspect for a moment, we can see that a railway seat or a hotel room cannot be stored for later use. If it is not available when it is required, or not used when it is available, the opportunity for raising revenue is lost. The same seat or room may be required on an alternative day but it cannot be put into store on one day and sold on another. This attribute does not mean that the marketing of service products presents insurmountable differences. Rather, it means that the marketing mix elements must be combined in a suitable manner.

Consider, for instance, the problems of SNCF (the national railway system of France) or British Rail. Many of the services to and from Paris or London are stretched to their limits for only a few hours each day while commuters are travelling to and from work. For the remainder of the day their trains travel far from full. To utilise this wasted capacity and to obtain a contribution towards profits, SNCF and British Rail both offer lower priced off-peak facilities.

It is not only the consumer or industrial goods manufacturer who attempts to establish his customers' needs and then tries to meet them profitably. British Airways developed the Shuttle service between London and Glasgow after extensive research into customers' requirements. It was found that for short journeys customers were much more interested in availability of service, punctuality and rapid embarkation and disembarkation than they were in in-flight meals or drinks. In response to this set of perceived needs, British Airways developed Shuttle, a service that guarantees a seat, provided that the passenger appears at an appointed time. In-flight ticketing dispenses with both pre-booking and lengthy check-in procedures.

In all these examples, as is the case for many other service products, commercial success can be measured conventionally in terms of profitability. Clearly, the lack of profit from a service product raises the same questions as does the lack of profit from either consumer or industrial goods. Is the service right? Am I promoting it in the appropriate way? Is the price too high or low? Is it being sold in the right places? In some service sectors, these questions are more easily posed than answered. Professional services in medicine, dentistry, accountancy, architecture and management consultancy are of this type. For service products of this kind, constraints are imposed in terms of promotion and pricing. Advertising a particular expertise is often forbidden, and prices may not be freely set. Nevertheless, they can and do compete with each other by innovating within the marketing mix structure, through their choice of place of business, for example, or in the mix of services that they provide.

There are other forms of service products which provide purchasers with less direct benefits. For example, building societies offer the benefits of being able to determine where you live and in what type of house; they also often afford an additional bonus in a capital gain through price inflation of property. Together with banks, they also offer the facility, through numerous plans, to save for any one of a number of eventualities. Their marketing to potential users will emphasise derived benefits rather than the product itself.

Let us consider those service products for which profitability cannot be used as an efficiency measure. Primarily, these are service products in the social or welfare field. For example, the motor car has brought untold benefits to society. It has also given rise to many serious problems, amongst them the dangerous combination of drinking and driving. Injuries due to collisions between vehicles are also a hazard in our society and the likelihood of serious injury occurring is increased by the reluctance of many people to wear seat belts. Can marketing help to reduce drunken driving, or encourage the wearing of seat belts?

Question 5
Does the marketing of services differ from the marketing of products?

The principles of marketing can be applied here by identifying the "consumers" and their needs. Commercial organisations attempt to make a profit and satisfy customer needs by means of a profit objective. Reaching this objective or failing to do so is in fact the measure of their efficiency. Relating this to the social/welfare context, we can use as a measure of efficiency the success or failure in reducing social problems. Thus, fewer road deaths at hours notorious for drinking and driving can be used as a measure of success. It is by no means perfect. There can be many extraneous influences at work as well but, despite this, it is better than no measure at all.

In addition to both commercial and social/welfare service products, there is often the dimension of service within a service product. Many companies engaged in the marketing of physical products have found that they can develop profitable diversification spin-offs by marketing their "know-how". Thus, a Dutch company engaged in the production of dyestuffs found that there was a small but highly profitable market for the production knowledge and application techniques that they had acquired over the years. A separate company was set up to exploit these skills - a service product spun-off from an industrial product. Similarly, British Rail have established a successful consultancy company which advises other countries on how to develop rail services.

Product services

We must also consider our second major aspect of service (see Figure 6). Many consumer and industrial goods are sold on the basis of service either before the sale is made, or after the sale, or indeed both. A British minicomputer manufacturer's sales staff spent a considerable amount of time with prospective customers determining their specific needs before attempting to sell them any particular computer. Highly trained systems analysts studied the prospective company in terms of the tasks done by company employees. In this way, they traced the flow of information, decisions, organisation inputs and outputs. Using these studies, the manufacturing company made recommendations not only for the applications of its products, but also for improvements in the client company's operations. Following the sale, and depending upon the size of the computer and its type of application, the company provided maintenance engineers to service the equipment. This detailed attention to product services built them a most successful business in a highly competitive market.

Very similar supplier/customer relationships exist to a greater or lesser degree for most capital goods products. In ship-building, the before-sales service often extends into a complete bespoke service with extensive after-sales activity to maintain and service the product, although batch production can reduce some of the expenses involved.

Figure 6

The Product Service Package

Consumer goods can also be subject to both before and after-sales service facilities. Indeed, for Germany's VW/Audi, the reduced after-sales service requirement has been made a major sales feature. VW promote computerised servicing diagnosis, and Audi prolonged servicing intervals. Washing machine manufacturers offer service insurance packages to consumers across Europe whereby, for an annual payment, the appliance will be serviced regularly and replacement parts supplied without charge.

A major Norwegian house builder has been developing a before-sales service which extends well beyond a choice of sanitary ware and paint colour finishes. Within the constraints of local authority planning permission, and customers' budgets, a complete design service is offered to purchasers once a building site has been purchased. The customer can specify the number and size of rooms and, to a degree, their location. Sales have boomed.

Service is not confined to products. Many suppliers have found that the way they pack, deliver and process customers' orders has a considerable impact on the customer which usually results in increased sales. A study of actual consumer uses of a product, its relative importance to the business and the effects on the business of failure to supply, can only result in a better supplier/customer relationship.

However, service costs money which must be recovered, either in higher product costs, a service charge, or through greater contribution from increased sales. Such service must be seen as an element in the marketing mix. A few moments' thought will show that product service is a substitute for, or a complement to, other elements in the marketing mix. Service is likely, for example, to affect both the price and the place elements of the mix. A leading Italian manufacturer charges a higher price for his machine tools because of a technical differentiation which reduces the servicing frequency and therefore the servicing bill. Mass distribution of newpapers, bread and milk on a door to door basis undoubtedly increases the price of the product. It also makes life a lot more convenient.

The marketing of services

The implication of these various examples of service products and product services is that exactly the same principles of marketing apply as in the case of physical products. It is always important in any organisation not to think in terms of products or services *per se*. Rather, it is necessary to ask, "What *benefits* do our products or services provide?". Customers do not buy products or services, they buy the benefits that those products or services provide. This is not just a semantic point; it is an important distinction which can be vital to the long-term survival of the firm. There are many examples of companies who have taken a narrow view of their business and defined it purely in terms of the products or services that they provide; as a result, they were forced out of business when competitive products or services were introduced which provided the same benefits but in a more cost-effective way. (The distinction between products and benefits and its implications for marketing practice are discussed in detail in Question 12, "What Products Should We Market?").

When it comes to devising a market strategy for an organisation in the service business, the same factors should be considered as with any other firm. Who are the customers? What are their needs? What benefits do they seek? How sensitive are they to the various elements of the marketing mix?

There are clear signs that the marketing concept is being increasingly accepted by companies in many service industries where previously it was thought inappropriate or not applicable: banks, building societies, design consultancies, even professions where their regulations allow the concept to be implemented. Indeed, with the growing recognition

Question 5
Does the marketing of services differ from the marketing of products?

that all organisations are in service marketing to one degree or another, it may be that the distinction between different types of marketing will soon no longer be made.

Application questions

5.1 Compare the way in which you choose your lawyer or hairdresser with the way in which you choose a car or a brand of soap. What are the essential differences between marketing a service and a physical product?

5.2 Think of a product where the availability and quality of before or after-sales service was an important element in your decision to buy. How did the manufacturer inform and persuade you of the importance and quality of the service?

5.3 Does the product range offered by your organisation present any opportunity for you to develop a "product service"? How could new forms of "product service" be initiated? Who should assume responsibility for this?

5.4 If your organisation offers a "service product", how do you market it? Are there particular difficulties associated with marketing a "service product"? How could these difficulties be minimised or eradicated? How could your present marketing strategy be extended? Are there any aspects of product marketing which you could apply?

Question 6
Is international marketing different?

Overview

International marketing is the performance of the marketing task across national boundaries. The basic principles of marketing therefore still hold good. However, the environment in which international marketing takes place is different from the domestic environment; the control which it is possible to exercise over the four 'P's is different; and there is a different dimension of complexity to planning the marketing function in an international context.

The most critical determinant of the way an organisation markets abroad is the method chosen to enter a foreign market.

The key questions in international marketing are concerned with whether to market abroad, where to market abroad, what to market abroad and, finally, how to market abroad.

Marketing principles

Perhaps the best way of beginning to answer this question is to remind ourselves that marketing is the way in which an organisation matches its resources with the wants of its customers against the background of a dynamic environment. International marketing is simply the performance of that marketing task across national boundaries. All the different activities involved in the marketing task still have to be undertaken. Marketing research has to be carried out. Appropriate products must be developed and realistic pricing, packaging and branding policies adopted. Sales forecasts must be made and effective communication with customers established. Distribution policies have to ensure that the product gets to the right place at the right time.

So, in principle, international marketing is no different from domestic marketing.

Yet, in practice, whenever an organisation begins to operate outside its domestic market, it is in its marketing operation that difficulties are most likely to occur. This has forced marketing practitioners to pay increasing attention to the subject of international marketing, and they have begun to focus more and more on the *differences* rather than the *similarities* as a means of improving performance.

International marketing has three unique elements:

– there are different environmental variables;

– the control which it is possible to exercise over the four 'P's is different;

– there is a different dimension of complexity to planning the marketing function in an international context.

Let us look at each of these unique features in some detail to see how they affect marketing activities.

The international environment

The different factors involved include the following:

Tariffs are taxes on imports levied either on value or on quantity in order to earn revenue and to protect home industries. They affect the price of exported goods, making them less competitive than locally produced goods. Companies affected by tariffs often react by using marginal cost pricing policies (where the price charged reflects not the total production cost but only the costs incurred in providing an additional quantity of goods); by modifying the product; by repositioning the product in a higher priced market segment; or by shipping completely-knocked-down for local assembly, thus attracting a lower rate of duty.

Quotas, which are direct barriers to imports, are much more serious because the firm has less flexibility in responding to them. Apart from attempting to get a fair share of quotas, virtually the only response is to set up local production if the market size warrants it.

Exchange control means that foreign currency is in short supply and that the government is rationing it rather than letting higher prices ration it. If a company is manufacturing in a country with exchange controls, it has to comply with strict government regulations in order to obtain currency for imported supplies. Unless the company can do this, it may be forced to use domestic supplies, despite possible higher costs and inferior quality. It should be borne in mind too that a country with exchange controls is rarely concerned with the profitability of an individual organisation: currency fluctuations can either wipe out a company's profit or create a windfall virtually overnight.

Non-tariff barriers, in the form of customs documentation, marks of origin, regulations concerning the constituents of the product, packaging and labelling laws and so on, can similarly have a dramatic effect on a company's freedom over the management of the four 'P's.

Political instability, boycotts, customs unions and other environmental factors can also have a drastic effect on a company's marketing policy.

One German company selling perfume in Latin America lost most of its market share when the tariff was raised from 20 per cent to 50 per cent. The options discussed by the local management at an emergency meeting were to continue paying the high duty and change the product positioning to a high price segment; to import the primary ingredients and manufacture locally; to ask for a lower price from the home factory; or to give up the market completely. Eventually, the company realised that it had to take a longer term view which took account of the potential in the *total* Latin American Free Trade Area (LAFTA), and that this should have been done at the market *entry* stage rather than after a heavy investment had been made in only one market. The company went on to set up manufacturing facilities in one of the LAFTA countries, and South America is now a profitable market for its products. However, this company had learned the hard way that it just did not enjoy the same degree of control in its marketing overseas as it did in its home market.

The cultural environment

When a marketing operation covers different nation states, there are always problems related to variations in customs and habits. Such problems are magnified greatly when it comes to differentiating between cultures. Intuitive skills can make a great contribution to successful marketing programmes in the home market, but behaviour which relies on the same cultural criteria in foreign markets can lead to the most elementary and expensive marketing mistakes.

Seven elements of culture which need careful attention can be readily identified:

Material culture   The extent to which

culture is reponsive to increased productivity and its consequent rewards, as well as the current state of material wealth and its impact on purchasing inclinations and abilities.

Language The most obvious perhaps, but an aspect of culture which requires very careful attention in, for example, the choice of brand names and in the communication of ideas.

Aesthetics This again demands most careful understanding if promotional activities, including such aspects as packaging and product design and so on, are not to be mishandled.

Education This determines whether or not written communication is possible. High levels of illiteracy mean that instructions on packaging are pointless, and that training programmes for distributors and agents must take careful cognisance of the problems which result. The conduct of marketing research will also pose problems. The main danger lies in the difficulty of correctly interpreting data in an unfamiliar cultural context.

Religion Like language, religion is a readily identifiable aspect of cultural difference which we find both within and across national boundaries. Its taboos and predilections must be ascertained and their impact on economic behaviour studied with care.

Attitudes and values Attitudes and values, most especially towards marketing and sales, will need to be ascertained and understood. Different cultures respond differently to the acquisition of conspicuous wealth, to the prospect of change in life styles and to the taking of social risks.

Social organisation The nature of social organisation can be seen most clearly in the family. Certain cultures are respecters of age and status whilst others have developed a more meritocratic stance. Some have a greater respect for womenfolk than others. Some operate through a greatly extended concept of family, whereas in others the family has almost broken down as an effective social institution even for bringing up children.

Successful inter-cultural marketing activity is built upon an understanding of how local culture interacts with the four 'P's. Closer to home, a similar understanding is required of the different segments of any market we might wish to reach. The distinction here is that in an alien culture we need to proceed with analysis and forethought; but then, so do we in any segment with which we do not feel a close affinity.

International control

Without doubt, the most critical determinant of the way you market abroad is your *method of entering* a foreign market. This, above all else, decides the degrees of freedom you have over the management of the four 'P's.

Straightforward *exporting* can be either indirect or direct. Indirect exporting is when a third party arranges the documentation, shipping and selling of a company's goods abroad; this usually represents the smallest level of commitment to international marketing. As foreign sales grow, however, the company begins to make a limited commitment, usually in the form of taking on the documentation task itself. It is often at this stage that overseas agents or distributors are appointed to carry out the selling task abroad, with the result that the company is now a direct exporter, although it is likely that the commitment is still limited to marginal production capacity with no additional fixed investment.

If the company feels that it needs a more aggressive marketing approach, it is likely to undertake a limited fixed investment. This usually takes the form not just of increased production capacity but also of a marketing subsidiary abroad.

Foreign production can take the form of licensing, contract manufacturing, local assembly or full manufacture either by joint ventures or wholly owned subsidiaries. With licensing, the company is hiring out its brand name, technical expertise, patent, trademark, or process rights. The licensee manufactures and markets abroad for the licensor. Whilst this avoids the need for a heavy investment, it can lead to an overdependence on the licensee, who quickly builds up both manufacturing and marketing expertise. Associated Engineering, the largest engine components manufacturer in the world, and Pilkington Glass are two examples of organisations who successfully employ the licensing method of production.

Contract manufacturing entails using someone else's production capacity and is usually only possible for technically simple products like food. It is a useful way of getting round tariff barriers as well as of gaining experience of a foreign market without the need for investment in capital and labour.

Similar advantages apply to local assembly. As well as enabling a company to avoid paying the higher tariffs on assembled goods, local assembly helps employment and enables the company to gain experience of the market. It also allows a stricter degree of quality control.

Sometimes, laws forbid one hundred per cent foreign ownership of assets, especially in the less developed countries. Many companies, therefore, set up joint ventures either with a foreign government or with local partners. This is certainly a way of sharing risk and of gaining experience using local expertise; its major disadvantage lies in the loss of complete control, and hence freedom of action, especially in the field of marketing.

One hundred per cent ownership of foreign production plants represents a major commitment to international marketing and should only be undertaken after much research. Most overseas manufacturing is established only when the geographical situation of the markets leaves no alternative. ICI built a polyethelene plant in the south of France because this was the only way to get into the market. Likewise, GKN's big stake in the German components industry gave them a market share which could not be achieved by direct export from the UK.

From this discussion, it will be clear that there is a big difference between the marketing task of a company selling to a middleman as a final customer, with little concern about what happens to the product after the sale, and the task facing the company that assumes full responsibility for all stages of marketing right through to final user satisfaction. Regardless of the level of involvement in foreign marketing, companies are more and more finding it necessary to become marketing oriented in their international efforts.

The important point is that each of the options described above should not be considered as a series of steps to be followed en route to becoming a multinational company (in which all opportunities are assessed from the worldwide viewpoint and in which the terms "home" and "foreign" are meaningless) but more as strategic alternatives. And, since the method of market entry is the major determinant of the degree of control a company has over its marketing, each of the different options should be carefully considered before a decision is made.

Management decisions

Each management must resolve the following issues, illustrated in Figure 7:

- *Whether* to market abroad. Geographical extension may be more desirable than product diversification, depending, of course, on circumstances. However, the decision to sell abroad should not be taken lightly.

- *Where* to market abroad. This is one of the major decisions for international marketing. Choosing foreign markets on the basis of proximity and similarity is not necessarily the most potentially profitable option to go for.

- *What* to market abroad. The degree to which products should be altered to suit foreign needs is a fundamental problem in inter national marketing.

- *How* to market abroad. This is concerned not just with the issue of how to enter a foreign market, but also with the management of the four 'P's once a company arrives. And, finally, there is the difficult question of how to coordinate the marketing effort in a foreign country.

Figure 7

The Key Questions in International Marketing

Whether to?   Where to?

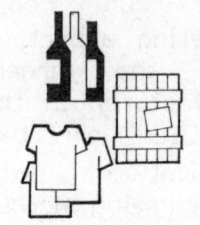

- Direct
- Agent/Distributor
- Local Manufacturing

What to?   How to?

Application questions

6.1 What existing arrangements does your organisation have for reaching international markets? What are the advantages and disadvantages of these arrangements? What alternative arrangements could be explored?

6.2 What additional markets is your organisation moving into? On what criteria should the organisation decide to go into a new market, and how should it approach the task?

6.3 What is the justification for your organisation restricting its activities to the home market? Should other markets be considered?

6.4 Explain how the cultural and environmental differences of other countries are taken into account in your marketing efforts overseas. Is this provision adequate? What problems have been encountered because insufficient attention was paid to these factors? What could your marketing department do to reduce the risk of marketing overseas?

Unit II   The behaviour of customers

Question 7   Who are our customers?

Question 8   Are all our customers the same?

Question 9   Why do customers behave the way they do?

Question 10   How can consumerism affect marketing?

Question 11   Is marketing unethical?

Question 7
Who are our customers?

Overview

The first stage in planning and implementing an effective marketing strategy is to define in precise and actionable terms just who the organisation's customers are or could be. Knowing where sales are coming from, and the source of profits, is the key to understanding current market positions and to assessing the potential for the future. A number of questions immediately present themselves. For example, are the customer and the consumer the same? What measures can be used to define a market? The answers to such questions are vital to a rich and full understanding of the organisation's markets.

The nature of our market

We have seen how marketing can be defined as the matching of the organisation's resources with the needs of the customer. This presupposes both the identification of those *needs* (a subject to be considered in the next Question) and the identification of the *customers*. The nature and identity of the organisation's customers is not always given the attention that it deserves. Some indication of the importance of this knowledge can be gained from the following data, taken from a UK company's survey of the soap market:

- 24% of the customers of its best selling product accounted for over 82% of its sales;

- 61% of the sales of the product were to women up to the age of 35;

- the sales of the company's product accounted for 18% of the total industry sales.

The company management felt that this survey data could provide some useful cues for marketing action. Clearly, the data had to be interpreted. Only a small percentage of customers, for example, accounted for a majority of sales, and a majority of these customers were under the age of 35. The reasons for this pattern of purchasing - why some people bought in great quantity and others not at all - still had to be explored. (The "why" of customers' behaviour is examined in Question 9). But the initial identification of customers provided the basis for future investigation and action.

Customers and consumers

First, we should distinguish between *customers* and *consumers*. This difference is more than semantic. In many cases, the customer is acting as an intermediary or an agent for the final user of the product. Consider the case of the industrial purchasing officer buying raw materials, such as wool tops, for conversion into semi-finished cloth. This cloth is then sold to other companies for incorporation into the final product, say a suit or dress, for sale in consumer markets. Here we can see that the requirements of these various intermediaries and the end-user himself must be translated into the specifications of the purchasing officer to the raw materials manufacturer. Consequently, the market needs that this manufacturing company is attempting to satisfy must in the last analysis be defined in terms of the requirements of the ultimate user, the consumer - even though the direct customer is quite clearly the purchasing officer.

A similar situation exists with the housewife who in her weekly shopping trip is acting as an agent on behalf of her household. She is the customer, her family are the consumers. Her motivations and her actions, like the purchasing officer's, can be explained, partly at least, by her perceptions of the needs of the consumers on whose behalf she is acting.

The distinction between customers and consumers can also be seen operating in the service sector, as when a conference organiser acts on behalf of an organisation in setting up the venue for an internal conference, arranging speakers and so on. Here the organiser is the customer for the different promotional and administrative services needed; the organisation is the consumer.

Given that we can distinguish between customers and consumers, the next questions to be faced are: who are our potential customers (as distinct from our actual customers) and who are our "lost" customers? The answers to such questions can often provide an organisation with more valuable insights for marketing strategy than a simple analysis of existing customers alone. Being able to identify potential customers is the first stage in converting them to actual customers. A definition of the potential market for any product or service must be grounded upon a clear view of what basic customer needs the product meets or is intended to meet. Do these people use alternative products or do their needs go unsatisfied?

It is common practice in marketing to refer to the market share that a product or brand currently holds. This is essentially a measure of the proportion of the total sales of similar types of products that the product accounts for. Thus, Gerber babyfoods could be described as having a percentage share of the Belgian or British market. This share could be expressed either in terms of the value of the market, often called the "sterling" share, or it could be expressed in terms of units sold. Either way, it is a measure of actual sales as a proportion of an actual market rather than a measure of actual sales as a measure of the potential market. The difference between these two measures gives some indication of the scope for extending the market penetration of a product.

Past or lost customers are equally difficult to identify but, like potential customers, a knowledge of who they are could be invaluable in increasing an organisation's marketing effectiveness. When, in answer to Question 27, we discuss the methods of marketing research, we will see that there are ways in which both potential and past customers can be identified. Investigation can then be made into the reasons for their behaviour in relation to the company's product.

Describing the customer

Knowing who our customers are implies an ability to describe them in terms appropriate for marketing action. Depending on the nature of our business, we might usefully describe industrial customers in terms of their level of purchases from us, the size of their total turnover, or the sort of business that they are in. For consumer markets, geographical location, age, occupation, education, marital status or income are typical measures of markets. Such measures are termed demographic characteristics. One of the benefits of demographic characteristics is that they are commonly used bases for the majority of data collection exercises such as censuses. They have the additional advantage of being relatively straightforward to measure. However, convenience should not be allowed to obscure the possible irrelevance of demographic measures to specific market circumstances. This is a point which we

Question 7   Who are our customers?

will develop in the next Question, "Are all our customers the same?".

It is essential to be able to describe the organisation's markets in terms which will act as guidelines for marketing strategy. Knowing the precise ages of a market, for example, is of no use to the organisation if it is unable to capitalise upon this fact in terms of advertising or distribution strategies. Nevertheless, basic demographic data can provide a valuable source of initial market information, even though the company may then wish to look beyond that data. The table below, for instance, demonstrates national differences in ownership of various household appliances.

Table 1   Some national differences in the ownership of household appliances

Percentages of households owning in 1976

	Refrigerator	Deep freezer	Electric cooker	Gas cooker	Cooker hood	Kettle	Food mixer	Dishwasher	Coffee maker
Austria	91	30	60	40	20	19	70	4	21
Belgium	88	31	22	78	17	11	77	12	18
Denmark	92	70	52	48	-	28	67	18	31
Finland	94	62	80	20	24	-	54	8	20
France	91	21	26	74	15	12	68	13	19
West Germany	93	37	68	32	22	30	75	12	32
Great Britain	83	29	42	58	23	86	45	6	22
Italy	92	28	6	92	11	21	8	18	11
Netherlands	96	30	94	6	21	5	63	4	24
Norway	86	69	87	13	27	26	78	14	30
Spain	74	15	40	47	8	6	38	8	8
Sweden	92	66	97	3	30	15	61	18	32
Switzerland	91	35	74	26	31	10	78	12	31
Bulgaria	62	-	-	-	-	-	-	-	-
Czechoslovakia	80	21	88*	-	-	-	-	-	-
East Germany	73	12	71*	-	-	-	-	-	-
Poland	68	18	42	-	-	-	-	-	-
USSR	54	-	-	-	-	-	-	-	-
Yugoslavia	47	-	75*	-	-	-	-	-	-

\-   No data available

*   All cookers

Source: Official Surveys, Market Research agencies,
          Various journals, Euromonitor estimates

European Marketing Data and Statistics, 1978/79, Euromonitor Publications, London

It will be apparent that the problem of identifying our customers is complicated by the scale of the markets in which the organisation operates. Philips of Eindhoven, for example, have a pretty clear idea of who their customers are for heavy electrical equipment stations. On the other hand, the same company faces greater problems in defining their market for domestic electric light bulbs. A market which can be measured in terms of tens of customers is generally easier to define than one measured in terms of tens of millions of customers.

The 80/20 rule

As a market increases in size, there is almost always encountered a phenomenon known as the *80/20 rule* or the *Pareto effect*. This simply means that it is usual for a small number of customers to account for the largest part of the business. It may not be 80/20, it could be 82/18, but there is rarely a proportional balance between the customers and the purchases they make from the organisation. In many manufacturing companies, this relationship can be used as the basis for describing a large market in terms of the importance to the business of individual customers. If we draw a graph to show the proportion of customers that account for a certain proportion of sales, then we might expect to find a relationship of the kind shown in Figure 8.

In this diagram, an organisation's customers have been categorised simply as 'A', 'B' or 'C' customers according to the proportion of total sales that they account for. The 'A' customers, perhaps 25% of the total, account for 80% of the sales; the 'B' customers, say 55% of the total, account for 15% of total sales; and 'C' customers, 20% of the total, account for the remaining 5% of sales. This type of classification can be extremely useful when it comes to developing a strategy for taking particular products to particular markets. Exactly the same phenomenon can often be found if we plot the proportion of our products that provide a given proportion of profits (to be discussed in Questions 12 and 13).

The Pareto effect is found in almost all markets from industrial compressors to banking, postal services or dog food. The marketing man in consumer markets will frequently concentrate his efforts on the "heavy half" because a small percentage of committed users of the product account for a large percentage of sales. In the direct mail business, for example, it is an accepted principle that customers who have bought a product, any product, through direct mail in the past are the prime market for selling additional, even different, products to in the future.

Knowing the customer sounds easy enough. However, detailed analysis of exactly who he or she might be is vitally necessary if effective matching of company resources with customers' needs is to be accomplished.

Figure 8

The 80/20 Rule or Pareto Effect

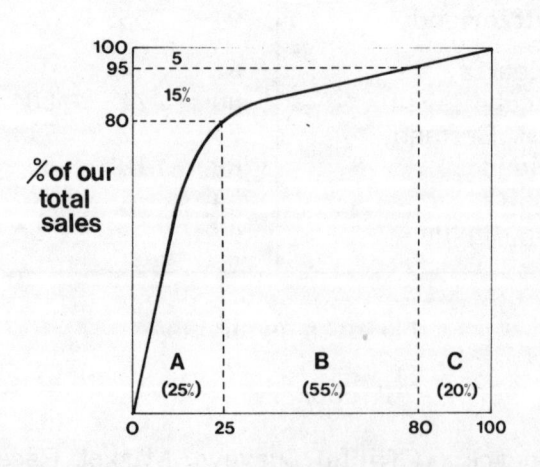

Question 7   Who are our customers?

Application questions

7.1 Who are your organisation's customers, and who are its consumers? What needs do these two groups have in common and what needs are exclusive to one or other of them? How does, or should, your organisation market its products to both groups?

7.2 Think of a product or service you buy for which your organisation is one of the relatively small number of large customers. How does, or should, the manufacturer attempt to maintain and increase the volume of your purchases?

7.3 Think of three products or services:

(a) one for which you are both customer and consumer;

(b) one for which you are customer but not consumer;

(c) one for which you are consumer but not customer.

What fundamental differences are there between the needs of customers and consumers?

7.4 Identify an item where you recently switched brands. Why did you do this, and how might the manufacturer of the original brand regain your custom?

Question 8

Are all our customers the same?

Overview

Recognising that customers differ from each other in terms of who they are and why they buy provides opportunities for market segmentation. Segmentation, it is suggested, can provide the key to profitable marketing in competitive markets. The means whereby groups of customers are distinguished from each other is clearly important and attention has to be paid to the choice of criteria for segmentation. Customers can be categorised on many dimensions, but only those criteria which relate in some way to purchasing behaviour and which are themselves actionable are of any use to the marketing strategist.

Market segmentation

Once an organisation's customers, actual and potential, have been identified, the question arises of whether the organisation can satisfy their wants. The problem would be easily solved if all customers presented the same requirements or, put another way, if their wants could be satisfied by the same product sold in the same way. However, as we saw in the previous Question, there are differences in demographic characteristics between customers and closer examination reveals that other more subtle differences exist as well; these include taste, life style, and so on. These differences amongst customers mean that an undifferentiated campaign to a mass market will seldom meet with widespread success. On the other hand, few organisations are in a position to be able to cater for highly specific individual requirements within the market place.

Fortunately, it is often found that when a market is subjected to scrutiny, the members of that market fall into natural groups or segments within which customers exhibit the same broad characteristics. These segments form separate markets in themselves and can often be seen to be large enough to warrant a separate marketing strategy. Looking at markets in this way is termed *market segmentation*.

A segmented approach to marketing can bring many advantages to an organisation. In the first place, many companies have found that if they can identify a viable sub-market they can cater exclusively for the needs of that segment and gain a degree of dominance that would probably not be possible within the total market. One German firm in the specialist instrument field took this view and discovered that it was more profitable to have a 50% share of a DMk 50 million market than to have a 5% share of a DMk 250 million market. They realised, as many other organisations in all fields of enterprise have recognised, that market segmentation strategies can be the key to profitability in competitive markets.

Recognising that customers are different can enable the marketer to achieve a closer matching of customer needs with the firm's product or service offering. Thus, the matching process that is at the heart of marketing is in fact facilitated by adopting a segmentation approach. Segmentation strategies have an additional value in that they allow the company to relate its strengths and weaknesses to its marketing approach by ensuring a concentration of resources in those areas where the company has the greatest advantage.

Identifying customer groupings

Two approaches to segmentation suggest themselves:

- market segmentation through an analysis of the characteristics of the customer;

- market segmentation through an analysis of the responses of the customer.

Segmentation by customer characteristics poses the initial question, "Who are our customers?". We saw in Question 7 that demographic features can be a useful way of describing customer differences and can indeed be used as the basis for a segmentation strategy. For example, a French commercial bank might decide to develop particular services that are angled at the young and newly married in the joint annual income bracket of Fr40,000-Fr60,000. But demographic characteristics are not the sole criteria whereby we can characterise markets. In consumer markets, for example, it might be appropriate to use personality factors or "life style" types as the basis for segmentation. The Pan-European marketing campaign for Martini, for example, has been aimed at penetrating a particular segment of the market that enjoys, or aspires to, a particular life style. Israel's Pan-European campaign to develop sales of avocado pears also describes a particular life style. Similarly, industrial markets can be segmented by descriptive characteristics. A UK manufacturer of marine engines might set up approaches to the sale of marine systems to the warship market which contrast with those employed towards the container ship market.

Segmentation on the basis of responses asks the question, "Why do they buy?". This approach can involve an examination of shopping patterns to determine how many customers shop at the retail outlet closest to their home or how sensitive customers are to price changes. An approach which is becoming increasingly popular is to examine the attributes that the customer is seeking from a product or service. This is called benefit segmentation and is based on the notion that the reason a customer purchases a specific product is to acquire the "bundle of benefits" that he or she perceives it to contain.

These two approaches to segmentation are by no means mutually exclusive. On the contrary, many organisations combine both approaches to provide a richer and fuller description of their market segments. The UK toilet soap market can be looked at in a number of ways. It can be analysed in terms of the age and the life styles of consumers. These descriptive criteria may form useful bases for segmentation. Benefit segmentation, on the other hand, provides additional dimensions to the segments. Because individuals will have different requirements when it comes to benefits, we can see that the rationale for segmentation under this scheme is the grouping of customers on the basis of the similarity of their perception of the benefits that a particular product contains. In the case of toilet soap, for example, market research might reveal that there is a segment that seeks mainly hygiene-related benefits, such as cleanliness, deodorant properties, freshness, etcetera. Another segment might be largely concerned with the cosmetic properties of the soap, such as skin care and scent. Still another segment might be seeking "value for money" as the main benefit and therefore would be guided more by the unit price of the soap. The identification of these different benefit segments would then enable the design of marketing strategies aimed specifically at them.

As the principles of segmentation are universal, similar examples can be cited from industrial and service markets. One British insurance company, for example, has directed its product development towards a target market consisting of highly taxed individuals with surplus investments. The new products extend the concept of unit trust business into comprehensive unit-linked packages which offer a particularly attractive return on investment. This venture into segmentation has enabled the company to develop and exploit new opportunities over and above the basic life assurance market.

Segmenting industrial markets, on the other hand, is complicated by the fact that it is rare for a single individual to be responsible for a purchasing decision. This responsibility is usually shared by several people who work together as a formal or informal purchasing committee. This purchasing committee usually consists of the following members: the works manager who wants reliable, functionally superior products; the user who wants the product that is simplest to use; a buyer who wants the cheapest product; and a finance director who wants the product that will deliver the best return on capital. Industrial market segmentation must take into account potential conflicts of interest between the members of this purchasing committee. Different promotional messages must be devised which will be consistent with each individual's interests. Since the various members of the purchasing committee are not all interested in all product benefits, segmentation demands that the message be adjusted to suit the audience.

The computer business is one which provides excellent examples of successful market segmentation. Several companies involved in computer manufacturing have grown very rapidly by means of identifying groups of users with specialist requirements. The companies have then gone on to develop products which meet these users' needs more cost effectively than the larger general computers which until recently were the only models available.

Criteria for segmentation

Whatever the means whereby we distinguish between our customers, the criteria that we use for categorisation must be appropriate to the specific product/market situation. In other words, why segment a market on the basis of age of customer (in the case of consumer and service markets) or on the basis of plant throughput (in the case of an industrial market) if those characteristics have no relationship to potential purchasing behaviour? Clearly, the characteristics must be related to behaviour. When segmentation is based on the benefits that the customer is seeking to acquire from a product, the criteria must be limited to those benefits actually related to purchase. Once we know the nature of those benefits and the particular combinations that the market seeks, then we are better poised to promote our product offering to those customers who are most likely to be attracted to it.

For a strategy of market segmentation to be successful, there are a number of requirements that must be met (see Figure 9):

- First, for a segment to be viable it is necessary that it can be distinguished from other segments. At the same time, the customers within each segment must have a high degree of similarity on the criteria adopted for segmentation. In other words, customers must be different on some dimensions, thus allowing segments to be isolated within the overall market, but customers within each segment must be similar on certain specific dimensions.

- Second, the criteria used to differentiate between customer groupings - market segments - must be relevant to the purchase situation. These criteria should be related to differences in market demand.

- Third, the segment should be of a sufficient potential size to ensure that any marketing investment made within it will result in an adequate return.

- Fourth, an identified market segment can only be exploited if it can be reached. It must be possible to direct a separate marketing strategy to each segment. This means that the customers

Question 8 Are all our customers the same?

in each segment could have different television viewing or reading habits, different retail shopping patterns, different responses to prices or different expectations as to the benefits to be derived from the product.

Figure 9

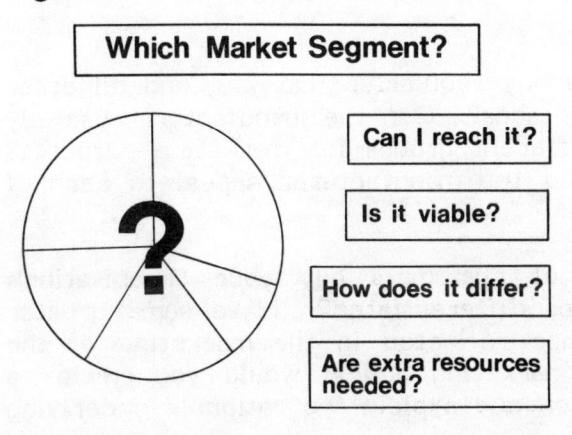

Which Market Segment?

Can I reach it?

Is it viable?

How does it differ?

Are extra resources needed?

As has already been indicated, the realisation that customers are different has led to many successful marketing innovations by a wide variety of companies. Building societies, for example, offer different rates of interest for customers with short- and long-term financial needs. Educational institutions segment their markets successfully by using criteria of educational qualifications and career aspirations. Manufacturers of components for computers divide their market and vary their terms of sale according to the requirements and circumstances of different customer organisations. These and other examples provide a testimony to the value of the market segmentation.

Segmentation in action

A Danish brewer of lager developed a new approach to its product strategy after a fresh look at its markets as a result of a segmentation analysis. The company knew that national differences existed in terms of preferences for beer and lager and it had some idea of what the criteria for preference were. Scandinavians liked a light, dry drink; the Germans and Dutch preferred a fuller, sweeter beer. Such knowledge was useful but it did not provide great insight into why some beers did better than others in some markets. The company knew also that the majority of beer was consumed by a minority of drinkers.

Evaluating its existing knowledge, the company believed that there could well be "gaps" in the European market where minority needs, which were not being currently met, could be filled by a product aimed just at them. The questions were: who were these people and what attributes should the product possess to ensure an appeal amongst these potential consumers?

It was decided that a multi-country study should be conducted in Denmark, Sweden, Holland and Germany to ascertain the nature of current preferences and to relate them to identifiable market segments. This was done through an attitude survey which questioned existing drinkers on their preferences for beer and lager along a number of dimensions such as strength, brightness, dryness and so on. At the same time the survey accumulated data relating to demographic characteristics such as age, income, occupation, etcetera. Information was also collected which was designed to give an indication of the life-styles that these drinkers associated with the consumers of various existing brands of beer and lager.

The research established that people have "images" of the type of person who drinks particular drinks. Thus, one drink might be seen as being "masculine", another as "friendly", another as "sophisticated", and so on. The segmentation study revealed that amongst occasional drinkers there was a need, particularly displayed by younger respondents, for a "potent but convivial" drink at a price that was not excessive but high enough to give a connotation of quality.

The outcome of this research was the successful development and launch of a "German-type" beer with special packaging in the form of a foil top and a label that was closer in its format to a bottle of Chateau wine. The promotion appeal was very much oriented towards the status aspirations of the younger, sophisticated end of the market and the price was about 25% higher than the regular beers in the market. This is just one example of the profitable exploitation of a market segment, based on a careful analysis of market characteristics and the opportunities within that market.

Application questions

8.1 Think of a consumer product which you buy regularly. Do you, and all other buyers of the product, buy it for the same reasons? Can the manufacturer usefully classify his customers, or consumers, into different groups for marketing purposes? On what basis would he do this? How could the manufacturer appeal to each of the groups which you have identified?

8.2 How many different, discrete types of customers buy your organisation's products or services? How are these groups differentiated? Have some greater potential than others? If so, is this balance reflected in the marketing of the organisation? If you were responsible for marketing policy, would you employ a segmentation approach? Outline your approach and explain the rationale underlying it.

8.3 Apply a "benefit" segmentation to your organisation's market. How do you/could you communicate with each segment which you have identified? How do the major points being conveyed to each segment differ? Are there ways in which your organisation could make more direct use of benefit segmentation?

Question 9

Why do customers behave the way they do?

Overview

Marketing success depends on understanding, and being able to explain, the way in which customers behave in terms of purchase decisions. If we can understand how and why our customers buy, we are in a better position to combine in the most appropriate way the different elements of the marketing mix.

There is now a considerable body of knowledge available covering the mechanisms of customer choice in consumer, service and industrial markets. This knowledge can be summarised and distilled in the form of "models" and theories of behaviour which can afford an effective basis for marketing action.

Why do people choose?

In a recent product test, two well-established brands of margarine were tested against each other in 400 French households. One was the brand leader and the other was a much smaller brand in terms of market share. Half the sample were given the two brands in plain foil wrappers simply marked "X" and "Y". The other half received the two brands in their usual, familiar wrappers. All 400 housewives were asked to state which brand they preferred overall. In those households where the brands were given in the anonymous wrappers, there was approximately a 50/50 split in choice. Neither brand emerged as the clear leader. However, amongst those households where the brands' true identity was revealed, the preference was 65/35 in favour of the brand leader.

Why?

A manufacturer of British defence equipment selling to the Middle East has found that price is of minor importance; that quality is taken for granted; that performance is assumed to be as specified; but that the critical determinant of the purchase order is the ability to establish a personal rapport with the buyer. On occasion, orders have gone to the most expensive tenderer where the performance levels have been lower, rather than to a cheaper competitor's bid.

Why?

These examples are not quoted because they necessarily demonstrate anything odd or out-of-the-ordinary on the part of the particular customers cited. Rather, they demonstrate the complexity of the mechanics of customer behaviour.

How do people choose?

The study of customer behaviour in marketing is essentially the study of how people choose. What are the influences that affect choices and how do they differ from person to person or from product to product? These are questions that the marketer must answer if he is to build an effective marketing strategy; for it is indisputably true that if we know more about how a customer chooses, then we are in a much better position to present products or services that will lead to his or her choice being our offering.

This approach contrasts with the

stimulus-response point of view, whereby the consumer is viewed simply as a "black box". Exponents of this view maintain that as long as one knows that for a given stimulus there is the likelihood of a certain response, then what goes on in between does not matter. Such a view is too crude and limited for the development of creative marketing strategies. It postulates the customer reacting rather like one of Pavlov's dogs. If we expose him or her to a sales visit, for example, an order does or does not result. Now, in reality, we know that sales visits by themselves rarely generate orders because there are so many other elements at work as well. If there is a connection between sales visits and orders placed, it will probably not be a direct one. It is more likely that a visit might influence the customer's attitude towards the product or service and that influence, along with many other factors, might then affect choice behaviour in the way we wish.

Accordingly, it is often the case that today's marketing practitioner is looking for models of customer behaviour which attempt to describe and explain the influences of several and hopefully all marketing actions upon choice. These models need not necessarily be very elaborate or complex but they do need to be grounded upon a secure theoretical foundation. This need for theory should not dismay the practical marketer; it has often been observed that there is nothing so practical as good theory.

The requirement for a deeper understanding of choice mechanisms applies equally to industrial and service markets as it does to consumer markets. There is often a feeling that industrial buyer behaviour is somehow more rational or straightforward than the behaviour involved in the purchase of consumer goods. This has repeatedly been demonstrated not to be the case. The marketer encounters the same patterns of interplay of behavioural factors in the marketing of machine tools or printing inks as he does in marketing toothpaste, canal narrowboat holidays or education.

Models of buyer behaviour

Over the years, a considerable body of theory and knowledge has developed about customer behaviour. If the theories are taken to offer a complete picture of how the customer's mind works, it will soon become clear that they stand in opposition to each other. In other words, if the psychoanalytic explanation is believed to offer a complete explanation of behaviour, then the economic view which stresses the importance of "utility" in purchasing behaviour cannot also be correct.

However, the prudent marketer will not seek a global explanation of why customers behave in the way they do; rather, he will be content to derive insights and knowledge from the different models which have been built up. In doing this, he will usually be able to find a way of understanding more clearly the motivations operating in his own particular market, whether it be in the industrial, consumer or service sector. He can then proceed to build on this understanding to develop a marketing approach which will meet his customers' specific requirements.

The models described below summarise some of the main theories which have been used to explain customer behaviour. They may be employed or rejected as the individual marketer sees fit; it should be noted, however, that they have all provided insights which have proved invaluable in different marketing situations.

The rational, economic model The idea of the rational customer is based largely on the writings of theorists in economics. In their attempt to understand how a customer allocates his resources of disposable income, they propose a model whereby the customer seeks to maximise his satisfaction or "utility" as return for payment.

This approach to customer behaviour

suggests that choice behaviour is determined by the utility derived from a purchase compared with the financial outlay necessary to acquire the item. The model ignores all the many non-price factors that marketing practitioners know to exist in given situations. One example of this is the economists' concept of the demand curve, which postulates that, in most situations, as the price of a product goes up, the demand for it will fall. This does indeed happen in many cases but there are many exceptions to this trend (see Question 21, "What price should we charge our customer?" for some examples and discussion of this).

The Pavlovian learning model According to this model of behaviour, learning is largely an associative process and most behaviour is conditioned by reward and punishment.

The modern versions of the Pavlovian model offer a number of insights useful to marketers. The model suggests, for example, that repetition and reinforcement are desirable attributes in advertising. In addition, it implies that in order to achieve its objectives, an advertisement must arouse strong drives in the customer, whether these are hunger, thirst, cold, pain or sex.

The Freudian psychoanalytic model This model is well known in at least some of its aspects and is widely used by advertisers. Its basic thesis is that the individual human being is a divided kingdom, where behaviour rarely allows of a simple explanation. The individual maintains a precarious balance between emotion and rationality, between instinctive drives and socially acceptable behaviour.

Using this model, the marketer can construct his message so that it appeals to the parts of the psyche which are not accessible to the consciousness but which are still likely to determine behaviour. One disadvantage of this model, of course, is that it is difficult to make generalisations about any particular market segment. However, very effective advertising campaigns have been devised which appeal to the customer's private world of hopes, fears and dreams.

The social-psychological model In this model, man is seen as primarily a social animal, open to influence from the broad culture in which he lives and from the sub-cultures with which he has chosen to identify.

In using this model, the marketer would draw on the importance to the individual's attitudes and behaviour of culture, sub-cultures, reference groups (that is, social groups to which the individual relates in his or her behaviour) and face-to-face groups.

The organisational buyer model The previous models concentrate on the drives, forces and influences which mould the individual customer. However, the organisational buyer (such as the purchasing agent) can be seen to respond to a rather different set of circumstances. These customers are buying not on their own behalf but on behalf of an organisation; their motivation, therefore, may be regarded as particularly complex.

This model suggests that organisational buyers are not impervious to personal appeals of the kind outlined earlier. However, they are also concerned to meet the needs of the organisation as satisfactorily as they can. They are, therefore, open to a dual approach by the marketer.

Behaviour in action

Whatever insights into customer behaviour are accepted as being useful for the individual marketer, it is a good starting point to regard such behaviour as comprising two related processes: perception and decision making.

Perception

All buying decisions are based on the perception and interpretation of information. However, perception is not a straightforward process: selection and distortion of information invariably occur when a customer perceives information.

Two main phenomena affect perception and should be thoroughly understood by the marketer. These are selectivity and subjectivity. *Selective perception* is a psychologist's term which means simply that people do not pay attention to all the information available in any communication. They pay attention only to those things which are important to them, be it price, styling or masculinity.

Subjective perception means that no two people will interpret the same communication in the same way. This phenomenon is the main reason why eye witnesses are frequently so unreliable. In the area of customer behaviour, customers are inclined to read into an advertisement what they normally expect from that source. If the customer has had a bad experience with a pre-prepared and packaged meal, all commercials for such products are likely to be viewed with suspicion. Customers selectively distort information in a manner which is consistent with previous attitudes.

Decision making

The decision-making process comprises two basic elements: beliefs and choice criteria.

All customers hold *beliefs* about the presence or absence of certain benefits among the brands available in a particular product class. It is known that customers do not notice all brands available in a given class of product. For example, if one were expected to decide rationally which deodorant to use, information on thirty or forty available brands would have to be processed. We know, however, that this never happens. Instead, what seems to take place is a phenomenon described as "bounded rationality". This is a short listing of acceptable brands. Out of the total set of deodorants, a customer in fact will make a purchase decision based on a group, or sub-set, of five or six brands which might possibly meet his or her needs. He or she has relatively little information about the other brands in the product class. The customer uses his beliefs about some of the benefits located in the smaller group to make a purchase decision.

A second factor influencing the purchase decision is the customer's *criteria for choice*. Potent, convivial, high quality, for example, are all potential choice criteria for one class of product. Choice criteria are simply those attributes of a product that the customer defines as important and desirable. These attributes must also allow distinctions to be made. That is, a shopper must be able to compare an attribute, such as freshness, in one brand to the freshness of another brand. Customers may find safety in a car an important criteria; but, if they are unable to discern a difference in the levels of safety between motor cars, safety cannot be numbered among their choice criteria.

Choice criteria are derived from the multitude of experiences a customer is able to relate to the product. There are also certain outside variables such as social class, ethnic origin and religious persuasion, which can help determine and mould choice criteria. This concept is probably the single most important aspect of buying behaviour. If a marketer understands his prospective customer's choice criteria, he can then set about the business of designing products consistent with them.

Many marketers have found that the division of choice criteria into "functional" and "non-functional" categories is a useful basis for marketing action. Functional criteria relate to the physical properties of a product - the colour of a suit, for example. Non-functional criteria relate to the non-physical properties associated with the product - the connotations which are evoked for the customer. Style, image and tone are often very important to the customer; they should be of equal concern to the marketer.

Having chosen the sub-set of products, and appropriate choice criteria, the customer is now in a position to make his decision. By comparing the products in his sub-set with the choice criteria, the consumer can arrange the various brands in an order of preference.

Customer behaviour: a review

The points made about customer behaviour can be summarised as follows:

- The first element in the buying process is the nature of the beliefs which the customer holds about the presence or absence of certain benefits among the brands available in a particular product class.

- For any particular type of product, the customer has various choice criteria. Choice criteria are simply those attributes of a product that the customer feels are important and desirable.

- These choice criteria are then used to select five or six most suitable brands from the entire product class. This smaller group of products, or sub-set, limits the purchase possibilities.

- Depending on how each of these brands in the sub-set meet the choice criteria, they can then be arranged in order of preference. Once this process is complete, the customer is in a position to make his purchase decision.

However, all these steps involve information, and information involves perception. Consequently, perception is an integral part of customer behaviour. There are two basic phenomena affecting perception:

- Selective perception refers to the fact that people tend to notice only those things which are important to them. The choice criteria are the important attributes and customers pay attention only to information about important attributes.

- Subjective perception, on the other hand, refers to the fact that different people are apt to interpret the same situation differently, depending on their fundamental attitudes.

And that, in outline form, is the way buyers behave. While the description is in no way foolproof, it does help a marketer to develop products and strategies that are consistent with customer-buying patterns.

Application questions

9.1 What is your organisation selling, both in the "functional" and "non-functional" sense? What is the customer buying? How can these answers be brought closer together?

9.2 What criteria does the potential customer use to decide whether or not he is in the market for your type of product or service? How does he decide between alternatives once he is committed to a purchase? Why is your own market offering chosen? What could you do to increase the likelihood of purchase of your market offering?

9.3 What is the model of buyer behaviour operating in your market? Who needs information and at what stage of the buying process is different information needed? Is there any way in which your organisation could improve its communications with potential customers?

9.4 How does your organisation encourage existing purchasers to purchase its products or services on future occasions? Is your organisation providing the right information in the right form to the right people?

Question 10
How can consumerism affect marketing?

Overview

Customers' complaints express dissatisfaction with the way in which organisations match their resources with customer needs. As such, they constitute a criticism of marketing practice. Accordingly, organised customer protest, (known as consumerism) must act as a spur to redoubled marketing effort, as encouragement to the organisation to devote even more care and attention to understanding what consumers need. This involves increased attention to segmentation of markets and the development of more suitable products or services for the different segments.

It is equally important that marketing should take care to present the true economic facts about products or services offered. The avoidance of exaggerated claims and a clearer indication of what can reasonably be expected in return for a certain price are important steps in the right direction.

Caveat emptor

In a perfectly competitive market place, all the products or services offered by an organisation would meet the needs of its customers and consumers at the requisite level of profits. As the situation is at present, however, consumers complain with an increasingly strident voice about the way businesses operate. What conclusions are to be drawn from this? Are the major companies not based soundly on a marketing philosophy? Or are the strident voices not representative of the wishes of the vast majority of customers?

Consumerism, the name given to a widespread of activities in the past decade, focusses our attention on the problem. Is marketing failing to do its job well, or are a small collection of agitators making something of nothing? The truth in most cases is probably to be found in the 80/20 rule: 80 per cent of the problem is poor marketing, and 20 per cent is populist agitation.

Traditionally, it has been argued that a bad product will sell only once. Its customers will reject it after unsatisfactory performance, and any organisation which persists in offering such products or services cannot long survive. Consumerists increasingly argue that a passive approach of this kind amounts to shutting the stable door after the horse has bolted. They usually want to see it made illegal for such products or services to be offered on the market in the first place. Most countries have passed a significant amount of legislation in support of this position. Up to the end of the nineteenth century, the doctrine of "caveat emptor" or "purchaser beware" was widely accepted, although customers and consumers had always enjoyed a certain amount of protection as a result of regulations imposed on traders. However, since the end of the nineteenth century, the responsibility for the quality of the product or service sold has fallen more and more on the shoulders of the vendor.

Caveat vendor

In most countries within the EEC today, customer groups have succeeded in obtaining massive legislative support. Sweden is perhaps the most extreme example, with its Consumer Ombudsman and Market Court. However, the UK has its own Director of Fair Trading and an impressive array of legislation, including the Competition Act which became law in April 1980, and gives the Director of Fair Trading increased powers of intervention. As an illustration of legislation which supports customers' rights, we can perhaps take the concept of "implied terms of sale". In 1973, a statutory responsibility was laid upon a supplier of goods in the UK to ensure that any goods were indeed good for the purpose for which they were promoted and sold. This reversed the dictum, "caveat emptor", to "caveat vendor", or "seller beware".

Although many businessmen resisted this trend, it is difficult to see why they should feel that a change of this kind damaged their interests. No marketer, surely, would doubt that trust was an important element in his relationship with his customer. That customer groups, or politicians with or without populist agitation, had to lobby and get laws passed to secure this sort of relationship with suppliers is an indictment of marketing activities throughout Europe and beyond.

The marketing of children's toys provides an example of how customers, consumers and company objectives can all be satisfied by careful business practice. The successful toy companies of today are those which inform parents that their products are not potentially dangerous, not coated with lead paint, and not destroyed the hour after they are first pressed into active service. Fisher-Price is one of the most successful toy manufacturers. Since 1968, it has eschewed child manipulative promotion, carefully tested its products with children for durability, safety and purposeful play, and charged the prices necessary to make and market "good" toys. Sales and profit margins are impressively good.

Consumerism's way to better marketing

Consumerism is pro-marketing; it wants the marketing approach to business implemented in a sincere rather than cynical spirit. The cynical implementation, which consumerists claim has been all too widely practised, is no better than high pressure salesmanship or misleading puffery. The sincere implementation of the marketing approach entails respect for each individual customer served. Indeed, the consumerist argues eloquently that the sort of relationship found between a manufacturer and a customer in, say, a capital goods market should be created in consumer markets. And, in so far as that is both economically feasible and what the consumer really wants, marketers must surely want it also.

Broadly, consumerists argue that recognition of the following consumer rights would ensure that a more satisfactory relationship would be built up between organisation and customer (see Figure 10).

Figure 10

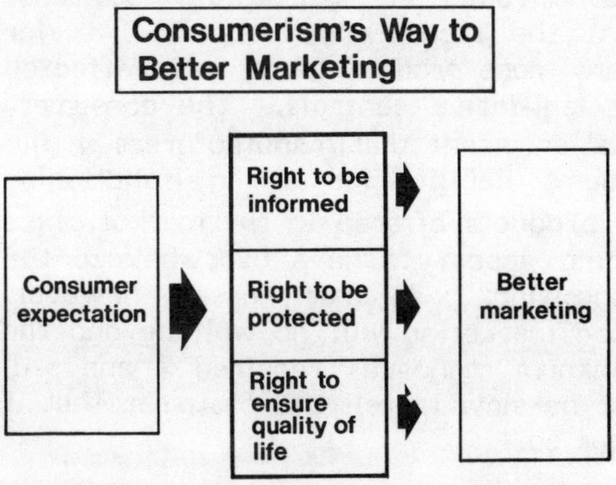

Consumerism's Way to Better Marketing

Consumer expectation → Right to be informed / Right to be protected / Right to ensure quality of life → Better marketing

The right to be informed of the true facts involved in any buyer-seller relationship. Some of the key aspects, which have already been subject to legislation or regulation in Europe, include: the full cost of credit/loans taken up, often known as "truth-in-lending"; the true cost of an item, under the slogan "unit pricing"; the basic constituent elements of products, known as "ingredient informative labelling"; the freshness of foods, discussed generally as "open-dating"; and "truth-in-advertising".

The case against producers is that they either mislead through exaggerated claims or fail to tell the whole truth about their products or services. Consumerists believe that the individual has the right to know these truths. Again, who can doubt that this demand, if sincerely felt, should be met? Who would be unwilling to tell an industrial purchaser the answer to basic questions about any merchandise offered for sale? What other information would our customers like? Can we not track it down before they clamour?

The right to be protected is also a major plank in the consumerist platform. All too often at present, consumerists argue, consumers' trust in organisations is abused. Safety standards (which are monitored by government agencies) and the quality of medicines (which are subject to statutory controls) are exceptions which all businesses could learn from. It is certainly the case that the trend within the EEC is for many more product fields to be affected by legislative controls. The consumerists' argument that manufacturers should assume liability for any malfunctioning of products offered in the market place would appear to have overwhelmed the opposition. In most cases, however, good marketing will go well beyond the minimum standards required - and will not be slow to tell the customer that it does so.

The right to ensure quality of life is perhaps the most difficult demand for the marketing activity to satisfy. Nonetheless, if a meaningful segment of the market needs to perceive the products it purchases as furthering the quality of life, then that is a need that should be respected. The non-biodegradability of packaging, for example, has been shown on occasion to offend substantial numbers of customers. If a sufficiently large group of these customers is prepared to meet an organisation's research and development costs, along with the costs involved in changing to a preferred alternative, then good marketing should lead the organisation to work with these customers towards a change in its methods of packaging.

It should be emphasised that none of these rights is unfamiliar to the marketer of industrial or consumer products. He has been accustomed to responding to similar demands. What is different today is that the process of marketing is no longer done on the initiative of the marketer in a framework of caveat emptor. The framework is no longer paternalistic. Today, the customer works through representative institutions, even unions - and the cry is caveat vendor.

Consumerism will affect marketing by bringing into being a more informative approach to all forms of marketing communication. It must, and will, give rise to a greater integrity in the advertising and promotional puffery of our profession without, one hopes, making life too dull, too much like a company share issue prospectus. It will give rise to a greater concern amongst all levels of business management with the long-term social implications of the materialistic bias of our society. Does the continual emphasis on immediate material expectations bear some responsibility for the level of delinquency in our society? What are the implications for tomorrow of our present pattern of usage of raw materials or pollution of the environment? The outcry in France over the pollution of the sea shores by manufacturers was a recent instance of protest against pollution; rapid action followed.

The consumerist argues that in present-day Europe we can certainly afford to trade off some of today's advantages for the longer term interests of society.

Consumerism as an opportunity

The social emphasis of consumerism, particularly its demands for an enhanced quality of life, is no threat to profitable enterprise. In considering this point, organisations might find it helpful to draw an analogy with changing attitudes to social factors at work. From the mid-nineteenth century, manufacturers were compelled by law to ensure that unsafe machinery was fenced in; considerable cost was, of course, incurred in carrying this out. Within the office, modern times have seen a concern to obtain office furniture and equipment designed to promote comfort at work; again, the introduction of such equipment has been an expensive business. It may well be that, in the long term, fewer accidents and a happier workforce will help improve an organisation's overall profitability. Even if this does not happen, however, the organisation should bear in mind that society expects the cost of safety at work to be included in the price of a product or service. Consumerism, like safety at work, presents an opportunity for the organisation to adjust its approach in accordance with changing social standards. As an articulate expression of customer needs, consumerism demands a marketing response.

One of Britain's most successful consumer movements is the Campaign for Real Ale (CAMRA). Britain has always been a beer drinking nation; traditional beer, however, was fragile, difficult to transport, store and serve. The breweries' response was to introduce conditioned beers that were chilled, pasteurised and filtered for fermentation; they were then transported around the country in kegs or large tankers. The phasing out of real ales aroused a strong protest amongst certain sections of the community and eventually led to the founding of CAMRA, a lobby with a powerful voice.

Although CAMRA's attacks on lager have not stopped this segment of the market from growing, CAMRA has been successful in preventing the big brewers from phasing out real ales and cask conditioned beer. CAMRA's good beer guide which directs thousands of beer drinkers to pubs serving real ale has also revived interest in small traditional brewers. As a result of CAMRA's activities, the brewing industry has had to respond to the tastes of a small (only 14 per cent of sales) but vocal part of the beer-drinking segment. The case of CAMRA illustrates well how the voice of dissatisfied customers can present a marketing opportunity rather than a problem.

Consumerism calls out for the reformulation and development of products and services to meet the requirements both of short-term satisfaction and longer-term benefits. A closer look must be taken at the system of marketing values which asserts that immediate consumer satisfaction and longer term consumer welfare may be opposing goals for an organisation's marketing activity. It is now necessary - and good marketing practice - to promote products which provide consumers with both short- and long-term satisfaction.

In consumer goods markets, for example, marketing specialists have devoted most of their efforts to promoting desirable and pleasing products. They have tended to ignore the long-term disadvantages to society which often accompany such products. Consumerism has reminded us vociferously of these disadvantages and, in a very real sense, has given us the opportunity to be better citizens. It is possible now to design and sell a motor car that is considerably safer than its equivalent in 1960. At that time, attempts to sell safety were conspicuously unsuccessful even though car makers emphasised safety factors in their promotional literature. It is possible now to design and sell an effective flameproof fabric for children's wear because an awareness of the need for it has been created. Consumerism, in other words, opens up market opportunities which the astute marketing-based organisation will wish to take up. Other examples which can be cited are phosphate-free detergents, reduced lead content petrol, degradable plastic containers for a host of products, synthetic tobaccos, new nutrient based breakfast cereals and low polluting manufacturing systems.

In precisely the same way, retailing organisations have made great use of the popularisation of "unit pricing" to help them build their business. Use of this system involves informing customers of the price charged per standard unit, whether this is 100 grams or one ounce. A major supermarket chain introduced unit pricing as a key service to its customers, inviting them to exercise their own judgements about relative prices compared with relative quality. New trade was developed and existing customers affirmed that they found the service of considerable value. It was, they reported, something they frequently tried to do themselves, but found too difficult on the basis of a fresh exercise for each shopping trip.

The articulate customer movement known as consumerism is here to stay as a force acting on organisations in their market place. If respectfully used, it can provide a significant further input of information in the process of matching the resources of the organisation with the needs of its customers.

Application questions

10.1 When were you last disappointed in a purchase you made? Should you have been "protected" by official regulations, or did you deserve your disappointment? What sort of protection would have been reasonable? How would it have affected the marketer?

10.2 In what ways does your organisation respond to consumer reactions? Is there adequate guidance for how such reactions should be taken into account? In what ways could your organisation's procedures be improved?

10.3 How can your organisation use consumerism as a form of free marketing research? What new business opportunities does consumerism offer your organisation?

10.4 Does your organisation consider consumerism as something which increases manufacturing costs or as something which leads to increased long-term profitability? Suggest some reasons for this attitude. Identify ways in which your organisation could make consumerism work for it rather than against it. What changes would the organisation have to make in order to gain from consumerism? How could these changes be brought about?

Question 11

Is marketing unethical?

Overview

Many aspects of business activity have been subjected to searching criticism in recent years. Marketing in particular has been criticised heavily for its allegedly unethical foundations. It has been accused of using dubious means to sell goods and services to people who have no basic need of them. Critics of marketing have also argued that it contributes to materialism in society, that it elevates consumption to be an end in itself and that it leads to a wasteful misallocation of resources.

This Question presents a summary of arguments and counter-arguments commonly heard in the debate on the ethics of marketing. It also sets this debate within the context of the social and economic systems in which marketing is practised. It is suggested that marketing systems develop to meet society's requirements and, as these requirements change, so our marketing systems must adapt to the changing environment.

Is the consumer defenceless?

In recent years, dissatisfaction has been expressed by increasingly large numbers of people at the structure of a society which seems to have consumption as both its means and its end. Capitalism presents an unacceptable face, some believe, in as much as it promotes the growth of an acquisitive and materialistic society.

In the late sixties and early seventies, there was a growing consciousness of the problems that the age of mass consumption brought with it. A quite new awareness of alternatives that might be possible, indeed necessary, became apparent. This movement quickly found its chroniclers: books like Charles Reich's *The Greening of America*, Alvin Toffler's *Future Shock* and Theodore Roszak's *The Making of a Counter Culture* appeared on book shelves throughout the world. The message articulated in these and other testaments of the movement was basically a simple one: that people could no longer be thought of as "consumers", as some aggregate variable in the grand design of market planning. They were individuals intent on doing their own bidding.

Feelings such as these have led to critical examination of commercial activity of all kinds. As one of the more visible manifestations of such activity, marketing has been singled out for special attention. One criticism frequently brought against marketing is that it plays on people's weaknesses. By insidious means, it is claimed, marketing attempts to persuade the consumer that he or she must smoke this brand of cigarette or use this brand of deodorant; that without them their lives are somehow incomplete. This argument involves the notion of the defenceless consumer, a person who is like clay in the hands of a wily marketer and thus in need of protection. Such a view of marketing tends to exaggerate the influence that the marketer can bring to bear on the market place. It implies that consumers' powers of perception are limited in the extreme and that consumers' intelligence is minimal. It further suggests that skilful marketing can create needs.

This last point deserves close examination. Marketing may well be able to persuade people that they want a product; but that process should not be confused with creating a need. The sceptic might respond to this view by claiming, for example, that, "Nobody wanted television before it was invented; now it is a highly competitive market. That market must have been created". This argument confuses needs and wants. Clearly, nobody wanted television before it was invented; but there has always been a need for home entertainment. Previously, that need had been met by a piano, a book of parlour games, or something of that kind. Now technology has made available a further means of satisfying that basic need for domestic entertainment - television. Many consumers find that television better satisfies their need for home entertainment than did the piano.

A further example of how new technology can be used to extend an already existing market can be found in the spread of photocopying as the most common method of copying documents. The need to take copies of documents had already existed but had been largely met by the use of carbon paper. When photocopying was introduced as an alternative, it was soon recognised that the new method had many advantages over the old and that it enabled consumer needs to be met more exactly.

In these examples, as so often, the role of marketing has been to identify in as much detail as possible what the customer needs and then to persuade him or her that a specific product or brand will provide the most effective means of satisfying the expressed need. Underlying this view of marketing is the belief that consumers have certain perceived buying problems. They have needs which can be satisfied only through the acquisition of specific goods and services. Consumers seek satisfactory solutions to their buying problems, first, by acquiring information about available goods and services and their attributes and, eventually, by choosing that product which comes closest to solving the problem.

Any argument which depends on a view of the defenceless consumer must be rejected by a scrupulous marketer. The consumer is still sovereign as long as he is free to make choices - either choices between competing products or the choice not to buy at all. Indeed, it could be argued that by extending the range of choices that the consumer has available to him or her, marketing is enhancing consumer sovereignty rather than eroding it. It should be noted, too, that although promotional activity may persuade an individual to buy a product or service for the first time, promotion is unlikely to be the persuasive factor in subsequent purchases, when the consumer is acting from first-hand experience of the product. Although promotion may sell an unsatisfactory product the first time round, it cannot do so on future occasions.

Nevertheless, as we have observed, commercial activities of all kinds, including marketing, are being reappraised in the light of society's current criticisms. It is necessary, therefore, that we look very closely both at the ethics of marketing and at the kind of role which marketing assumes within the social and economic systems supporting it.

Some ethical concerns

Several specific issues have formed the focus of the debate on the ethics of marketing. The main issues to be discussed include: marketing's contribution to materialism; rising consumer expectations as a result of marketing pressure; and the use of advertising to mislead and distort. Let us look at some of the arguments involved in these discussions.

Marketing, it has been suggested, helps feed and in turn feeds on the materialistic and acquisitive urges of society. Implicit in such criticism is the value judgement that materialism and acquisitiveness are in themselves undesirable. Whether or not one holds

Question 11 Is marketing unethical?

with this view, there would seem to be a case here which marketing must answer. The prosecution in the case would argue that marketing contributes to a general raising of the level of consumer expectations. These expectations are more than simple aspirations: they represent on the part of the consumer a desire to acquire a specific set of gratifications through the purchase of goods and services. The desire for these gratifications is fuelled by marketing's insistent messages. Further, if the individual lacks the financial resources with which to fulfil these expectations, then this inevitably adds to a greater awareness of differences in society and to dissatisfaction and unrest among those in this situation.

The counter-argument that can be used here is that marketing itself does not contribute to rising expectations and thus to differences in society: it merely makes people aware of, and better informed about, the differences that already exist in society. Indeed, the advocates of the cause of marketing could well claim that in this respect its effects are beneficial since it supports, even hastens, pressures for redistribution. The defence in this case could also usefully point out that materialism is not a recent phenomenon correlated with the advent of mass marketing.

Much of the criticism levelled at marketing is in fact directed at one aspect of it: advertising. Advertising practitioners themselves are fully conscious of these criticisms. One booklet published by the world's largest advertising agency, J. Walter Thompson, was entitled: "Advertising - Is this the sort of work that an honest man can take pride in?". Within that publication were summarised six of the major arguments used by the critics of advertising.

"That advertising makes misleading claims about the product or service advertised.

That by implication or association it offers misleading promises of other benefits which purchase and use of the product will bring.

That it uses hidden, dangerously powerful techniques of persuasion.

That by encouraging undesirable attitudes it has adverse social effects.

That it works by the exploitation of human inadequacy.

That it wastes skills and talents which could be better employed in other jobs."

Supporters of advertising would point to the fact that advertising in all its forms is heavily controlled in most western societies, either by self-imposed codes (such as the British Code of Advertising Practice) or by legislation (such as the Trade Description Acts). It could also be claimed, on behalf of advertising, that you might be able to persuade people to buy something once through subtle advertising claims, but that sustained patterns of repeat purchase cannot be built up if the product itself is not perceived by the consumer to provide the gratifications he or she seeks. For example, we might be persuaded that Martini is indeed "The Right One", as its promoters claim, and we might give it a trial. However, if it fails to do the things we want it to do (that is, meet the needs we wish to satisfy) we will quickly turn to drinking something else and/or seek to gratify our needs in another way.

The debate about the ethics of marketing often confuses marketing institutions with the people who work in them. Clearly, there are dishonest businessmen who engage in activities that are detrimental to their fellow citizens. These activities include dubious trade practices, misleading advertising, unsafe products and various unethical practices that are harmful to consumers. However, it seems a grave error to criticise marketing institutions because of the practices of a small number of unethical marketers. It is clear, for example, that there are advertisers who engage in deceptive practices designed to mislead and possibly defraud consumers. Nevertheless, the institution of advertising can be used not only to inform consumers about potentially beneficial new products, such as new energy saving technologies, but also to promote non-profit community services, such as theatres and symphonies. This argument can, of course, be applied to all marketing activities.

Marketing and society

Any critical appraisal of marketing as an activity must take place within the context of the social and economic systems in which it is practised. A leading marketing scholar, the late Wroe Alderson, suggested the concept of *marketing ecology* as a useful approach to interpreting marketing's wider role. By this he meant the study of the continual adaptation of marketing systems to their environments; his suggestion was that the marketing systems in existence at any one time are simply reflections of the contemporary value system dominant in society. In systems technology, this approach would involve seeing marketing as an "organised" behavioural system which sustains itself by drawing on the resources of the environment and which survives only by adapting to changes in that environment. The environment represents not only the immediate surroundings of our customers and suppliers but also the wider phenomena which are embodied in technological, ideological, moral and social dimensions.

The environment exerts a number of continual pressures on a marketing system. Technology alone constantly demands change in any marketing activity; shortening life-cycles in all product fields bear witness to its clamourous effects. Many commentators have claimed that the rate of technological development is one of the most forceful catalysts for marketing change. Even greater perhaps than this pressure, however, has been the impetus for change provided by a radically different moral and ideological climate in society at large. The basic purpose of business activities today has come to be questioned and not only by those committed to alternative systems of exchange.

As has already been briefly discussed in this Question, marketing has been caught up in the broader issue of the social responsibility of business. Although there is a wide range of opinion about the meaning of "social responsibility", the implication is always that the organisation must look beyond the profit motive. Recent studies have shown that the vast majority of company executives acknowledge the interests of employees and consumers as well as the interests of shareholders. Executives are now being asked to acknowledge the interests of a "fourth estate": that is, society.

Although unlikely to abandon the profit motive as the primary focus of their attention, company executives are now increasingly exploring ways of conducting business where "social responsibility" is a salient criterion of success. The positive acknowledgement of the social dimension of corporate activity is likely to result in the deliberate use of marketing and marketing technology as an agent of social change. Already we have seen the adoption of a marketing approach by government agencies in attempts to gain participation in local planning decisions, to care for the countryside, to discourage the smoking of cigarettes, and so on.

When we talk about marketing, we are referring to more than just a set of techniques and procedures. We are alluding to an organised behavioural system which is constantly changing as it adapts to the evolving requirements of society. It is indeed the case that society gets the sort of marketing systems that it needs.

Question 11   Is marketing unethical?

Application questions

11.1   Identify a product recently bought by you which did not exist ten years ago. Did the marketer create your need for the product, or did the product satisfy a need which existed already? Do you consider that you were manipulated by the marketer? If so, how could such a situation be avoided in the future?

11.2   Consider a marketing practice of your organisation which might be held by some to be unethical. Would you defend it and, if so, how? Would the organisation suffer materially if the practice were changed?

11.3   Think of a form of packaging or other marketing activity adopted by your organisation which could be considered socially harmful. What would it cost to eliminate the damage and would your organisation, or society at large, be willing to pay the cost? What prevents these changes being made?

11.4   Within your own organisation, in what ways do marketers form society or does society form marketers? Should any changes be considered?

Unit III   Product decisions

Question 12   What products should we market?

Question 13   How do products make profits?

Question 14   How can we select and develop new products?

Question 15   Can we test new products before they reach the market?

Question 16   How can we estimate how much product we will sell?

Question 12

What products should we market?

Overview

We have seen that the strategy which an organisation adopts towards its offering in the market place is the most important factor in determining the organisation's long-term success. Continued successful performance, however, also depends on the ability of organisations to base their product offering on a dynamic view of the market place. In other words, organisations must recognise that the marketing environment will change over time and will demand a changed response from them. That response will typically take the form of a programme of adjustment to their product-market strategy.

Benefits not products

"Customers don't buy products; they seek to acquire benefits". This is the guiding principle of the Marketing Director of one of Britain's more innovative companies in the hair care business.

Behind that statement lies a basic principle of successful marketing. When people purchase products, they are not motivated in the first instance by the physical or objective attributes of the product but by the benefits that those attributes bring with them. Let us take some simple examples. You, the reader, bought this book not because it was *n* pages of printed paper bound together, but rather because it contained a promise to bestow certain insights about marketing. Those who buy and who read books seek specific benefits that are not limited to the physical product, in this case the printed page. If those benefits are provided more efficiently by some other product or service, then the consumer is likely to use the new product in preference to the old. Thus, certain segments of the book-buying public may well find that other information technologies, such as the microprocessor, serve their information needs more efficiently than books can. If this happens, book publishers will lose part of their market.

In the service sector, different segments of the market seek different benefits from investment portfolios. The older person wants a high interest yield; the younger person wants to grow capital at a rate higher than inflation. For both segments, however, the decision to assemble a portfolio arises from a wish to acquire certain financial and economic benefits rather than to buy specific shares. To take an example from industrial marketing, a purchaser of industrial cutting oil is not buying the particular blend of chemicals sold by leading manufacturers of industrial lubricants; rather, he is buying a bundle of benefits which includes the solving of a specific lubrication problem.

This last example provides another guide to identifying what it is that people buy. People buy one product rather than another because they see in it the best way of solving a particular "problem". Here the word "problem" means a consumer need requiring satisfaction.

The difference between benefits and products is not just a question of semantics. It is crucial that a company wishing to develop its business profitably should define its scope of activity, present and future, not in terms of the products or services that it offers, but rather in terms of the benefits that it provides or the problems that it solves. If the company takes too narrow a view of its business, by defining its business as the manufacture of, say, fountain pens, then it may run the risk of concentrating upon becoming better and better at producing fountain pens whilst gradually the market is turning to other forms of writing implement. The alternative approach would be for this company to recognise that the benefits it provides are in the field of written communication and that, if better or more cost-effective means of providing those benefits come along, then people will naturally move towards the new product which makes use of such developments.

One famous marketing author, Theodore Levitt, called the narrow, product-based view of the business "marketing myopia". That particular ailment has been the cause of the decline of many previously successful companies. He pointed out that companies buy $\frac{1}{4}$" drills because they need $\frac{1}{4}$" holes. While the need for making holes may endure, the mechanical drill may soon be replaced by another technology. Marketing myopia results from confusing products with markets. You will recall our Swiss watchmaker in Question 1, who was confident that the development of electronic watches would not seriously affect his company's business: while some people may always have the need to know the time of the day, such people may not need a mechanical watch to do so. To overcome myopia of this kind, the organisation must constantly review its product range by confronting the question: "Does each product provide relevant and desired benefits for today's needs?". Answering this question objectively requires a knowledge of the market beyond simple head-counting and demographics. To answer the question, the organisation must regularly conduct benefit-needs research which includes the benefit segmentation analysis discussed in Question 8. Many organisations have proved the value of such research. In the male hair control market, for example, Brylcreem would have been replaced by hair sprays and other competitive products had its manufacturer not undertaken extensive research to reformulate and reposition the product to meet market needs.

It is easier than one might think to ask customers to describe the benefits that they derive from existing products. It is rather more difficult to elicit information on benefits that ideally the customer would like but which currently are not provided. It can be done, however, as one French manufacturer of floor polish has shown. Group discussions with housewives indicated that there were something like twenty benefits which, to a greater or lesser degree, were sought by users of this type of product. The benefits included "stands up to damp mopping", "provides a lasting shine", "no streaks", "non-slip", and so on. A further sample of housewives were questioned on what combinations of such benefits they most preferred. They were also asked to rate existing products in terms of how well they provided these benefits. What emerged from this study was a detailed basis for the development of a new product and the design of a whole new approach to marketing that product.

Matching products and markets

In Question 1 we defined marketing as the process of matching an organisation's resources with customer needs. The product is the vehicle whereby this matching is achieved. Because the product is central to the fortunes of the company, the need for a defined policy towards products is all important. Put at its simplest, the product will only continue to provide the means whereby *company* objectives can be met if it concurrently provides the means whereby *consumer* needs are met. Figure 11 illustrates this idea.

The art of successful product management, therefore, must be based on a clear view of just *how* the present and future product range will continue to meet these twin goals of satisfying

Question 12 What products should we market?

customer and company objectives.

As a first stage in successful product management, it is essential to think of the "product" as a variable in the marketing mix, in the same way that we might consider price or promotion.

Figure 11

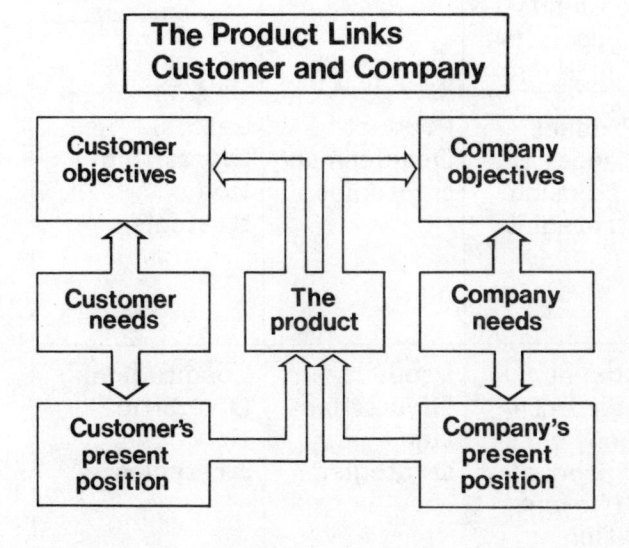

```
         The Product Links
         Customer and Company

  Customer                    Company
  objectives  <----------->   objectives
      ↕           ↕               ↕
  Customer      The           Company
   needs  <-- product -->      needs
      ↕           ↕               ↕
  Customer's                  Company's
   present   <---------->     present
   position                   position
```

Freedom to exploit the product variable largely depends on the internal resources of the firm, the market opportunities and the competitive threats. (The technique most commonly used to assess these factors is a Strengths, Weaknesses, Opportunities and Threats analysis (SWOT) which is discussed in more detail in Questions 14 and 29). Pertinent questions which help to establish the appropriateness of an organisation's current product market strategy include the following:

- What benefits do customers seek in this type of product? Does our product provide these benefits in greater proportion than competitors' products?

- What competitive product advantages are causing us to gain or lose market share?

- Does our product range still provide "value-in-use" to customers in relation to its cost to them?

- Does each product in our range still meet the corporate objectives set for it?

The answers to these questions will provide a firm basis for developing a product-market strategy.

Product-market strategy

What is "product-market strategy"? Very simply, it is the totality of the decisions taken within the organisation concerning its target markets and the products that it offers to those markets. "Strategy" implies a chosen route to a defined goal and suggests an element of long-term planning. Thus, the product-market strategy of the firm represents a decision as to the current and future direction of the firm. It looks forward from the market segmentation issues discussed in Question 8 towards the selection of new products to be described in Question 14.

Effective planning is the hallmark of the successful organisation. Product-market strategy is the means by which the company plans for growth. Clearly, the growth must have purposeful direction if future profits and cash flows are to be maximised. The two main directions of commercial growth plotted out in product-market strategies are *product development* and *market development*. Table 2 illustrates the concepts employed.

Some product-market strategies are less costly to pursue than others. The marketing director must develop his or her strategy with the cash flow and profitability requirements constantly in mind. It follows that a sound marketing approach will attempt, initially, to increase profits and cash flow from existing products and markets, as this is usually the easiest and least costly course to follow. Some examples, however, can illustrate the total pattern of strategy at work.

Table 2   Product-market strategies

| | PRODUCT ||||||
MARKET	*Present*	*Product Modification* - quality - style - performance	*Product Range* - extension - size variation - variety variation	*New products in related technology*	*New products in unrelated technologies*
Present	Market Penetration strategies	Product Reformulation strategies	Product Range Extension strategies	Product Development strategies	Lateral Diversification strategies
New	Market Development strategies	Market Extension strategies	Market Segmentation - product differentiation strategies	Product Diversification strategies	Longitudinal Diversification strategies
Resources and/or distribution markets	Forward or Backward Integration strategies				

Market Penetration Heinz extended the consumption of its canned soups (traditionally a winter purchase) by promoting the idea of celery soup, drunk hot or cold, as a suitable summer time purchase. In its promotion, the company emphasised the celery/summertime/slimming connotations.

Market Development A British hotel chain has opened up a new market by offering "Leisure Learning" weekends in its hotels.

Market Segmentation A German food manufacturer added a range of large size packs to his existing range which was selling well. This addition opened a new market segment among catering users.

Product Reformulation An Italian car manufacturer found that poor finish and subsequent rust were proving costly in terms of lost sales. A rust proofing programme has not only won back dissatisfied customers but has attracted new customers who began to be critical of their current car and switched to the Italian manufacturer because of the promise of extra quality.

Question 12   What products should we market?

Product Range Extension A European breakfast cereal manufacturer found that his new variety pack became very popular amongst children who were no longer "locked in" to one type until the pack was emptied.

Product Development Some companies manufacturing transistor radios have greatly increased their market by combining the radio with an alarm clock and/or a cassette tape player.

Lateral Diversification A successful French company in the materials handling market acquired a small warehouse design consultancy which then enabled the company to offer a complete package to its customers.

Longitudinal Diversification An Irish television rental company successfully launched an office equipment leasing company into an area hardly known before. Hitherto, office equipment was purchased. Leasing became an attractive and profitable alternative for both customer and the company.

Forward Integration A British wallpaper manufacturing company found that market share, profit and cash flow were all much improved by owning its own retail outlets.

Backward Integration A Dutch dairy producer found that moving back to own dairy herds smoothed out supply problems and helped to improve service to customers.

Application questions

12.1 Identify the benefits you bought when you made your most recent purchase for your home. Did the marketer help you see the benefits arising from ownership of his product or service, or did you have to imagine them for yourself? Was there any additional information which you wished that the manufacturer had provided? Had he provided any information which you felt to be inappropriate or misleading?

12.2 What benefits do your organisation's products or services provide? How will people acquire those benefits ten years from now? Will your organisation still be in a position to provide the benefits?

12.3 How could your organisation improve its position in the market?

(a) by moving back in the material supply chain?
(b) by moving forward closer to the consumer?
(c) by repackaging existing products?
(d) by introducing new products to existing markets?
(e) by introducing existing products to new markets?

At both a formal and informal level, how does your organisation identify, monitor and evaluate the possibilities? Identify ways in which you feel the relevant procedures could be changed or improved.

Question 13

How do products make profits?

Overview

Products make profits for the company by effectively providing customers with the benefits they seek within carefully controlled cost and revenue parameters. The concept of the product life cycle is a particularly useful tool for marketers. The marketer can use the concept, along with his carefully acquired knowledge of his particular market, to assess whether a product is in a stage of growth, maturity or decline. He can then go on to develop appropriate marketing strategies.

Decisions on product-market strategy must be made in the context of a product range portfolio which should contain a suitable balance of growth products, mature products and declining products. Only if such a portfolio is built up, will the organisation have a sound base on which to plan for future development.

The product life cycle

The successful development of any organisation depends both on the profit-making capacities of individual products and on the way in which these products complement each other in the market place. Let us first consider the way in which individual products generate profits.

The concept of the product life cycle

Marketing practitioners have made extensive use of the concept of the product life cycle ever since it first emerged in the marketing literature. In its simplest form, the concept suggests that any product or service moves through identifiable stages during its life and typically exhibits the generalised pattern of sales shown in Figure 12.

Introduction into the market marks a period of slow growth when profits are almost non-existent as the company still has to recoup the costs of product development and introduction. In this early stage, only a few people, known as "innovators", buy the product. If it is successful, the product then moves into its *growth* stage when large numbers of people (the so-called "early adopters") account for increasing sales. Repeat purchases grow and word-of-mouth reputation develops. Often, competitor organisations see a potential market, imitate the product and, by adding their weight to the promotional expenditure, accelerate an increase in the total sales of the product.

However, no market opportunity is

Figure 12

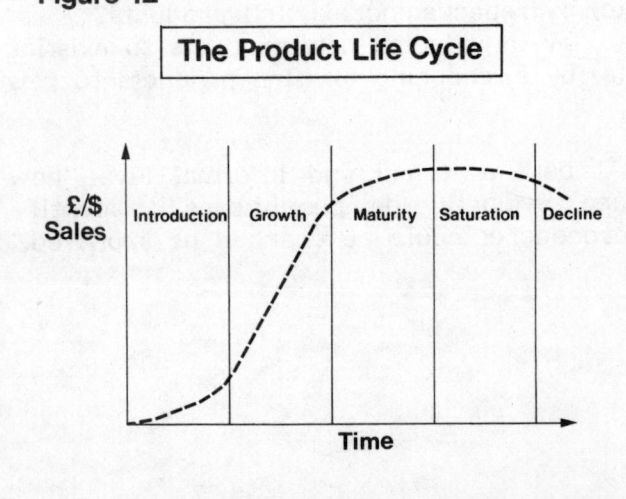

The Product Life Cycle

£/$ Sales vs Time: Introduction | Growth | Maturity | Saturation | Decline

infinite and, ultimately, the rate of sales slows as the product moves into its *maturity* stage of life. At this stage there are few new sales to be obtained. Repeat purchases from loyal customers, along with some customers won from competitors, are the only source of a possible increase in sales. As the product reaches the point of market *saturation*, there will normally be no further sales expansion unless the company modifies its marketing mix. Eventually, the product moves on to the *decline* stage of its life cycle where, despite often desperate actions, sales continue to decline as the product is replaced by a new generation of product innovations.

Uses of the concept

One of the main values of the concept of the product life cycle is that it enables the marketer to ensure that he adjusts his activities to meet the different requirements of his organisation's products at different stages of their lives. Clearly, before this can be done, careful analysis must be made of the individual life cycles of the different products offered and of the particular markets into which they are being sold. The importance of the concept lies not in offering hard and fast rules but in providing a framework for developing specific marketing strategies.

In using the concept of the product life cycle, it is important to distinguish the life cycle of the product *class* (for example, reprographic equipment) from that of the product *form* (for example, photocopying) and the specific *brand* for example, IBM). The concept applies differently in each of these three cases. The life of the product class, for example, tends to be much longer than the lives of the other two types; the product form seems to correspond more accurately with the "ideal" product cycle shown in Figure 12; and the product brand tends to follow an erratic course, largely because of changing competitive strategies. If the marketer takes care to make such distinctions, he may well be able, for example, to distinguish certain patterns of movement in sales of a brand and yet know that these may have no relationship to basic trends in the overall market for the product class or product form.

From a management point of view, the product life cycle concept is useful principally in that it focusses our attention on the likely shape of things to come if we take no corrective action. As we saw in Question 12 when considering the product-market matrix, there are several courses of action open to a company in its attempts to maintain sales of its products. Figure 13 illustrates how one company in the automobile lubricants field was able to maintain market leadership by "rejuvenating" the life cycle of a particular brand. As growth in sales began to slow for the brand, the company initiated a programme of product range extensions and market developments which successfully took the brand into additional stages of growth. At the same time, the company was aggressively seeking new products and even considering potential areas for diversification. This company had recognised the value of the product life cycle concept and had gone on to manage it to great effect.

An additional useful feature of the concept is that, when a drop in sales occurs, the organisation is encouraged to look not just at the promotion, place and price elements of the marketing mix but also to examine closely the product itself. Has it passed beyond its growth period? Should basic changes in formulation be considered? Again, an associated close analysis of the particular markets involved is necessary to arrive at an accurate assessment of the situation. When, for example, the manufacturers of Brylcreem found that sales were falling, they decided, after careful analysis of the situation, that the product itself was in need of re-formulation. Accordingly, they changed both the nature and the image of the product and succeeded in re-positioning it in the market.

In similar circumstances, other organisations have come to the conclusion that a product has reached the end of its profitable life cycle and should be allowed to die. That is, they have decided that the large amounts of money that could be spent on giving a declining product "a new lease of life" would be better spent on building up a new product. Several manufacturers of convenience desserts have followed this course of action.

Whatever the circumstances, the art of successful product management lies in assessing the stage of life which individual products have reached and in determining the most appropriate marketing strategies for those products.

Figure 13

Product Market Strategies and Product Life Cycle

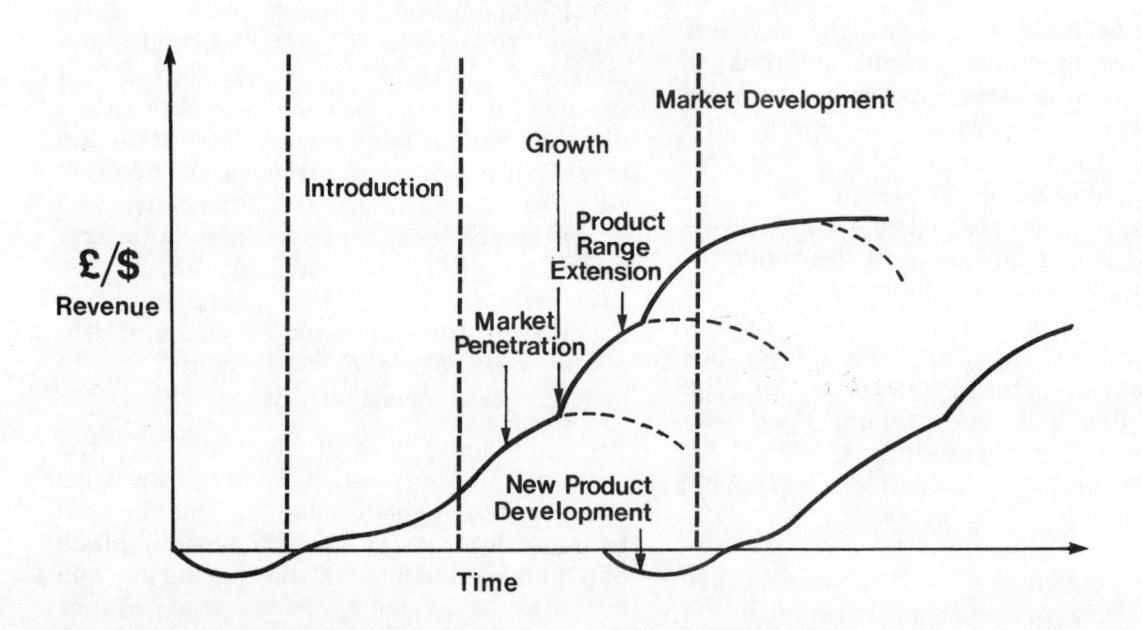

The product portfolio

The majority of companies offer more than one product and operate in more than one market. Decisions on product-market strategy, therefore, must be made in the context of a *product range portfolio* and the defined market segments to which this portfolio is marketed. At any particular time, the profitability of the firm will depend upon the individual profitability of each of the products in its portfolio. A review of a company's portfolio would typically reveal products at various stages of growth, maturity and decline. The precise balance of that portfolio would not only indicate today's profitability but would also provide a sound guide to tomorrow's profitability.

A product portfolio is in many respects similar to the investor's portfolio of stocks and shares. The investor may wish to achieve a balance between yield or income and capital growth. Some shares might produce more of the latter and less of the former, while others counteracted this pattern. Or the investor might attempt to achieve a balance in terms of risk - some shares having a higher risk of capital loss, against which must be balanced the prospect of higher returns.

The company will also seek to assemble a portfolio that will meet its objectives - be they objectives of growth, cash flow or risk. As individual products progress or decline, and as markets grow or shrink, then the overall nature of a company's product portfolio will change. It is imperative therefore that the whole portfolio is regularly reviewed and that an active policy towards new product development and divestment of aged products is pursued.

The Boston Matrix

One approach towards product portfolio review that has gained considerable recognition in recent years is the "Boston Matrix", named after its originators, the Boston Consulting Group. The thinking behind the Boston Matrix is simple, yet it has profound implications for the firm.

Usually discussions of product life cycles are conducted in terms of the sales of the product, or perhaps the profit accruing to it. However, there is a further consideration which may be of even more importance in product portfolio decisions, and that is cash flow. Profits are not always an appropriate indicator of portfolio performance: they will reflect changes in the illiquid assets of the company, such as inventories or capital equipment, and thus do not indicate the scope for future development available to the firm.

Cash flow is a key determinant of the firm's ability to develop its product portfolio. To emphasise this, the Boston Consulting Group developed a means of classifying products within the firm's portfolio according to their cash usage and their cash generation.

In their matrix, products are classified according to their positions on two dimensions: Relative Market Share and Market Growth Rate. *Market share* is used because it indicates the extent to which the product should be capable of generating cash. The measure of market share used is that of the product's share relative to the largest competitor. This is important because it reflects the degree of dominance enjoyed by the product in the market. *Market growth* is used as an indicator of the product's cash requirements.

Figure 14 summarises the categories employed in the matrix.

Figure 14

The Boston Matrix

Product Categories

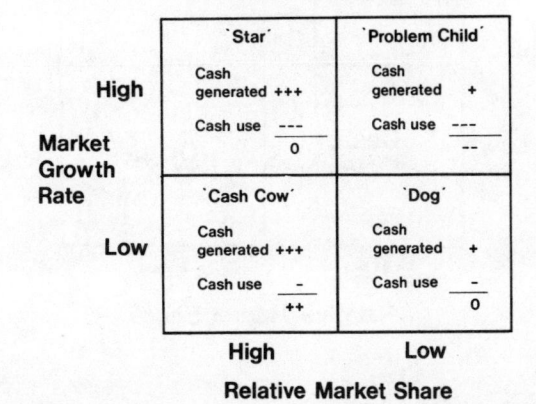

	High Relative Market Share	Low Relative Market Share
Market Growth Rate High	'Star' Cash generated +++ Cash use --- 0	'Problem Child' Cash generated + Cash use --- --
Market Growth Rate Low	'Cash Cow' Cash generated +++ Cash use - ++	'Dog' Cash generated + Cash use - 0

The graphic labels, "Problem Child", "Star", "Cash Cow" and "Dog", used to describe products in each of the quadrants give some indications of the market position and prospects of a product in those categories. Thus, the Problem Child is a product which has not yet achieved a dominant market position, or perhaps it once had such a position but has slipped back. It will be a high user of cash because it is in a growth market.

The Star is probably a relatively new product that is still growing but has already achieved a high market share. On balance, it probably is more or less self-financing in cash terms. The Cash Cows are yesterday's stars which have retained their high market shares, but are in markets where there is little additional growth. As the name suggests, the Dogs are those products which have little future and may indeed be a cash drain on the company. They are probably candidates for divestment.

The art of product portfolio management is to develop a mix of products that in cash terms will be more or less self-funding in total. Thus, over time in a well-managed business, one might expect products to move through the matrix as in Figure 15(a) below. The flow of funds within the firm might appear as in Figure 15(b).

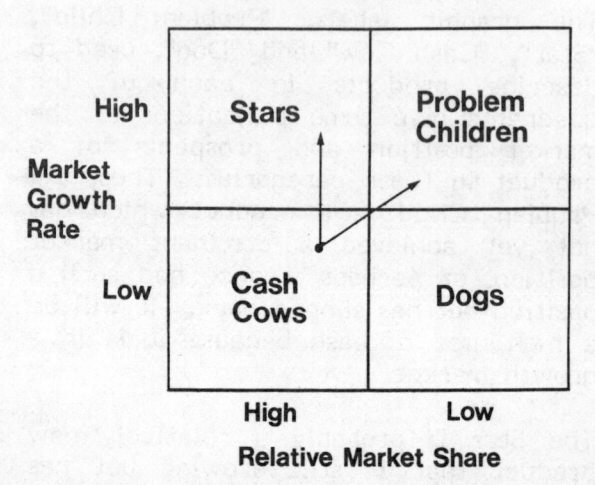

The Boston Matrix may be used to develop a forecast of how a company's portfolio might look in, say, five years time. In Figure 16, a manufacturer of office copiers and associated equipment has identified the current position of his product range and has also forecast the expected position in five years' time. The area of each circle is proportional to the product's contribution to total company sales volume.

Figure 15a
The Boston Matrix
Ideal Product Development Sequence

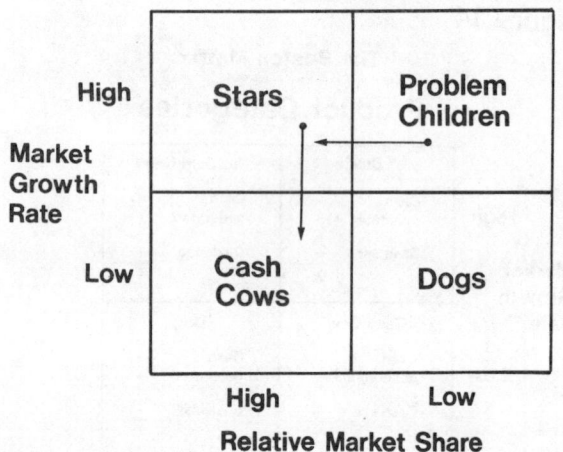

	High Relative Market Share	Low Relative Market Share
High Market Growth Rate	Stars	Problem Children
Low Market Growth Rate	Cash Cows	Dogs

Figure 15b
The Boston Matrix
Internal Flow of Funds

	High Relative Market Share	Low Relative Market Share
High Market Growth Rate	Stars	Problem Children
Low Market Growth Rate	Cash Cows	Dogs

Figure 16
The Boston Matrix
Product Portfolio Movement

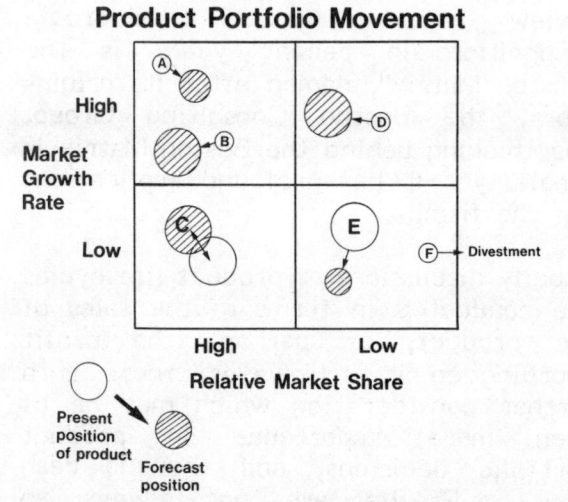

The definition of high relative market share is conveniently taken to be a ratio of 1 and above relative to the largest competitor. The cut-off point for high versus low market growth needs to be defined according to the specific circumstances prevailing in the markets in which this company operates, but here the company has taken a figure of 10%.

This analysis enabled the company to formulate a policy towards new product development, as well as to decide on

Question 13 How do products make profits?

the policies that needed to be pursued towards existing products in order that a balance could be maintained within the company's portfolio. Use of the Boston Matrix is particularly helpful in demonstrating to senior management the implications of different product-market strategies and highlighting potential weaknesses in current strategies.

Planning for profits

To ensure successful growth, all organisations must aim for a balanced product portfolio which contains:

- a substantial number of new products which will provide major profits in the future;

- a sufficient number of mature products to generate enough money to finance the growth products;

- a planned phasing out of products which in the past have been major products but which are beginning to be a drain on the company's resources.

An appropriate balance between products will provide management with a sound basis on which to plan for future development.

Application questions

Note: The word "product" is used in these application questions to include services. All the questions are as relevant to the marketing of services as they are to the marketing of products.

13.1 Briefly analyse and define your organisation's product portfolio in terms of the Boston Group's categories. Is the portfolio evenly balanced? How could it be improved: by elimination, by addition or by attempts to change the positions of existing products?

13.2 How would you define your organisation's products in terms of the stages outlined by the product life cycle concept? How much of your organisation's profitability is coming from products or additions to the product range being developed to replace yesterday's "breadwinners"?

13.3 Where do you see your organisation being in five years' time? Which products will have been phased out or re-launched in a modified form? What new products or product extensions will have been added to the range?

13.4 Who is responsible for the balance of the product portfolio in your organisation? Is there adequate provision for "managing" new product developments and product re-launches? How could product management in your organisation be improved?

Question 14

How can we select and develop new products?

Overview

The selection and development of new products is a process vital to the success of nearly all organisations. The process requires the company to take both a MACRO and a MICRO view of product-market development. The macro approach involves the use of techniques to identify the gaps between current company performance and company objectives and to develop appropriate strategies to fill these gaps. The micro approach assesses the product in terms of its fit within the product portfolio and its contribution towards company objectives.

The major sources of new product ideas tend to be customers, scientists, competitors, salesmen and top management. Where a more structured approach is needed, a number of techniques have been developed to facilitate idea generation. Once generated, the ideas must be subjected to rigorous evaluation and analysis procedures.

Product-market development: the macro view

As we have seen, it is vital that an organisation's product development programme should be firmly based within the corporate plan. Most organisations ensure that this happens by taking, first of all, a macro view of product-market development. In Question 12 we emphasised the need for explicit objectives within an agreed definition of the business. Once these have been established, viable strategies can emerge, involving either market development or product development.

The usual method of arriving at both the objectives and the possible strategies is to conduct a *marketing audit* of the company. A marketing audit involves a thorough evaluation of the company's internal and external operating environments. Internal factors are the company's basic *strengths* and *weaknesses*; external factors are the *opportunities* and *threats* over which the company has no direct control. The identification of strengths, weaknesses, opportunities and threats is called a SWOT analysis.

One example of a strength is established customer loyalty. Products with high market shares ensuring good profits with strong cash flow positions are also strengths. On the other hand, a large proportion of products in the decline stage of their product life cycles could be a distinct weakness. One of the values of an analysis of this kind is that the identification of a weakness provides an opportunity to rectify the situation, even to the extent of converting it into a strength.

The external factors may be viewed in a similar light. Opportunities and threats may be posed by political and regulatory events at home and overseas. The recent huge increases in oil prices, for example, have had significant effects on almost all businesses. Long-term social changes should be examined during the audit and so too should technological developments.

The marketing audit comprises the first three steps of the planning process outlined in Question 3:

1. gathering relevant information about the external environment and about the organisation's internal resources;

2. identifying the organisation's internal strengths and weaknesses vis-a-vis the external market opportunities and competitive threats facing the organisation;

3. formulating some basic assumptions about the future.

As indicated in Question 3, marketing objectives are based on the results of the marketing audit. The audit indicates where we are; the objectives indicate where we want to go. Clearly, organisations often find that there is a gap between what they are trying to achieve and what they can expect from current operations. A technique known as gap analysis helps an organisation to identify the direction in which it must move in order to attain its objectives. Gap analysis involves assessing which company products are currently meeting which customer needs and identifying additional requirements which are not yet being met. This procedure will often indicate one or more of the strategic alternatives (such as market penetration or product range extension) discussed in Question 12. It is illustrated in Figure 17.

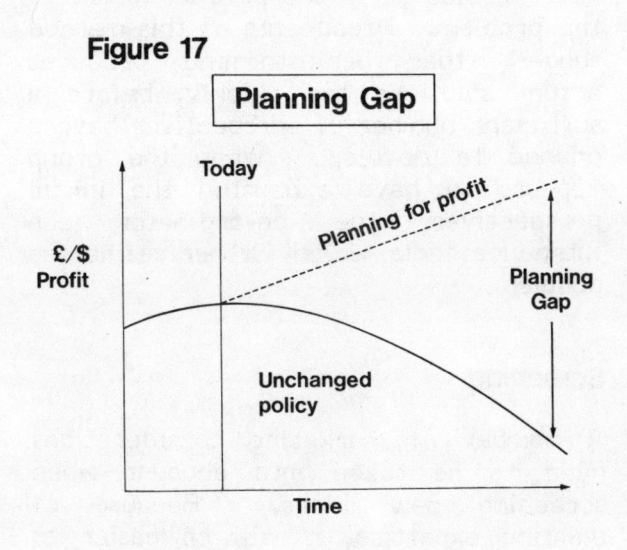

Figure 17

Planning Gap

[Graph showing £/$ Profit vs Time, with "Today" marker, "Planning for profit" dashed line going up, "Unchanged policy" curve going down, and "Planning Gap" between them]

Use of this technique ensures that the company evaluates systematically each possible strategy. Clearly, it is less expensive, in terms of R & D activity, production and marketing, to obtain growth from market penetration or market development strategies than from diversification policies which may necessitate a major acquisition on the part of the company.

New products: the micro view

After a marketing audit and gap analysis have clarified the place of new product development in a broad company context, the organisation must examine the micro considerations. These involve the range of factors that must be taken into account when a product is assessed in terms of its fit within the product portfolio and its contribution towards objectives.

New product development can usefully be seen as a process consisting of the following six steps:

Exploration The search for product ideas to meet company objectives.

Screening A quick analysis of the ideas to establish those which are relevant.

Business analysis The idea is examined in detail in terms of its commercial fit in the business.

Development Making the idea into hardware.

Testing Market tests necessary to verify early business assessments.

Commercialisation Full-scale product launch, committing the company's reputation and resources.

In the following discussion, we shall look at some of the main considerations involved in exploration and screening. New product testing will be described in the next Question.

Product conception and exploration

There are a number of sources of new product ideas but the major ones are customers, scientists, competitors, company salesmen and management. Customers, at all levels of distribution, are never reticent in this area and a number of profitable ideas have been suggested. A Yorkshire supermarket group suggested to manufacturers the idea of mushy peas as a new frozen foodline.

Scientists often look for commercial applications for their work. A great deal of sponsored work in universities is to this end. Competitors often introduce new products that prove successful and open the way to new opportunities. A French earth moving company successfully improved upon a unique sales feature of a competitor and moved ahead in market share.

Company salesmen by virtue of their proximity to the customer have first-hand experience of customers' unsatisfied needs - and of their complaints. This information can be obtained without too much difficulty by an appropriate reporting procedure. Top management knows the company's strengths and weaknesses and is in a good position to develop product policy. In their search for a profitable new product, they can use their familiarity with their organisation's situation to judge the relative importance of the different factors that must be taken into account. Thus, they may well direct the search amongst products which are complementary, use existing distribution channels and physical facilities, and so forth.

New product ideas are so vitally important for a growing company that a number of techniques have been developed and used quite successfully to ensure an adequate flow.

Attribute listing involves listing the attributes of an object and then modifying different attributes in a search for an improved specification for the object. For example, one might list the attributes of a hand food-mixer and consider modifications, such as nylon bearings, larger crank, or interchangeable beaters, to improve its performance.

Forced relationships is a technique in which product ideas are first listed then considered in relation to each other. An insurance company recently combined household effects insurance with personal effects insurance, thus giving a lower per unit cost for each insurance policy issued but a higher value per policy sold.

Brainstorming is often described as a creative conference, the sole purpose of which is to produce a large number of ideas. A group of six to ten people is given a brief outline of a problem and such technical information as may be required to determine any constraints. The group meets one or two days later simply to generate ideas. No criticism or evaluation is permitted; off the top of their heads, the group members generate ideas for subsequent evaluation. One major European oil company reported a successful brainstorming session to discover uses for a middle-distillate oil. In thirty minutes over one hundred ideas had been generated.

Operational creativity or *synectics* adapts brainstorming. Here, the brief is defined so broadly that participants have no clue as to the precise nature of the problem. Proponents of this method suggest that brainstorming produces actual solutions too quickly, before a sufficient number of perspectives have a chance to develop. When the group appears to have exhausted the initial perspectives, the co-ordinator can introduce facts which further refine the problem.

Screening

A number of marketing considerations need to be taken into account when screening new ideas. Because of existing expertise, it will be easier to sell a new product if it is *complementary to the existing range.* More-

Question 14   How can we select and develop new products?

over, the new product may well help sell more of the existing products. Price-quality relationships are important. To move too far away from a current relationship may upset existing customer images of the company and inhibit sales. A wide range of variation in qualities, sizes or flavours presents a number of problems, including customer confusion, excessive inventory holding and possibly excessive segmentation with high promotion costs.

If complementary products can increase total sales, then, conversely, substitutes may reduce total sales. The introduction of new products needs to be viewed in the context of the complete product range. Full advantage should be taken of distribution channel similarities. Using the capacity of existing salesmen, trade and retail contacts ensures both effective and minimum cost distribution and maximum market penetration. When additional gains can be achieved without a comparable increase in the means of gaining them, "synergy" is operating. Synergy can be summarised as the "2 plus 2 equals 5 effect". It would normally prove far less profitable to introduce a product requiring exclusive distribution facilities as, for example, if a dry goods grocery manufacturer were to introduce frozen foods rather than add another dry goods product which could be adopted without any fundamental change in distribution.

An even *level of demand* throughout the year is preferable to seasonal fluctuations unless the manufacturer produces products which have complementary patterns of seasonality. An uneven level of demand leads to problems of under-utilisation of labour and facilities. For similar reasons, a wide market can be preferable to one which is highly segmented and narrow.

A product which offers *protection* from competitive imitation is preferable to one with little or no protection. Protection may be offered by patents, by the need for large capital investment or by long development times. If the product itself is an imitation, the relative strengths and weaknesses of competitors should be assessed.

Since growth forms a basic objective for most companies, a new product should be one which demonstrates growth potential compatible with that required by company objectives. *Service requirements* must also be considered from at least two points of view. A technical product may well seem particularly attractive if the design eliminates much of the maintenance required by its predecessors or competitors. The second point of view would take into account the fact that the new product does have servicing needs and that the existing distribution channel may not have the ability to handle this work. This often proves a problem with diversification strategies.

For some products, the *protection considerations* may be just as important as the marketing factors and the organisation may need to consider such matters as location and size. Clearly, the use that can be made of existing plant capacity is important. The amount of additional investment is an equally important factor. Technical personnel are highly trained and specialist and their transfer competence to a new field must be considered. Also, a product requiring new raw materials may need new handling and storage techniques which may prove expensive.

Financial considerations relate to the product's ability to perform satisfactorily within the product portfolio when considered in terms of the company's economic objectives. Thus, cash generation and profitability are important. The risk of the investment, measured against current products and their development costs and income streams over time, must be considered in the light of company policy. Clearly, the product must pass the investment vetting used by the company in terms of payback, average return, net present value or internal rate of return.

Manpower requirements will vary both with size and complexity of the product project. Whatever these may be, the manpower considerations must be taken into consideration for planning purposes. The problems of industrial relations must never be overlooked, particularly when new technologies are introduced.

The *procurement factors* are important. National supply of materials may be preferable because of quality and reliability considerations. Known selling agents or vendors are easier to deal with. Supplier concentration may suggest that price and suitability problems can be expected if there are few suppliers. Erratic lead times in delivery of materials can cause havoc with production schedules if they are not previously known. At best, they mean high buffer stocks are needed as a safeguard against poor delivery. In a period of rapid inflation, price trends must be watched over time for cyclic or other crucial traits.

Testing

Arriving at any product idea is not easy; developing an idea to be ready for the market is even more difficult. To minimise failure, and to ensure early rejection where appropriate, it is beneficial to follow a rigorous evaluation and testing procedure. New product testing is examined in Question 15.

Application questions

Note: The word "product" is used in these application questions to include services. All the questions are as relevant to the marketing of services as they are to the marketing of products.

14.1   What was the most recent new product introduced by your organisation? How do you explain its success or failure?

14.2   What procedures were used to generate and develop the idea of your newest product? With the benefit of hindsight, how would you have changed these procedures?

14.3   In what respects is your newest product compatible with the rest of your product range? Are there other new products which would complement the range?

14.4   Has your organisation ever introduced a new product which was not compatible with the existing range? If so, how was the decision justified? With hindsight, should that decision have been taken?

Question 15

Can we test new products before they reach the market?

Overview

Whilst a steady flow of successful new products into the market place is a prerequisite for long-term corporate survival, the introduction of such new products is not without its hazards. Rigorous tests of market acceptability must be applied in order to reduce the risk of new product failure. Such tests must balance the cost of delay and the costs of information gathering against the benefits of reduced uncertainty.

New product testing can involve a number of stages. The CONCEPT TEST gives a broad picture of how acceptable the product concept is to its potential market. The QUALITATIVE SCREEN assesses the product's fit in terms of the company's objectives and resources. The ECONOMIC ANALYSIS examines the detailed economics of the project. The PRODUCT TEST assesses how potential customers react to the physical product when it is compared with competing products. The TEST MARKET reproduces the conditions of a full-scale launch on a much smaller scale.

New products: facing the risks

We have seen that new products are the life-blood of a company in its attempt to survive in a dynamic and competitive marketing environment. Marketing management must continually seek for viable and profitable new products, but it must be recognised that this is a task fraught with risk. For the majority of companies, the introduction of a new product into the market place involves a considerable investment, both in the development process and in the introductory stage when market acceptance has to be won if the product is to succeed. This investment can represent a considerable slice of a company's financial, physical and managerial resources and there can be no cast iron guarantee that the investment will yield an acceptable return.

In cases where a company has pinned everything on the success of a single new product, the product's failure to match expectations can lead to disaster. Consider the case of Rolls-Royce and the RB211. The company had committed major resources to an engine which, whilst technically unimpeachable, did not match the wants of a large enough section of the market to recoup the tremendous development costs. Hindsight would suggest that this was an unwise step to take. As it was, it almost led to the collapse of the company. In the consumer goods market, a major food manufacturer invested heavily in developing a new dessert. Careful testing indicated that the product would be acceptable to potential customers. The company proceeded to launch the product but found that retailers were unwilling to stock it as the type of packaging developed for the product led to problems in stacking. Since the main distribution channels planned for the product could not be used, the company was forced to withdraw it from the market, thus losing a substantial investment and upsetting its product portfolio.

This example can be matched by hundreds of others from consumer, industrial and service markets.

Research has indicated that, in some product areas, up to 80 per cent of all new product launches fail, in the sense that they do not meet marketing targets and are withdrawn soon after their introduction. Some product fields, such as grocery or cosmetics, are more prone to early deaths than others but, whatever the context, all the evidence seems to point to a high failure rate for new product introductions. It should be noted, however, that the criteria used by companies to judge success and failure in this context vary a great deal. One major food manufacturer undertook research on all products under development. Of four recent launches, three had been failures; but this was in the light of very stringent demands - the return on investment within twelve months along with a full volume of sales. Because of these high demands the products had been deemed failures - but most organisations would have counted them as major successes.

What then should be the role of marketing management in attempting to reduce the uncertainty that surrounds the new product launch?

There are no means of providing crystal-ball revelations about prospects for success or failure in this area; but some procedures can be very helpful in quantifying the risks implicit in a new product launch. This Question will explore some of these methods. However, before going on to do this, we should first look more closely at some other factors involved in the new product testing decision.

When the testing has to stop

It is always easy to postpone crucial marketing decisions by saying, "We need some more research". The problem with continually putting off the moment of decision is that delay costs money. In the first place, there is the cost (which can be substantial) of gathering further information. Secondly, there is the "opportunity cost" of foregoing profits which could be earned if the product was launched immediately and proved successful. However, these costs of delay must be balanced against the costs of proceeding too rapidly. These latter costs relate directly to the risk of failure in the market place; one would expect this risk to decline with every additional stage in the research and testing programme. We can view the trade-off between these two costs schematically as shown in Figure 18.

Figure 18

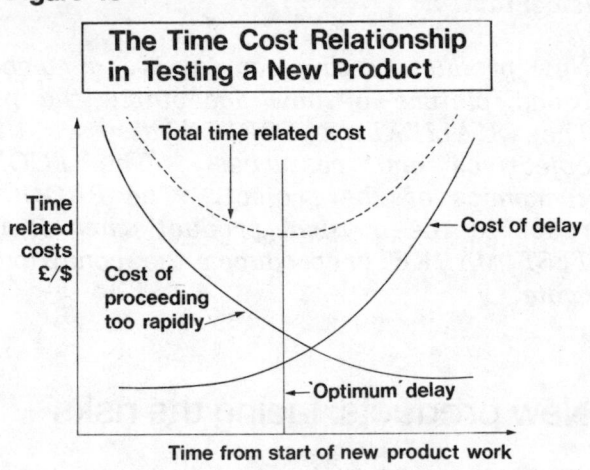

The Time Cost Relationship in Testing a New Product

Time related costs £/$

- Total time related cost
- Cost of delay
- Cost of proceeding too rapidly
- 'Optimum' delay

Time from start of new product work

Whilst our research technology is too primitive to allow us to determine where the optimum balance in this cost-benefit framework should be, the diagram serves to emphasise that the new product testing decision is a process of balancing the uncertainty surrounding a new product launch against the costs of reducing that uncertainty still further.

New product testing

Let us consider the means of testing available to a European manufacturer of sisal-based floor-coverings who markets his products to the "contract" market - a market where an intermediary, often either an architect or a purchasing agent, buys the product for use in offices, hospitals, schools, and so on.

Question 15 Can we test new products before they reach the market?

This is a fairly complex market where various types of floor-covering are available. It is a highly competitive market and, frequently, the floor-covering is specified on the basis of some total, overall scheme for interior decoration.

On the advice of marketing consultants, this company was attempting to formalise its new product testing procedures. Previously, they had tried to identify trends in styles and colours on the basis of past sales; and there had always been an attempt to perform a break-even analysis on the basis of projected costs and prices. Beyond this, new product testing was more a matter of technical assessment of product quality.

The consultants suggested a process of testing which involved several stages. (This process, which we shall go on to examine in detail, indicates activities which should take place, in one form or another, in all new product testing.) Each stage in the analysis provided the opportunity to pause and make one of three decisions: launch the product now, collect further information, or abandon the product now. The second two decisions were given the short-hand of PASS and REJECT.

In the case of the floor covering manufacturer, the sequence, illustrated in Figure 19, started with a test designed to give a broad picture of how acceptable the product concept was to its potential market. (This was accompanied by an initial appraisal of how the product might fit into the company's product portfolio.)

This *concept test* was administered by means of a dozen interviews, conducted by trained interviewers, with architects and purchasing agents representative of the target market. The purpose of the test was to expose them to details of the technical specification, possible colour range and recommended uses of the product. Sometimes artists' impressions of designs and colours were shown. The results of this stage of the test sequence were entirely qualitative but they served to eliminate all those products which were complete non-starters. It was scarcely possible to make a decision to launch the product at this stage.

The next stage was still qualitative; and in fact it was termed the *qualitative screen*. This screening process asked two basic questions in depth: is the product concept compatible with company objectives and is it compatible with company resources? Consideration of the first question involved such issues as: does the concept complement our existing market offering? is it compatible with the image that we seek and the segment of the market with which we identify? The second question raised issues such as: does the company have the capital to get this product to market and to develop an initial level of sales? does the company have the necessary knowhow and adequate physical facilities to handle the product successfully?

Figure 19

Stages of New Product Development

Concept Test →Pass→ Qualitative Screen →Pass→ Economic Analysis →Pass→ Product Test →Pass→ Test Market →Pass→ Full Launch (with Reject branches at each stage)

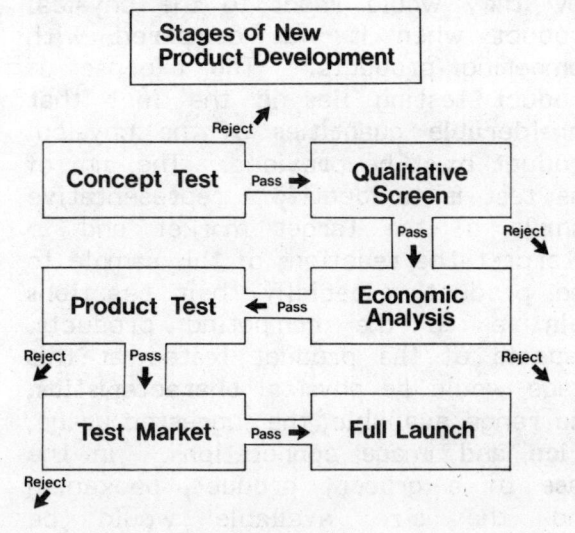

If the product concept survived this screening process, it was subjected to the next stage in the testing sequence: the *economic analysis*. This analysis was designed to examine the economics of the project under differing assumptions of costs incurred and revenue achieved. It was conducted at a fairly simple level as the company at that time had only a limited knowledge of how the market would react to products priced outside the narrow band with which the company was familiar. It was acknowledged that this stage of the testing sequence could be made considerably more sophisticated by applying the methods of investment appraisal that were in common use in other companies.

Once this stage of the testing had been successfully concluded, the company might feel sufficiently confident in the viability of the concept to move ahead to a full-scale market launch. Such a decision would have to be based on some highly positive results from the initial stages of the test sequence since the cost of setting up a production line, producing initial stock and developing and implementing a promotional programme would be substantial. More often a decision would be taken to go on to the next, and more expensive, stage of the analysis: the *product test*. The product test in this case was designed to gain impressions from a relatively large number of potential customers of how they would react to the physical product when it was compared with competing products. The expense of product testing lies in the fact that considerable quantities of the physical product must be provided. The aim of the test is to identify a representative sample of the target market and to interpret the reactions of this sample to the product, especially their reactions relative to the competing products. Aspects of the product tested at this stage would be physical characteristics, the range available, the suggested usage, price and image connotations. In the case of a grocery product, packaging and the size available would be important considerations. This company recruited a panel of architects and purchasing agents who were invited to compare, according to a number of appropriate criteria, the proposed new products with selected competitive products. The analysis of these results enabled a picture to be built up of how the proposed new product compared with existing products on a number of key dimensions.

It was at this stage that the company normally made the final decision as to whether or not to launch the new product. Clearly, there would still be some uncertainty about the new product's success but the sequential testing had enabled this uncertainty to be reduced to an acceptable level. The company could have gone on, as many companies do, to conduct a *test market*. The test market, as the name implies, is an attempt to reproduce the conditions of a full-scale launch but on a much smaller scale. Often a town, or geographical area, is chosen as representing the ultimate market; the product is launched in that town or area alone and its progress observed. As a test of this kind is very much an "experiment", it is necessary to ensure that conditions within the test market would be such that they could be fully reproduced on a national scale. For example, no extra promotional effort should be expended other than an amount proportional to the total to be spent in the proposed full-scale launch.

It should be noted, however, that test markets can never be completely reliable indicators of ultimate market performance. Quite apart from the problems of "grossing up" small-scale test market results to provide a global picture, there is always the possibility of unusual competitive activities which distort the results.

Whilst we have portrayed these stages of testing as a sequence, it should be clear that some of the stages could be conducted concurrently, as with the qualitative screen and the economic analysis. Whatever the sequence, the purpose of new product testing remains the same: to reduce uncertainty surrounding the new product to a level acceptable to the company whilst still enabling a launch to be made at the earliest possible time. The methods of product testing might vary from marketing situation to marketing

Question 15   Can we test new products before they reach the market?

situation but, whether the product be a new airline service, heavy-duty transformers, or a vinyl wallpaper, the principles are universal and the benefits considerable.

The consequences of inadequate research - or total lack of research - can be seen in many fields. Many hairdressers, for example, have extended their salons into beauty parlours by adding saunas, massage and other services. However, their anxiety to capitalise on fashion trends has not been accompanied by a thorough check on whether provincial High Streets will support services of this kind. In many cases, the new salons have foundered for want of clients.

Application questions

Note: The word "product" is used in these application questions to include services. All the questions are as relevant to the marketing of services as they are to the marketing of products.

15.1   What was the most recent new product purchased by you which was subsequently withdrawn from the market? How do you explain its failure? Could research have indicated that the product would fail? If you had been the brand manager responsible for the product, what research programme would you have recommended?

15.2   Consider the most recent new product launched by your organisation. Were all aspects of the product thoroughly researched? What research was done? What were the advantages and disadvantages of the research methods chosen? Would you have reduced the risk of the launch by undertaking any other research?

15.3   Who has responsibility within your organisation for the research and other decisions associated with a new product launch? Are any changes needed to make the new product launch less of a risk?

Question 16
How can we estimate how much product we will sell?

Overview

As we have already seen, the environment in which the marketing activity is set is constantly changing and needs continual monitoring. One result of this is that all estimates of sales take place against a background of uncertainty. Because of this uncertainty, sales estimation must be able to provide a flexible framework for marketing action and must recognise the probabilistic nature of sales levels. It is suggested that the central task of sales forecasting is the estimation of market potential and the share that our product might be expected to achieve. This task will be influenced both by the forecasting horizon and by the stability of the markets in which we operate.

The techniques of estimation include both MACRO and MICRO approaches. Macro approaches, which include the use of marketing models, enable the forecaster to deduce from a broad economic analysis the implications for a particular product/market. Micro approaches are based on building up an estimate of sales from an individual customer level.

Forecasting future sales

The problem of estimating the level of sales of any product, new or old, is ever-present and may only be imperfectly solved. Knowing in advance what levels of sales could be achieved, given a particular marketing mix and a particular marketing programme, would reduce considerably the complexity of the marketing decision. However, few people can claim the ability to predict the future accurately and in detail and the marketing decision-maker has to fall back on other, less precise, methods.

Even some of the most carefully prepared forecasts of future sales can be disproved by events. The wider environment in which the forecast is set changes in ways that are not always foreseen and thus not incorporated in the forecast. Energy crises, crop failures and drought, revolutions - these are just a few of the major events that can upset the forecast. It could be suggested that, if the world is so dynamic, what is the purpose of forecasting anyway? The answer is quite simply that any attempt to reduce the uncertainty that surrounds the future will, if used as a flexible input to a planning process, make us question the appropriateness of what we are currently doing. It must be recognised, however, that forecasts are useful only if they are indeed used in a flexible way. Sales forecasts can too easily become strait-jackets which inhibit the organisation's activities, as when they are seen as targets, endowed with all the sanctity that numbers tend to assume in a management context.

Forecasts deal with contingencies, not certainties. The head of planning in a large multinational chemical company says, "We have to have alternative plans that can deal with either/or eventualities". Establishing the nature of the "either/or" is the task of the market forecaster. Parallel to the need for flexibility is the need to recognise that the output of the forecast should be expressed in terms of a *range* of possible outcomes. Sales estimates share the imprecision of most forecasting methods. Beyond this, however, it must be recognised that the process whereby any sales level is achieved is essentially *probabilistic*. In other words, chance has a central role in the outcome of any marketing process. Our forecasts can, and should, be made to incorporate the probabilities that are implicit in the marketing environment in which we operate.

The successful use of forecasting can be seen in the case of a manufacturer of household durables. Prior to the start of each fiscal year, he worked out three different forecasts: "optimistic", "pessimistic" and "most likely". If taxation levels changed, competitive activity became particularly aggressive or some other phenomenon occurred to alter the market, the manufacturer could adopt an alternative plan without having to repeat the forecasting procedure. This approach enabled the company to react to market conditions with immediate flexibility.

But how do we start to grapple with the sales estimation problem?

Understanding market potential

The distinction between actual and potential customers (discussed in Question 7) is vital to successful sales estimation. The forecaster is concerned with establishing what proportion of the total market potential will be represented in his or her sales estimates. Market potential has been defined as the maximum possible sales opportunities for all sellers of a good or service. As such, it refers to the potential sales that could be achieved at a given time, in a given environment by all the firms active in a specified product/market area or segment. Thus, the concept of market potential extends our view of the market for our product in that we see the product as competing against alternative means of satisfying the same need. Successful sales estimation will therefore depend on determining the proportion of the market that can be achieved, given a specific marketing mix and marketing programme. This situation is illustrated in Figure 20.

Figure 20

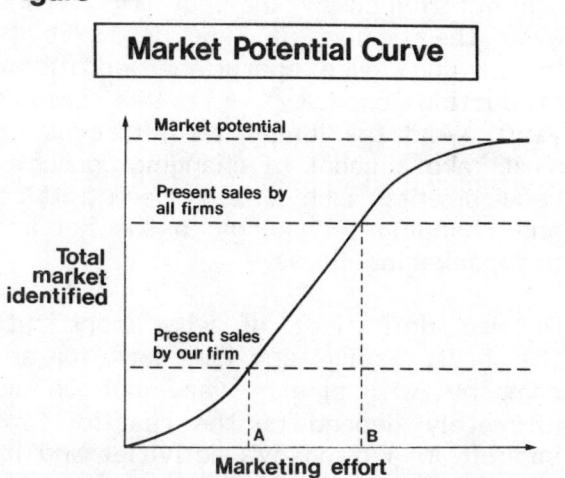

Market Potential Curve

A presentation of this kind, of course, gives a static picture of actual and potential sales at a given time and in a given environment; it could be influenced both by environmental changes and by changes in marketing effort by any of the firms (including ourselves) in that product/market area.

Looking at the sales estimation problem in this light, we see how it can be possible for estimates to become self-fulfilling prophecies, in that the estimate and the marketing mix/programme are dependent upon each other. In a sense, a given level of market achievement is predicated by what we believe to be potentially achievable.

The forecasting horizon

Clearly, the time period that we select for the forecasting exercise will influence our approach and our choice of estimation techniques. Most managers are accustomed to thinking in terms of short-, medium- and long-term forecasting, the actual length of these periods being determined by the organisation's planning requirements. As an example, a manufacturer of wine bottles in Spain knows that his short-term forecasting requirements are based on his need to plan production schedules on a weekly basis. His medium-term requirements are determined by the industry demand over the period of time it takes to install and make operational additional production capacity - in this case a year. And the longer term forecasting must take account of changing consumer requirements, such as easy-open bottles, and changing technology in the bottling and packaging fields.

Precise definitions of what constitute the short, medium and long term for any company will clearly vary but should ultimately depend on the reaction-time implicit in a company's activities and its organisation. The reaction-time for firms in ladies' fashion markets must necessarily be much shorter than for those companies engaged in the construction of hydro-electric power projects. Their definition of the forecasting horizon will vary correspondingly.

The firm's definition of that horizon will also be influenced by the variability of demand in their markets. For established products, that variability may not be pronounced, particularly if seasonal variations are allowed for. Even though on a week-by-week basis sales may seem to fluctuate widely, there will often be an underlying steady-state or a recognisable upward or downward direction in sales. The forecasting task for the manufacturers of beef stock cubes, a product in a steady-state that has lasted for many years, is quite different from that facing the Swedish firm Uddeholm as they launch on a completely untried market a new grade of stainless steel for use in the processing of fertilizers.

The techniques of estimation

Two broad approaches to market estimation have been employed by market forecasters in their attempts to estimate future sales levels. These may be termed *macro* (or aggregate product-market) estimates and *micro* (or individual product) estimates. These approaches are not alternatives but should complement each other in the information that they provide. Both approaches can use qualitative and quantitative methods of estimation, depending on their objectives.

The macro level of estimation

Let us first consider the macro approaches to estimation. Here, the emphasis is on observing the broad picture and, from that, deducing the implications for the product/market in which we are interested. Many business forecasters use leading indicators (that is, indices of related or even non-related activities) as aids in estimating changes in market conditions at a macro level. For example, in the United Kingdom, the Financial Times Ordinary Share Index has tended in recent years to signal changes in general economic conditions about six months in advance. Similar UK leading indicators, which would be classified as quantitative methods of estimation, are: new housing starts (a lead of about 10 months), net acquisition of financial assets by companies (leading by about 12 months) and interest on three month bank bills (with a lead of approximately 18 months).

Such indicators will only provide approximate pictures of general business conditions and cannot be guaranteed to offer consistent correlations. On the other hand, the forecaster may discern that there is a close fit between a seemingly unrelated activity and the sales performance of a particular product. One Danish manufacturer of garden furniture has established a satisfactory method of predicting sales on the basis of an apparent correlation between the rise in real wages in Denmark and the sales of his product, with a lag of 18 months. This does not necessarily imply any causal relationship - simply a statistical association - but it did seem to provide a useful aid to sales estimation.

Question 16   How can we estimate how much product we will sell?

There has been a considerable growth in recent years in the use of *marketing models* to provide a macro-type basis for sales estimation. Generally, these models are based on a number of statistically derived relationships drawn from empirical observations. Some of these can be relatively simple, embodying only a few relationships and requiring nothing more than a calculator to perform the manipulations. On the other hand, one Europe-wide oil company has recently developed a sophisticated energy model to guide it in formulating its strategy on synthetic fuels. The model covers all major energy forms, conversion technologies, transportation modes and demand. It also projects investment, financing and resource depletion to the year 2025 and even attempts to predict prices on the basis of supply and demand. A model of this kind attempts to *explain* the observed market behaviour in terms of marketing trends. This contrasts with the garden furniture example above where the correlation is not explained, only accepted as an observable phenomenon.

Not everybody shares this enthusiasm for large-scale models because of the problems of quantifying what are often qualitative and intangible relationships. Such relationships will often change considerably over time, thus making the model obsolete. Another factor weighing against the use of models is the considerable expense involved in collecting the necessary data. In many markets - as in the soup market, for example, it may be more cost-beneficial to employ less sophisticated estimation techniques.

An example of a qualitative macro estimation is the Delphi forecast (named after the Greek oracle which foretold the future). Here, a group of experts discuss a problem, such as, "what will be the major marketing features of the year 2,000?", and give their consensus of the answer to this problem.

The micro level of estimation

These macro approaches, it was suggested earlier, are particularly suited to forecasting which is intended, primarily, to depict broad market conditions. In themselves, though, they rarely provide a complete answer to the company's sales estimation problem. The micro level approaches to estimation which tackle the problem from the other direction, from the study of the sales prospects for an individual product, can often provide the missing pieces of the jigsaw.

Micro approaches are based on building up, from an individual customer level, an estimate of what total sales of the product could be in a given period. Quantitative micro methods rely heavily on surveys of actual and/or potential customers of a sort we shall be discussing in Questions 27 and 28 which deal with marketing research. Although the procedures involved may be very sophisticated, these studies basically rely on indications from respondents about their likely purchasing behaviour. For example, a German manufacturer of household electrical goods carries out a regular survey amongst a representative sample of actual and potential customers to ascertain the likelihood of their purchasing particular electrical appliances in the next twelve months. Using this device, he can track the way in which first time sales will move and also the way in which the replacement market is moving.

At the micro level, many companies rely on forecasts which are based solely on an analysis of past sales. In other words, past sales are charted with a view to identifying patterns and trends and thus enabling projections to be made. The nature of projections must be clearly understood: they are extrapolations from past behaviour and are based upon an assumption that what has happened in the past will be a guide to what will happen in the future. This need not be so. One British firm in the building products market expanded its production facilities on the basis of a sharp upturn in the early 1970s only to find that by late 1974 the market had collapsed. Although the collapse was only temporary, it lasted long enough to damage the firm's profitability and cast doubt on its chances of long-term survival.

An example of a qualitative micro estimate would be an estimate based on the judgement of members of the sales force concerning future sales.

Successful marketing management must be based upon reliable estimates of market demand. It would probably be true to say that companies pay rather less attention to this crucial input to marketing decisions than they should. Success in the markets of the future will almost certainly require a reversal of this neglect.

Application questions

16.1 Over what period of time do you forecast sales in your organisation? Are all relevant managers aware of the forecasts and do they all work towards them? What is the procedure for monitoring the extent to which forecasts are achieved?

16.2 In your organisation is there a variance between the forecast and actual sales? If so, how do you explain it? If not, how do you manage to achieve such accurate forecasts?

16.3 Is there any additional information which you would like to help you develop accurate forecasts in your market? In what way would the information help you? How could you obtain the information? What has prevented you from gaining the information in the past?

Unit IV   Place decisions

Question 17   What routes could lead to the customer?

Question 18   How can we get our products to the customer?

Question 19   What level of availability does our customer want?

Question 17

What routes could lead to the customer?

Overview

Where our customers buy our products is determined by the outlets at which those products are made available to them. The planning of the organisation's distributive activity should be based on a careful assessment both of the market requirements and the ability of the firm to meet those requirements. The MARKETING CHANNEL through which our products move is a network of institutions which themselves are linked by a series of mutually beneficial relationships. The marketing channel is itself dynamic, as are the markets that it serves. Accordingly, decisions regarding the choice of channel should be seen as an integral part of the firm's marketing strategy, subject to change and adjustment in the light of circumstances.

The marketing channel

This Question might be restated as, "What channels do our customers utilise when they acquire our products?". The *marketing channel* is the mechanism by which "the right product gets to the right place at the right time". As such, it is vitally important to the company's marketing effort, whether the company is operating in industrial or consumer markets or whether it is marketing products or services.

The marketing channel can be defined as the course taken in the transfer of a good or service from its original source of supply to its ultimate consumption. Consideration of the channel must take into account both the choice of the *route of exchange,* along with its administrative and financial control, and the *physical movement* of the product through that route. This latter point will be dealt with in detail in the next Question. Here, we shall go on to discuss the issues involved in marketing channel choice.

Many companies fail to pay much attention to the question of channel choice. Typically, it is not seen as being a variable in the marketing mix; and, frequently, the marketing channel will have taken its current form as a result of unplanned and haphazard development. Such disregard for this vital area of marketing decision making means that many opportunities for the profitable development of market potential are passed over. For example, one international chemical company selling to Europe through their own sales office direct to customers found that the use of a chemical merchant or middleman would reduce their selling costs and allow them to take advantage of a ready-made sales organisation.

Another company, a British shoe manufacturer producing better quality shoes, found that they could open up a new and profitable market segment by including their products in the catalogue of a national mail-order firm. Soon, they were selling the same shoes, at the same prices, to two, largely distinct, markets: to the up-market speciality shoe shop and to the wider down-market audience reached through the mail-order catalogue.

Here, then, are two examples of the benefits of taking a fresh look at marketing channels. Both involved a reappraisal of the route by which the customer acquired the product and a comparison of the costs and benefits of using alternative routes.

Many companies use multiple channels of distribution to get their products to the market place. These companies may, for example, sell to different markets by means of different outlets or they may approach the same market through a dual distribution channel, with some products taking one route and others taking another.

For example, L'Oreal markets its branded items such as Dop shampoo, Crystal colourants and Ambre Solaire suntan products through chemists, chain stores and supermarkets. However, only in the hairdressing salon will most customers come into contact with L'Oreal products such as Coloral colourant, Influence waving lotion or Kerastase conditioning. If the customer prefers not to visit the hairdressing salon, she is likely to buy for use at home products such as Elseve shampoo, Receital colourant or Elnette lacquer. Of this dual approach, the distribution through hairdressing salons reaches markets for sophisticated prestige higher-priced items, distributed through exclusive outlets where customers expect a certain amount of personal service. On the other hand, the customer who buys products for use at home is offered the type of point-of-sale service common to mass distribution outlets.

Alternatively, a company may habitually use one particular channel of distribution but may wish to consider the possibility of using a different one. Whatever the situation, it is a necessary and valuable exercise to look at the costs and benefits accruing through the use of any particular channel of distribution. The alternatives depicted in Figure 21, for example, have quite distinctly different cost and revenue profiles.

The cost/benefit appraisal must be undertaken in the widest possible context. It needs to consider, for example, questions of market strategy and the appropriateness of the channel for the product and customer requirements, as well as the level of comparative costs of selling and distribution.

Figure 21

What Routes Could Lead to the Customer?

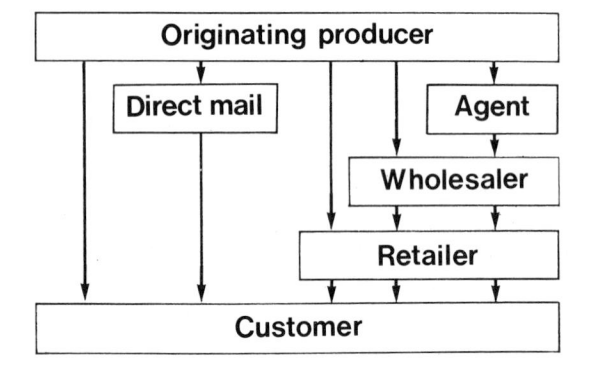

```
Originating producer
   │        │         │
Direct mail │       Agent
   │        │         │
   │        │    Wholesaler
   │        │         │
   │        │     Retailer
   │        │         │
        Customer
```

Criteria for the selection of channels

The needs of the customer

The ultimate purpose of the marketing channel is to reach the customer in a way appropriate to his or her requirements and to the firm's capabilities. But what are the requirements of the customer? While these will clearly vary from market to market, it is possible to identify general objectives which customers employ in deciding where to buy a product. These objectives can be summarised as optimising price/value considerations, maximising convenience, and ensuring availability.

The *price/value* dimension is present to a greater or lesser extent in all markets and it implies that the customer is seeking a certain level of value or utility from a good or service but that there is an implicit trade-off between that value and the price that is charged. In this way, one housewife at an Asda supermarket in the UK is optimising her own price/value balance whilst another housewife attempts to achieve a similar optimum by shopping at

Harrods. In industrial and service markets, the principles of price/value optimisation on the part of the customer apply in a similar fashion. Industrial purchasing officers, for example, employ standard evaluative procedures such as value analysis.

Convenience and *availability* are dealt with in some detail in the following two Questions but it should be emphasised at this juncture just what a key role they play in competitive markets. For example, the choice of supplier for providing the ancillary supplies to North Sea oil exploration and production companies has been largely determined by the customers' need to have a convenient and sure source of supply - even to the extent of paying a higher price.

The needs of the organisation

The selection of marketing channels must fit the needs and capabilities of the company as well as meeting the objectives of the customer. What sort of factors are involved here? In practice, we find that two major considerations are involved in the firm's channel decision, the first being the market and the second institutional factors.

Let us consider how these factors might influence the firm. Sometimes the firm's market segmentation policy will require that particular channels of distribution be used. If a company is marketing an insurance counselling service in Germany to individuals in the higher tax brackets, then it would probably not be appropriate to set up a network of door-to-door salesmen. The company may well prefer to use an indirect channel of distribution which might rely upon intermediaries such as bank managers and accountants.

Associated with the question of segmentation is that of coverage or penetration. In other words, how far do we wish to gain distribution penetration in our target segments? To gain maximum coverage may well require the involvement of an intermediary. A specialist book publisher, for example, was having only limited success in developing sales through mail order. Eventually he identified three major booksellers who had long-established positions as suppliers of libraries, overseas customers and others. The booksellers agreed to add the publisher's books to their list and actively to promote them to their customers. The publisher had to offer the usual trade discount but in return he had available a distribution network of a size and effectiveness that were beyond his own limited resources.

One of the problems with marketing channels which involve intermediaries (normally known as indirect channels) is that they almost always lead to a loss of close contact with the market place and to some loss of control over key areas such as customer service policy. Also, by implication, there is a loss of margin to the firm in that intermediaries necessarily absorb some of the margin that would either have been available to the firm or to the customer. On the other hand, they are often the only means of providing wider distribution without incurring the very considerable costs of maintaining a direct marketing channel. The intermediary performs a very necessary function in many markets by transforming what might be many small shipments from single producers to single customers into larger shipments comprising the products of multiple producers to multiple customers.

In some markets the intermediate function is performed by a wholesaler. In others, a distribution service company (for example, Pickfords, BRS, or SPD in Britain and Europe) will provide the means of gaining the benefits of large-scale distribution at a fraction of the cost of going-it-alone.

It would be a mistake, however, to view relationships with channel intermediaries purely from an economic point of view. The marketing channel through which the offering of the firm reaches the market place is a dynamic system, membership of which has considerable implications. In most channels, one member will often emerge as the leader, determining the policy of other members of the channel and even sometimes extending its control over them. *Vertical integration* is a common phenomenon in marketing channels. This process could involve a company in absorbing those firms who are its sources of supply (that is, backwards integration) or in extending its control of its markets (that is, forwards integration). Such a movement backwards or forwards need not always require ownership of the firms involved. Marks and Spencers, for example, is a retail operation in the UK which through its massive buying power exerts an almost total control over many of its suppliers. When you sell 100 per cent of your output to one customer you are to all intents and purposes "owned" by them. The motor car industry has a very similar relationship with its component suppliers.

Even where integration through ownership or control does not exist, the institutional pressures within the channel can be considerable. Who should hold the inventory in the channel? How should the available margin be split? Can intermediaries lower down the channel be relied on to follow through desired marketing strategy and promotional plans? The likelihood of conflict is enhanced if each level of the channel attempts to maximise its own return. In situations such as this, the return enjoyed overall in the channel may be reduced.

Determining channel strategy

Given these considerations, and assuming that we are in a position to choose rather than be chosen, what are the circumstances that might prompt a reappraisal of an organisation's channel strategy?

The introduction of a new product, or even a merger with another company, should involve a careful analysis of the costs and benefits of utilising present channels compared with possible alternatives. Likewise, a change in our marketing strategy might involve similar consideration. For example, an Italian manufacturer of specialist outdoor and climbing gear decided that the need for greater promotional and service support at the dealer level required a move from intensive to selective distribution. Or, again, the identification of new potential market segments might require a channel reappraisal. The market, too, can change, necessitating a reaction by the distributing firm.

One firm that was adversely affected by too rigid a policy towards channels was an old established Belgian company in household products such as polishes and scourers. The company had traditionally sold its products through hardware wholesalers who distributed the products to hardware shops. When approached by a leading supermarket chain to produce "own-label" brands for them, the company refused on the grounds that such a move might not be well received by their existing outlets - the hardware shops. The problem was that hardware shops were a declining feature of the Belgian retailing scene and much of the business that had formerly gone to these stores had been captured by the supermarkets. Thus, the company was locked into a channel of distribution that was accounting for an ever-falling share of the market.

Situations like this can be avoided if channels of distribution are viewed as a variable in the marketing mix and subjected to a regular and searching review.

Question 17   What routes could lead to the customer?

Application questions

17.1 How do your organisation's products and services reach your customers? What do you see as the advantages and disadvantages of these channels?

17.2 Who is responsible for deciding the channels of distribution to be used for your products and services? How are the requirements of customers reflected in these decisions? Are there any cases where the channels used may not be the most appropriate? How could a situation of this kind be rectified? Is there any case to be made for marketing personnel being more closely involved in these decisions?

17.3 Is there any opportunity for your organisation to integrate its channels of distribution? What integration would you recommend? What advantages would result?

17.4 If your organisation were new to the market, what channels of distribution would you establish? How would your recommendations differ from the existing channels? What prevents your organisation from making these changes?

Question 18

How can we get our products to the customer?

Overview

Getting the product to the customer cannot be viewed by marketing management as the concern of others. The distributive activity of the firm is as much a part of its marketing mix as are pricing, promotion and product decisions. Indeed, in some markets, the impact of the distribution effort upon sales can exceed that of the other mix elements. Seen in this light, the means by which the product reaches the customer assumes a vital importance in marketing strategy. The implications of this view of distribution's marketing role are wide-ranging and involve a reappraisal of attitudes as well as of the means of distribution generally employed.

It is also suggested that the key to the successful development of the firm's distribution effort is the adoption of a total systems approach whereby an integrative view is taken of the various activities involved in distribution.

The importance of distribution

Our previous discussions of the marketing mix emphasised the need to understand the impact of the mix elements on an organisation's marketing effectiveness. However, it is often the case that organisations concentrate on three elements - product, price and promotion - and leave the fourth element, *place,* to look after itself. In the quartet of the 'P's, place is the shorthand description for the means by which the matching process between the needs of the market and the offering of the firm is actually achieved. It is clearly an activity of some importance since it represents the addition of time and place utility to the product. Without this added-value the product is worthless.

The distributive activity has been given a number of different names. Physical Distribution Management (PDM), Marketing Logistics and Materials Management are some of the descriptions that have been used in discussions of this neglected area of management. Accompanying these different titles there has often been confusion surrounding the exact nature of the distributive task within the company. This confusion may in part explain the neglect that has typically been shown by marketing management. There has been a tendency in many organisations to treat distribution as something of a necessary but mechanical activity that incurs costs and is something to do with transport. Too few companies have seen their distribution effort as potentially contributing in a vital and positive way to company profitability through its revenue-generating capability.

Let us see how one British company in the food business released the profit potential that was latent in its distributive system. With a sales turnover of £100m a year from four major lines, the manufacturer was using a combination of 15 public warehouses and company-owned facilities to distribute 100,000 tons of goods each year. The company had separate sales and order processing organisations for each line, with a total annual warehousing and transport bill of over £3m. In recent years this figure had been growing alarmingly and yet turnover in real terms was static. A review by a team of consultants showed that there was little co-ordination between the distribution and marketing functions in the firm and that there was a considerable overlap in the selling and distributive activities. This overlap could be traced back to the somewhat complex organisational structure that had resulted when the present company was formed from a merger of three companies.

This audit of the company's activities resulted in a complete reappraisal of the way it sold and distributed its products. A single direct-sales force was set up, thus reducing the numbers of orders processed by almost 50 per cent; and a consolidation of deliveries reduced transport costs by 20 per cent. In addition, the number of warehouses was cut to seven, a move which both reduced the total inventory holding in the system and cut storage and handling costs by 40 per cent. The end result was a vast improvement in delivery performance, and hence sales effectiveness, plus an overall reduction of one-third in total distribution costs.

Similar examples can be cited from markets as diverse as fuel pumps and baby foods. As more and more companies take a fresh look at the role of distribution in their marketing effort, they are coming to the conclusion that there is considerable scope for profit enhancement through improvements in distribution. When it is considered that studies have estimated that the average European manufacturing company spends 21 per cent of its sales revenue on distribution-related activities, it is not difficult to imagine the benefits of such a reappraisal.

These benefits need not always come from cost savings in distribution. Frequently, profitability can be improved by spending more rather than less on some aspects of the total corporate distribution activity. International Computers, for example, have found that it pays to ship their computers from the UK to continental European customers by air freight rather than by surface transport. Although the costs of transport are clearly higher, savings are made on packaging and port charges. Furthermore, faster deliveries mean lower inventory carrying costs for goods in transit as well as improved cash flow as a result of a reduction in the time before customers can be invoiced.

The logistics concept

If the marketing requirements of the company are to be consonant with its distribution capabilities, the meeting point between these two activities must be identified and subjected to scrutiny.

A scrutiny of this kind may well call for a reappraisal of the conventional view of marketing and distribution in the company. If the performance of the marketing department is judged in terms of sales and market share, there will be a tendency to push the costs of distribution into someone else's cost centre. Indeed, if distribution costs are not in the marketing budget, this tendency is perfectly understandable. For example, one Dutch company in the machine-tool business experienced spiralling manufacturing costs because of the policy adopted by the marketing manager who insisted upon cutting delivery times by half. He had not thought through the implications of such a policy for production scheduling and for the requirements for stocks of sub-assemblies.

To overcome the problems caused by this compartmentalisation of company effort, a new, integrative approach to marketing and distribution has been developed. This orientation is known as the *logistics concept*.

The logistics concept involves a systems approach to management. It suggests that the movement activity in a company is so wide-reaching and pervasive in its effects that it should be considered as a total system. The logistics concept rejects the traditional situation where marketing, production, distribution, purchasing, and so on, operate solely within their own areas, oblivious of each others' activities, and concentrate on optimising their own performance.

Instead, the concept suggests that it may be necessary for some, or all, of these areas to operate sub-optimally in order that the whole system may be more effective. Thus, for example, the marketing manager must be prepared, if necessary, to accept a lower level of service than he would like; or the production manager must be prepared to schedule shorter runs with more changes. Some individual objectives must be sacrificed if the overall effectiveness of the system is to be enhanced.

The logistics mix

Moving this concept from the realms of theory to those of practice involves a consideration of the areas of major concern to logistics management. There are five key decision areas that together constitute the *logistics mix:*

Facility decisions These decisions are concerned with the problem of how many warehouses and plants the organisation should have and where they should be located. Obviously, in the short term, most organisations must take the location of existing plants and warehouses as given; but the question assumes importance in the longer term and when new plants or warehouses are being considered.

Inventory decisions A major element in many companies' total distribution costs is the cost of holding stock. Thus, decisions such as how much inventory to hold, where to hold it and in what quantities to order are vital issues. Inventory levels, as we shall see in the next Question, are also instrumental in determining the level of service that the company offers the customer.

Communications decisions It must always be remembered that logistics is not only about the flows of materials through the distribution channel. The flow of information is just as important to an efficient logistics system. Here we are talking about the order processing system, the invoicing system, the demand forecasting system, and so on. Without effective communications support, the logistics system will never be capable of providing satisfactory customer service at acceptable cost.

Unitisation decisions The way in which goods are packaged and then subsequently accumulated into larger unit sizes (such as a case load) can have a major bearing upon logistics economics. For example, the ability to stack goods on a pallet which then becomes the unit load for movement and storage can lead to considerable cost savings in terms of handling and warehousing. Similarly, the use of containers as the basic unit of movement has revolutionised international transport and, to a certain extent, domestic transport as well.

Transport decisions Last, but seldom least, are those decisions surrounding the transport function of the firm. The transport decision involves such issues as what mode of transport we should use: should we transport by road with our own vehicles or should we lease them? Should we ship overseas by air freight or by container ship? The organisation of delivery constitutes another major issue: how should we schedule our deliveries? How often should we deliver? Perhaps because it constitutes one of the more obvious facets of the distribution task, transport has received rather more attention within the firm than have the other four decision areas of the logistics mix.

Together, these five areas constitute the total costs of distribution within a company. It is frequently the case, however, that a decision taken in one area will have an effect on the other four areas. Thus, a decision to close a depot, a facility decision, will affect the transport costs, the inventory allocation and, perhaps, data processing costs. Managing the logistics function involves a continual search for such situations, the intention being to secure a reduction in total costs by changing the cost structure in one or more areas. This is the principle of a *cost trade-off* amongst the elements of the logistics mix.

One important feature of this logistics mix concept is that transport is seen as being just one element amongst five. Conventionally, in many companies transport *is* distribution; yet viewed in this total sense, it may account for only a small proportion of the total logistics costs.

The systems approach

One major problem of conventional approaches to distribution is that responsibility for the task is spread over many discrete functional areas. It has already been suggested that too heavy an emphasis on compartmentalistion within the company leads to a sub-optimal situation overall. In one Swiss engineering company, responsibility for stock levels throughout the system was in the hands of the production department. At the same time, the purchasing manager was pursuing policies which conflicted with production policy; the distribution manager operated an inflexible delivery system; and the marketing manager was driven to despair by the erratic service levels that resulted. All this arose from a failure to take a systems approach to the logistics function within the company.

Accepting the integrative systems-based approach which characterises the logistics concept implies a recognition that an inter-relationship exists between the parts of the whole such that action affecting one part can well affect all the others. Any action, therefore, must be considered in the light of its effect on all parts of the business and on the overriding objectives of the company. Thus, the company can be viewed as a number of interlinked sub-systems which must somehow be united if overall effectiveness is to be maximised. The distribution planner who accepts this approach must be concerned with the flow of materials through the whole business process, from raw materials through to the finished goods arriving at the customer's premises.

Figure 22 brings together those aspects of the company's operations which involve flows, either of materials or information. These flows are the core concern of an integrated approach to logistics management.

While physical distribution management is concerned only with those flows from the end of the production line to the consumer, the integrated approach of logistics encompasses the total flow of materials and related information into, through, and out of the corporate system.

Distribution's role in tomorrow's markets

Recent years have seen a slow-down in the growth of many markets, unpredicted shortages of materials, shrinking margins and spiralling costs. In circumstances such as these, an integrated distribution effort can make major impacts on marketing performance and on the total costs of corporate operations. There are signs that, in some markets, distribution is being asked to provide the key to long-term survival. The Chairman of Monsanto's European operations states, for example: "We in Monsanto increasingly regard distribution as having the same significance and making the same contribution to our success as skilful advertising, aggressive selling, efficient manufacturing and innovative research and development". Such views are not confined to those businesses where distribution costs represent a high proportion of total costs. In consumer markets and in service industries there is a growing awareness of the crucial role of distribution in the firm's marketing mix. No longer is distribution seen as being purely a cost centre and an inevitable source of profit erosion; instead, we are witnessing a growing emphasis upon integrated distribution strategies within the marketing context.

Figure 22

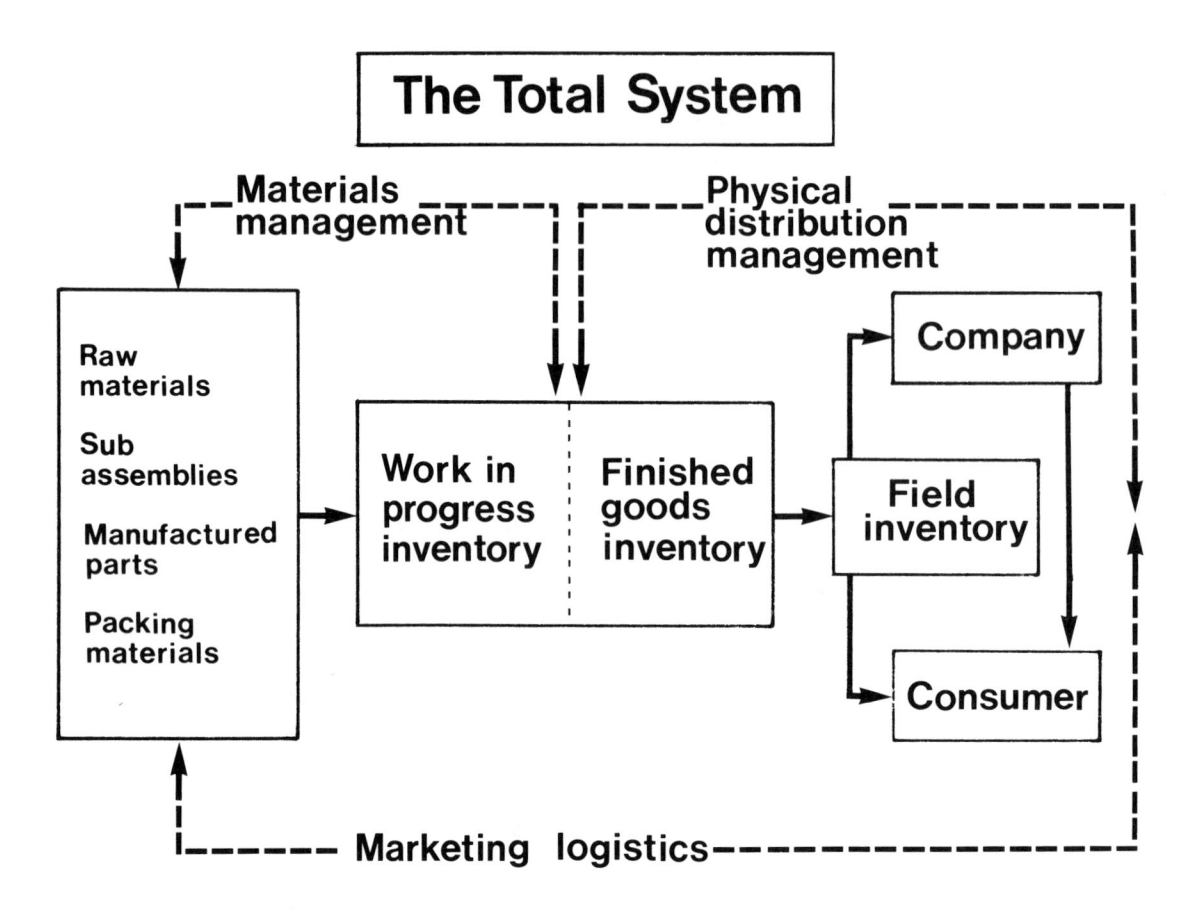

The Total System

```
                    Materials                Physical
                    management               distribution
                                             management
    ┌──────────────┐         ┌──────────┬──────────┐         ┌──────────┐
    │ Raw          │         │          │          │         │ Company  │
    │ materials    │         │          │          │    ┌───►│          │
    │              │         │ Work in  │ Finished │    │    └────┬─────┘
    │ Sub          │         │ progress │ goods    │    │         │
    │ assemblies   │────────►│ inventory│ inventory│───►│ Field   │
    │              │         │          │          │    │ inventory│
    │ Manufactured │         │          │          │    │         │
    │ parts        │         └──────────┴──────────┘    └────┬────┘
    │              │                                         │
    │ Packing      │                                         ▼
    │ materials    │                                   ┌──────────┐
    │              │                                   │ Consumer │
    └──────────────┘                                   └──────────┘
              
                    ──────── Marketing logistics ────────
```

Application questions

18.1 How is the logistics system managed within your organisation? In what ways could the integration of the logistics system be improved? What would be the consequence of such improvements?

18.2 Is logistics management adequately represented at board or senior management level in your organisation? How could representation be improved? Where you can identify changes, how could they be achieved?

18.3 What co-ordination takes place between the logistics and manufacturing functions within your organisation? What problems arise because the co-ordination is inadequate? How can problems encountered be minimised?

Question 19

What level of availability does our customer want?

Overview

Having discussed the overall concept of the logistics system in the previous Question, we now turn to one particular aspect of logistics: customer service. Service is defined here as the provision of "availability", a major determinant of sales in all markets. The task implicit in the management of customer service is to achieve a balance between the costs of service and the direct customer benefits. The appropriate level of availability depends not only on profitability but also on the nature of the product-market competition and the channels used. The customer's perception of logistics performance is described as the "customer service package".

Customer service: costs and benefits

One of the most important outputs of the firm's logistics system (discussed in the previous Question) is *customer service*. This may be defined in many ways. The brewers of Oranjeboom Beer in Holland measure it in terms of how frequently their sales outlets are out of stock. The National Westminster Bank in the UK considers their customer service offering in terms of the location of their banks, the availability of cash dispensers, the provision of budget accounts, and so on. Monsanto Chemicals European Division, based in Brussels, defines customer service in terms of the percentage of orders that they are able to fulfil within a specified period of time.

Another way to look at customer service is to see it simply as the provision of *availability*. If the company's product is not available at the time the customer needs it, and in the location he or she specifies, then the probability of making a sale is much reduced. In product/market areas where competing products are only weakly differentiated (as in the case of, say, sugar or butter) availability will be the largest single determinant of sales. Research has shown that in many product fields availability considerations will overcome brand loyalty. For example, if a particular brand is out-of-stock, many consumers will abandon their search for the brand and switch to the next most preferred brand. For an industrial company selling sockets holding stock of unusual sizes enabled them to charge high prices for immediate delivery. This policy helped establish the company's reputation for immediate delivery and encouraged engineers to contact them whenever their normal suppliers were unable to give prompt service.

However it is defined, customer service is essentially the added-value that availability contributes to the marketing effort behind our product offering.

Clearly, the provision of customer service in all its forms will involve the company in fairly large expenditures. In fact, it can be demonstrated that once the level of service (defined here as the percentage of occasions the product is available to the customer, when and where he wants it) increases beyond the 70/80 per cent mark, the associated costs increase far more than proportionately.

The implications of this cost relationship are worth some attention. In the first place, many companies are simply unaware of the level of service at which they are operating. They do not have any laid down service policy; and, even when the company does have a declared service policy, it is often the case that service levels have been arbitrarily set. Offering a 97 per cent level of service instead of a 95 per cent level may have only a slight effect on customer demand, yet it will have a considerable effect on logistics costs. For "normally" distributed demand, this 2.1 per cent increase in the level of service would lead to a 14 per cent increase in safety stock requirement alone.

This disturbing feature of logistics costs is at the hub of the question: What level of availability should we offer? The answer is simply put - at least in theory. Management must be certain that the marketing advantage of an increase in service more than outweighs the additional costs. However, it is not a simple matter to ensure that this happens. What little empirical research there is has tended to suggest an S-shaped response curve to logistics service. At very high levels of service, the customer just cannot distinguish between small increments in the level of service.

The fundamental need is for marketing management to recognise the cost implications of a service strategy. Indeed, it is possible to go further and suggest that by offering logistics service the organisation is, in fact, absorbing a cost that would otherwise have been borne by the customer. For example, if Nestle deliver orders to Albert Hijn, the Dutch supermarket chain, twice a week instead of once a week, they are relieving them of a necessity for holding stock. Similarly, if the manager of an Albert Hijn store knows that when he places an order with Nestle they will rarely be out of stock on that item then again his stock holding can be lower. The cost of holding stock can be as much as 25 per cent of its value a year for the retailer. By their service offering Nestle are absorbing some of this customer cost.

Marketing and sales managers who insist on offering maximum service to all customers, no matter the location of these customers and the amount of profit involved, are, therefore, quite probably doing their company a disservice. By carefully reviewing customer service policy, and perhaps even introducing differential service levels for different products or for different customers, marketing can enhance its contribution to corporate profitability.

What is the right level of availability

In most product/market situations, logistics service will be a key element in a company's marketing mix - as important in its effects as, say, promotion or price. As a good deal of money is likely to be spent on the provision of this service, the company must become concerned to measure the costs and benefits of the various service alternatives available. Companies should also bear in mind that service usually means that customers' costs are being absorbed. It is within this framework that the company must ask itself whether the customer response will be worthwhile.

Service can provide new possibilities for market segmentation. A market can be segmented by the response of its members to the level of service offered. Whether a segmentation of this kind is meaningful and viable will be determined by the nature of the market and the product. Examination may show that too high a level of service is being offered in terms of the benefits which accrue. Thus, a drop from a 99 per cent level of service to a 95 per cent level may not noticeably affect sales, but it will almost certainly have a marked effect on the logistics system costs.

Somewhere between these costs and benefits a balance has to be found. Usually, it will be at that point where the additional revenue returns for each increment of service are equal to the extra cost involved in providing that increment.

To attempt to identify this point of balance, certain information inputs are required.

1. How profitable is the product? What contribution to fixed costs and profits does this product make and what is its sales turnover?

2. What is the nature of the product? Is it the kind of product where stock-outs at the point of supply would result in loss of sales? Does the product have characteristics that result in high stock-holding costs?

3. What is the nature of the market? Does the company operate in a sellers' or a buyers' market? How frequently is the product purchased? Are there ready substitutes? What are the stock-holding practices of the purchasers? Which markets and customers are growing and which are declining?

4. What is the nature of the competition? How many companies are providing an alternative source of supply to our customers? What sort of service levels do they offer?

5. What is the nature of the channel of distribution through which the company sells? Does the company sell direct to the end customer, or through intermediaries? To what extent does the company control the channel and the activities of its members as they affect stock levels and order policies?

This basic information provides the raw material for the service level decision. To take an example, the level of service offered is less likely to have an effect on sales if the company is the sole supplier of the product and there are no substitutes. One UK food manufacturer carried a low price, low margin product line only because it was believed to complement the whole range of his products and because it would typically be sold along with high margin products. A distribution cost analysis revealed that many delivery locations were unprofitable because they bought only the low margin items. The food processor also discovered that in some cases his standard of service was too high. As a result he discontinued the delivery of "balance" consignments of goods not available when the first delivery against their order was made: customers were asked to include these items on their next order. Furthermore, the frequency with which orders were delivered was reduced, particularly when the delivery location was relatively distant from the depot. (It had also been found that no delivery locations situated more than 55 miles from the depot were profitable.) This action led to encouraging small and other unprofitable accounts to use wholesalers.

In many situations the offering of a high level of service (say, 90 per cent instead of 85 per cent) would, from a short-term point of view, reduce the total profitability of the product.

The customer service package

Experience in the market place suggests that, from the customer's point of view, customer service is a subjective phenomenon that comprises a host of tangible and intangible features. The customer's perception of service is formed by all the points of contact that the customer has with the company in his or her search for solutions to buying problems. Customer service can in fact be seen as a *package* in the sense that, whilst diverse, the constituent parts all have an effect on the customer's perception of logistics performance. Considering service offering as a package has a number of advantages, chief of which is that it forces us to take a global view of the customer's service requirements and thus encourages us to develop cohesive and integrated service policies. Inherent in this approach is the idea that the service package can vary from customer to customer, from market to market or from area to area. Thus, some of our customers may warrant special delivery service, or greater technical back-up or more formalised procedures through which they can provide feedback on their specific requirements. The service package can be designed with any of these requirements in mind and need not be the same for all customers or all segments of the market.

It is not easy to assess how the market will respond to a proposed customer service package. The concept of marketing experimentation is well established in other areas of the business. We are used to thinking of test markets for new product launches, advertising testing, and so on. The development of similar experiments to identify cost-effective service policies is more unusual. However, a number of companies have conducted experiments of this type and found the results to be extremely valuable.

One company manufacturing a wide range of grocery products in the UK had developed good cost data which enabled it to estimate accurately what the cost implications of different levels of service would be. What they could not predict, however, was the likely effect of those various service levels on sales revenue. They tackled the problem by identifying two areas of the UK, each served from a different depot and nearly identical to each other in terms of sales, retail structure and demography. In one of these areas they deliberately reduced the level of service in terms of safety stock maintained at the depot; in the other area no change was made from the existing level. The outcome of this experiment was that there was no significant difference in sales between the two areas. But there was, of course, a major reduction in the stock investment of the test region. The experiment indicated, therefore, that a lower level of service was considerably more cost effective.

In this experiment only one variable in the customer service package - stock levels - was subject to variation. However, similar tests could be developed which would enable the company to move closer to that balance between costs and benefits which is the ultimate aim of customer service management.

Application questions

19.1 What is your organisation's policy on customer service levels? How does the service level compare with that offered by your competitors? What is the rationale underlying this policy?

19.2 If your service levels were reduced by 10%, what costs would be incurred and benefits gained by your organisation? How could such a cut be achieved? Would such a reduction be to your advantage: (a) short term; (b) long term?

19.3 With the benefit of hindsight, what would you consider the optimum service level for each of the markets you supply? How could any changes identified be achieved?

Unit V   Price decisions

Question 20   What price should we charge our customer?

Question 21   What margins should we allow to our distributors?

Question 20

What price should we charge our customer?

Overview

Pricing decisions are of paramount importance in marketing strategy. Like the other elements in the firm's marketing mix, the price of the product should be related to the achievement of marketing and corporate goals. Thus, the role of price must be established in relation to such factors as the product life cycle, the requirements of the total product portfolio and sales and market share objectives.

The procedures and methods adopted to meet these goals are as dependent on the market and competitive circumstances as they are on costs. Indeed, the market-oriented approach to pricing, described in this Question, sees costs as a constraint which may determine a lower limit to the firm's pricing discretion rather than as a basis on which price is determined.

The price decision

In the economists' view of the world, price is regarded as the chief determinant of the level of sales of a product. Price is central to many of their models and the mechanism whereby prices are set has become a major field of study. At the governmental level too, the price of goods and services is subjected to great scrutiny, in this case because of the implications for inflation and general social welfare.

In the light of this external interest in prices, it is perhaps all the more surprising that many organisations adopt relatively unsophisticated approaches to the determination of price. Surveys in several countries have shown that the price decision in the firm often tends to be automatic, to be based upon some rudimentary formula or rule of thumb. Only infrequently, it would appear, do pricing decisions form part of an overall integrated marketing strategy where price is related in some specific way to the achievement of defined objectives.

The pricing decision is important in a number of ways but, clearly, its main importance lies in its direct and indirect effects on profits. It directly affects profits by determining the revenue that can be obtained. Its indirect effects lie in the way in which it influences demand, thus affecting the quantity sold, and the way in which it interacts with the other elements of the marketing mix. We can see from this latter consideration the importance of ensuring that the price set is appropriate to the company's marketing programme.

The way in which price can interact with the other elements of the marketing mix can be seen in the recent introduction of a ticket-selling scheme by London's West End theatres. From mid-afternoon, theatre-goers can obtain half price tickets (if seats are not already all reserved) from a single kiosk situated in the centre of the city. Fears that the already existing market for theatre tickets would be undermined were soon recognised to be ungrounded. Many customers were happy to pay the full price for theatre seats in order to eliminate the uncertainty and inconvenience of having to queue for tickets on the day of performance. The scheme by which reduced tickets are sold appeals successfully to a market not already reached.

Relating pricing objectives to marketing strategy

If an integrated marketing strategy is to be achieved, the pricing decision must be taken in the light of the objectives underlying that strategy. This implies, first and foremost, that the price of the product must fit the *market position* planned for that product. 'Market position' in this context means the place that the product occupies, in comparison with its competitors, in the eyes of the organisation's customers or potential customers. Sometimes this position will be determined mainly by the perceived physical attributes of the product; for example, a grade of industrial steel may occupy a particular market position by virtue of its product characteristics. On other occasions, the market position of a product may be considerably affected by perceptions of less tangible attributes; for example, a toilet soap may have connotations of gracious living associated with it. Because price is one of the marketing mix elements that will contribute to a product's market position, it is necessary that price should be consonant with that position. In the above situation, for instance, it would hardly be appropriate to set a rock-bottom price on the toilet soap.

The price of the product must also relate to its *life cycle* and to the organisation's strategic views on that cycle. Let us take an example of a Norwegian manufacturer of a new type of Kraft paper. On the launching of that product, he is faced with a decision as to pricing policy. He could go for an initial high price or *skimming policy* or for a lower price aimed at gaining maximum *market penetration*.

A skimming policy, as the name suggests, is based on entering the market at a high price and then later, if necessary, lowering the price to gain acceptance in other price segments. It is a strategy appropriate to several circumstances; for example, if the company feels that it has a sufficient lead over its competitors in the introduction of the product and can take advantage of this lead to achieve an accelerated rate of recovery on its investment. It is important in a situation of this kind for the innovating firm to be aware that a skimming policy can provide encouragement for other manufacturers to enter the market. The key to success in these situations is to plan for a steady reduction in price once an initial market penetration has been established and cost recovery is under way. Such price reduction will normally be made easier by the unit cost reductions that should occur once cumulative output starts to grow; this is known as the experience effect.

On the other hand, our Norwegian paper manufacturer could take the opposite route by going for a penetration pricing policy. Here, the price is deliberately set low with a number of objectives in mind. An initial low price makes it very difficult for would-be competitors to imitate innovations, particularly in technological product areas. A penetration policy also ensures maximum adoption of the product in its early life, thus leading to a more rapid experience effect. The problem associated with such a policy is chiefly the "opportunity cost" of possible additional revenue foregone.

The appropriateness of either of these policies will be determined to a large extent by the elasticity of demand in the market place; that is, the responsiveness of demand to relative price levels. In some markets demand does not seem to be affected by price - up to a point at least. In such circumstances, we say that demand is inelastic, as it is, for example, in the market for technical journals sold mainly to libraries. On the other hand, some markets are more sensitive to price as, for example, in urban bus services. Price elasticity by itself does not explain the response of markets to price levels but it should at least be included as a criterion in the choice of pricing strategy. Our Norwegian paper manufacturer, for example, would need to be sure that, in the markets at which his product was aimed, the choice of, say, a skimming strategy was compatible with the underlying price elasticity.

A further consideration facing the paper manufacturer is the competitive situation. The Kraft paper market is an established one, with a relatively large number of manufacturers supplying diverse markets around the globe. There are established price brackets for specific paper types and, within these brackets, there are a number of firms competing. Thus, the question must be asked: are we a price "maker" or a price "taker"? In other words, does our position in the market provide us with room to manoeuvre on price? In markets where the competitive product offerings are relatively undifferentiated, this becomes a very real consideration.

Finally, the paper manufacturer (and every other company) must recognise that pricing policies have a strategic importance in the context of sales and market share objectives and the revenue requirements of the rest of the firm's product portfolio. If, for example, the chosen marketing strategy was to establish as quickly as possible a sizeable share of the market, then sales maximisation through a penetration pricing policy would seem to be indicated. In this case, the company might even decide that the benefits of market share over-rode the need for initial profitability; that is, that market share should be bought by a deliberate pricing policy. On the other hand, in the case of an established product well into the maturity stage of its life cycle, the product might be viewed as a source of cash for financing the growth of other products. In these circumstances, the pressure would be to maintain price, and even to increase it, at the expense of sales and market share.

The firm's market profile is likely to have a great influence on pricing decisions. A British manufacturer of car radios, for example, was considering what price to set for an extension to its product range. The firm had considerable accumulated production expertise. It also had an outstanding distribution network; this was particularly important in its market since retailers may have considerable influence on their customers' choices. In addition, the company had built up a reasonably high reputation for its radios. In order to avoid damaging its reputation, the company was obliged to offer a price towards the upper range which would imply high quality. It was felt that a reduced price would not necessarily lead to an increase in the volume of sales. On the contrary, there was considerable evidence to suggest that price is seen by many consumers as an indicator of the product's quality.

In this latter context, we are seeing price in its true strategic role (see Figure 23), as a variable that enables the achievement of corporate marketing objectives across the complete product portfolio. The pricing decision on a specific product should be viewed in relation to the strategic requirements of the company's global market strategy as well as in terms of the product's own needs.

Figure 23

| Influences on Pricing Policy |

Low — High
Price

What are our competitor's prices?

Where is the product in its life cycle?

What is our market positioning policy?

Is the market developing, saturated or declining?

Pricing procedures and methods

Cost-oriented procedures

Given that pricing objectives have been established, how might the decision on a specific price be taken? The conventional profit-maximising model of the economist tells us that price should be set where marginal cost equals marginal revenue - in other words, where the additional cost of producing and marketing an additional unit is equivalent to the additional revenue that its sale would generate. In its theoretical form, the logic is indisputable; as a practical pricing tool, however, its use is somewhat limited. Why is this? It is because the economist's model requires a knowledge of the demand curve facing the product in the market place; it is based on a notion of cost behaviour strictly limited to the short-run; it does not take cognisance of any strategic objectives of the firm save profits; nor does it recognise that long-run goals can, and frequently will, be met by sacrificing short-run goals.

In practice, we more often encounter pricing procedures which are based on simple, although often equally unsatisfactory, precepts. Many of these procedures are what might best be termed "cost-oriented". One frequently encountered approach, based on costs, is the *target return on costs* method; this is commonly known as the "cost plus" method of setting prices. Using this approach, the company would set itself a target level of profits to be achieved at a given level of sales, such that an adequate return on costs would be obtained. A specialist book publisher in France uses this method, for example, when it makes a decision to produce 1,000 copies of a book at a total production and marketing budget of Fr.30,000. The firm requires a 20 per cent return on this investment - that is, Fr.6,000. Thus, the required level of total revenue must be Fr.36,000, which, on a sale of 1,000, implies a price of Fr.36.0. This method is based in effect on a breakeven analysis of the form illustrated in Figure 24.

The problem with this approach is that it assumes that if 1,000 copies of the book are produced, they can then be sold at the given price; whereas in fact the price itself is likely to have some effect on sales. Another problem occurs in some cases in the determination of total costs. This is particularly true in multi-product companies where many costs are common between products. The allocation of overheads between products can be difficult to determine; the allocation chosen is frequently arbitrary for the individual product. There is also the danger that the method might lead us to seek a return on "sunk" costs; that is, those fixed costs which represent outlays made in the past and which should have no bearing on the price.

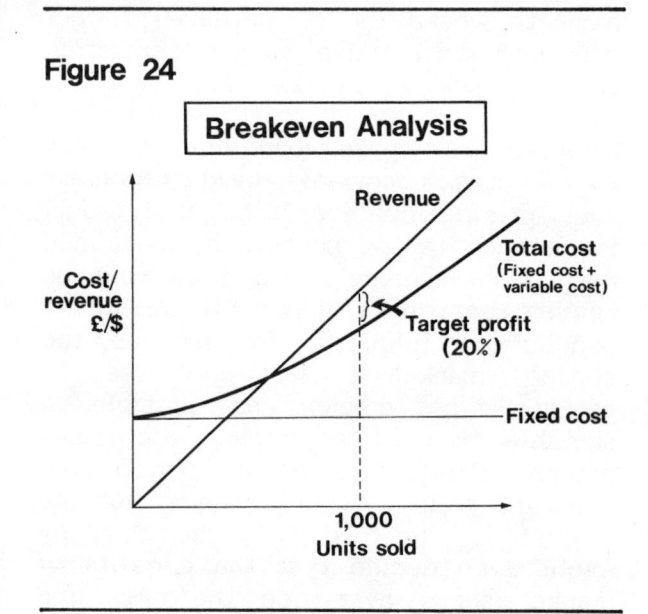

Figure 24

Breakeven Analysis

[Graph showing Cost/revenue £/$ on vertical axis and Units sold on horizontal axis, with curves for Revenue, Total cost (Fixed cost + variable cost), Target profit (20%), and Fixed cost, with 1,000 marked on the horizontal axis]

The market-oriented approach

The *market-oriented approach* to pricing stands in contrast to those methods which are based mainly on costs. In this approach, costs are viewed solely as a constraint on the lower limit of pricing discretion. The emphasis here is placed on such notions as what the market will bear, competitive activity and price/quality perceptions, as well as the overall strategic marketing goals of the sort outlined earlier.

The idea that a product should be priced according to market considerations rather than cost considerations is not new; it is surprising, however, to find that many companies enter a pricing decision by first talking about costs. In a sense, this is understandable: costs are tangible inputs to any decision process and appear to be easily quantifiable. Market factors are usually harder to pin down. Getting a feel for what the market will bear can really only come through experience in a product field. Few companies know enough about their markets to enable them to construct demand curves. It is more likely that the organisation will be able to identify broad bands within which the price will be acceptable to the majority of the chosen market. Some researchers have developed operational methods for determining what these price bands might be. They simply ask a representative sample of the target segment whether they would buy the product at a certain price and, if they answer "no", they are questioned with a view to finding out whether the refusal is due to the price being too high or too low (in the sense that the quality of the product might be in doubt). These researchers have reported that the consumer intent on a purchase enters the market not with a set of demand schedules in mind, but simply with two price limits. He has a lower limit below which he would distrust the quality of the product or service and an upper limit beyond which he would judge the article unduly expensive.

This latter point emphasises that the concept of price has a qualitative dimension. In other words, in many markets price is used by the customer as an indicator of quality. For example, Stella Artois is a Belgian beer marketed under licence in Britain. A major promotional campaign was based, amongst other things, on the premium price of the product. The advertisements suggested that this was a high quality product and they deliberately emphasised the fact that the price exceeded that of competitive products. Other manufacturers too have found that raising the price can have a beneficial effect on sales if the market cannot accept that a relatively low-priced product can in fact meet the claims that are made about it. Thus, the traditional view of price and demand being inversely related need not always hold good in a particular section of the market.

The market-oriented view of pricing attempts to relate the price of the product to the value that the customers believe they will derive from its purchase. This principle also holds good in industrial markets. For example, the Glacier Metal Company in Britain uses a method of pricing, known as *product analysis pricing*, which is based on the concept that the price the buyer pays for a product must be directly related to the various utilities that the user is seeking from the product. Here cost is seen solely as a lower limit beyond which the long-term price should not fall.

In almost all markets, the competitive structure of the market influences the price decision. Often, pricing discretion is limited by the fact that a going rate exists within a market and, unless the organisation occupies a dominant position in that market as a price-leader, this single fact will of necessity determine the price at which the company must operate.

For the marketing manager, these various aspects of the pricing decision can be seen as providing a framework for manoeuvre. The framework of the pricing decision for the individual company is illustrated in Figure 25.

As we have seen, even this range of manoeuvre might be circumscribed by competitive factors. In addition, it is often necessary to take into account the effects of state regulations and controls on the marketing environment in general and the pricing decision in particular. Overall, it will be apparent that the pricing decision is one which has so many ramifications both for profit and for strategy that it should be taken only in the light of careful analysis of the many factors outlined above.

Figure 25

```
                    ┌─────────────────────────┐
                    │  The Framework for the  │
                    │    Pricing Decision     │
                    └─────────────────────────┘
```

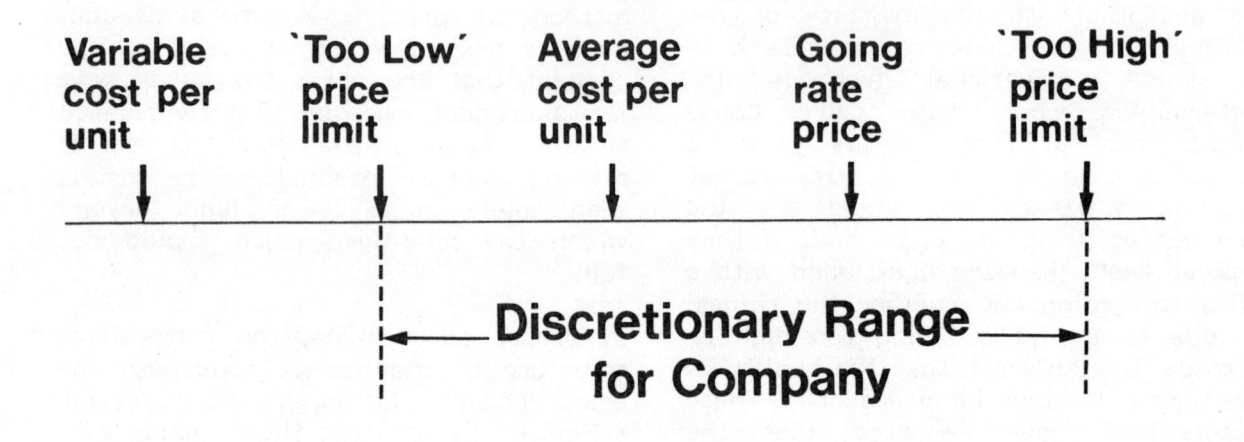

Variable cost per unit	'Too Low' price limit	Average cost per unit	Going rate price	'Too High' price limit
↓	↓	↓	↓	↓

|←——— Discretionary Range for Company ———→|

Application questions

20.1   When the most recent product or service was introduced into your organisation's range, how was the price established? In retrospect, was this decision correct? Was there any additional research which could have helped you establish the correct price?

20.2   Do customers' perceptions of your prices coincide with your declared pricing policy? If there is a variance, how can it be explained and rectified?

20.3   How do your prices compare with those of your competitors? Is this intended organisation policy? How is your pricing policy justified?

20.4   How should your prices be altered: (a) in times of inflation; (b) as your product or service enters different phases of its life cycle? How would you justify these recommendations? How could these changes be implemented?

Question 21

What margins should we allow to our distributors?

Overview

The margins given to intermediaries in the marketing channel should be viewed in terms of the VALUE-ADDED by them as product or service passes along the channel. In return for the performance of various functions necessary to the efficient completion of the exchange process, the firm will be willing to make available some of the total channel margin available to it. The various types of margins that are commonly encountered are trade, quantity, promotional and cash discounts.

It is suggested here that the overall policy towards distributor margins should be considered in the wider context of the need of the firm to achieve its declared marketing goals. Likewise, the question of margin levels must take into account the financial policy and capital structure of the firm.

Reward structures in the marketing channel

Questions 17, 18 and 19 have shown the vital importance of the choice of marketing channel to the success of the marketing effort. The intermediaries that constitute that channel perform a number of functions that enable the exchange transaction between producer and consumer to be carried out. In return for the functions that they perform on the firm's behalf, these intermediaries naturally seek a reward. Put in its simplest terms, this reward amounts to the margin between the price of the goods at the factory gate and the price the customer eventually pays. It is common to refer to this margin as the *value-added* by these intermediate functions. In perfectly competitive markets the nature of the reward for this value-added would be determined solely in terms of economic criteria; that is, an intermediary would earn an amount equivalent to the worth of the service he provided. If a higher reward were to be demanded, other intermediaries would enter the market or the functions performed at that level would be performed elsewhere, thereby bringing the reward structure back into balance.

The actual situation in most markets is, however, quite different to this. Instead of perfectly competitive market structures, one usually encounters *vertical marketing systems,* where varying degrees of control and integration are administered by the more powerful members of the channel. This situation need not result in a loss of economic strength. Indeed, it may often lead to improvements in total channel efficiency. In the fragmented and unintegrated market structure implied by perfect competition, the typically small size of intermediary units will not allow for economies of scale in purchasing, handling and distribution. A fragmented structure can also lead to each individual unit in the channel attempting to maximise its own reward - a tendency which could result in a less than optimal situation in the channel overall.

Ideally, the reward structure in the marketing channel should involve an acceptable rate of return on investment being earned at each level in the channel. This return would reflect the services and the functions that are performed at those levels - in other words, the return would be a real reflection of value-added. What occurs in practice is, of course, often less than this ideal. It has been suggested that the ultimate objective of marketing channel management should be to achieve a situation where all members of the channel gain, a "win-win" situation. In practice, of course, the reward structure does not always give an acceptable rate of return to each level in the channel. The purpose of this Question is to examine ways in which "win-win" states might be achieved.

Available discount options

Most organisations have a number of devices for compensating the intermediaries in the channel. These will usually take the form of a number of discounts against some nominal price list. The most commonly encountered forms are:

1. *Trade discount* This is the discount against the list which the company will give to a channel intermediary in return for the service he makes available. Thus, a wholesaler might purchase goods from the manufacturer at a 20% discount, in return for which he will provide such services as bulk breaking, storage, and retail order-filling. In turn, the wholesaler will offer a trade discount to the retailer. In some cases, the wholesaler will be bypassed and the discount normally passing to the wholesaler will either be retained by the manufacturer or passed on directly to the retailer. In some markets, such as groceries, the retailers have taken on the functions of wholesalers and demand an increased discount to reflect this fact. The precise level of the trade discount is an issue to be explored later in this Question.

2. *Quantity discount* A quantity discount is one which is offered in relation to the size of the order: the greater the order the greater the discount. A manufacturer offering this discount does so in order to encourage larger purchases than might otherwise be made. A discount of this kind can be to the benefit of both parties.

Let us take the example of a Dutch manufacturer of household electrical appliances who offered to wholesalers a discount of 5% on orders for Fl.6,000 or more, a 7% discount on orders for Fl.10,000 and a 12% discount for orders over Fl.15,000. These discounts were in addition to the normal 20% trade discount. The rationale for such additional discounts on price was simple. In the first place, the competitive environment demanded that discounts over and above the normal trade discount be given on larger orders. In addition, the company believed that there were a number of economic advantages associated with a quantity discount structure. The first of these was that they felt that the wholesaler would be encouraged to buy more and thus sell more. Secondly, by ordering in larger quantities, the wholesaler would carry a greater proportion of the total costs of holding inventory - costs that would otherwise have to be borne by the manufacturer. Thirdly, the company felt that the encouragement to purchase in larger quantities could well lead to a decline in the number of orders placed by an individual wholesaler in a given period. This would have the effect of reducing the manufacturer's costs of meeting order.

Naturally, the wholesaler would want to be sure that the size of the discount more than compensated for his increased inventory carrying costs. A successful quantity discount scheme is a good example of a "win-win" situation.

3. *Promotional discount* In a number of markets, other institutions join the manufacturer in promoting the sale of that manufacturer's products. Promotion might take the form of advertisements in various media informing the public that products are available at particular outlets. Alternatively, and this is

frequently encountered in fast moving consumer goods markets, the promotion may be in the form of in-store displays, "money-off" offers, competitions, and so on. This latter form of promotional activity has come to be known as *below-the-line promotion* and in some markets is more important than the more traditional media promotion.

It might be argued that these various types of promotional activity benefit both the channel institution and the manufacturer. However, in a number of situations the channel institution requires an additional discount in order to become involved in activity of this kind. This often happens when a particular channel member holds a great deal of power. Thus, in the UK, a manufacturer of convenience food products has to offer an additional discount to the large supermarket chains in order to persuade them to participate in a promotion that he is planning.

4. *Cash discount* Organisations often attempt to encourage the prompt payment of accounts by offering a cash discount to their customers.

A typical example is a Belgian manufacturer of office equipment whose terms were thirty days credit but who offered a discount of $2\frac{1}{2}\%$ for payment within ten days. In inflationary times, when the management of cash flow becomes as important as making a profit, the speedy payment of accounts by customers is vital to the manufacturer. With a cost of capital of 20% or more, this office equipment company, with Fr.600m annual sales, was facing an average account payment period of forty days; in other words, some accounts were always overdue. Forty days represented approximately Fr.96m accounts outstanding at any one point in time (40/250 x 600) which represented an opportunity cost of Fr.19.2m a year (96 x 20%). Clearly, the $2\frac{1}{2}\%$ incentive to settle within ten days was having little effect. The customers were in effect using their trade credit as a source of working capital; and, even at a discount of $2\frac{1}{2}\%$ foregone, it was cheap at the price.

The problem of the level and structure to be used in determining cash discounts is difficult to solve. There is a limit to the extent to which the firm can eat into its own margin in order to increase the discount for prompt payment. Likewise, in competitive markets, it is difficult to reduce the period of credit - or even to persuade the customer to respect the period of credit offered.

Margin management

As we have just seen, there are a number of problems surrounding the allocation of margins amongst channel intermediaries. In a dynamic marketing channel, there will be constant pressure for the improvement of margins at all levels. The ultimate effect of this is often a shortening of the channel, with the functions of some intermediaries being absorbed by others.

Because of this pressure, the question of margins must be seen at a strategic as well as a tactical level. In those markets where there is a proliferation of products (say, breakfast cereals in Europe) the problem of gaining distribution has to be solved by offering the largest part of the total margin available to the retailer. Strategic implications such as these will often determine the policy towards margins.

This whole area of *margin management*, as it is coming to be called, can be viewed as a series of trade-off decisions which determines how the total channel margin should be split. The concept of the total channel margin is simple. It is the difference between the level of price at which the organisation wishes to position its product in the ultimate market place and the cost of the product at the factory gate. Who takes what proportion of this difference is what margin management is about. The situation is illustrated in Figure 26.

It can be seen that the firm's channel requirements will only be achieved if it carries them out itself or if it goes some way towards meeting the requirements of an intermediary who can perform those functions on the firm's behalf. The objective of the firm in this respect can be expressed in terms of a willingness to trade off margin in order to achieve marketing goals. A trade-off of this kind need not lead to a loss of profitability; indeed, as Table 3 suggests, the margin is only one element in the determination of profitability.

Here, profitability is more precisely defined as a rate of return on net worth, net worth being share capital and capital reserves plus retained profits. It can be seen that by improving the utilisation of capital assets (capital management) as well as by using a higher gearing it is possible to operate successfully on lower margins if this means that marketing goals can more effectively be achieved.

Table 4 gives an example of two Spanish producers of welding rods. Company A operates on a low retained margin (2%), passing the rest of the margin on to other intermediaries in the channel. Company B operates on twice the margin (4%).

Figure 26

The Main Factors Involved in Margin Management

Firm's Marketing Goals
e.g. Sales
    Market share
    Return on investment

⬇

Firm's Channel Requirements
e.g. Distribution coverage
    Inventory holding at point of sale
    Promotional & sales support

⬇ ⬆

Intermediaries' Requirements
e.g. High stockturn
    Maximum margin
    Return on investment

Table 3 The role of margin management in the determination of profitability

Stage 1:

$$\text{MARGIN MANAGEMENT} \times \text{CAPITAL MANAGEMENT} = \text{Rate of return on capital employed}$$

$$\text{i.e. } \frac{\text{Net Profit}}{\text{Net sales}} \times \frac{\text{Net Sales}}{\text{Total Assets}} = \frac{\text{Net Profits}}{\text{Total Assets}}$$

Stage 2: FINANCIAL MANAGEMENT

$$\text{Rate of return on capital employed} \times \text{Gearing ratio} = \text{Rate of return on net worth}$$

$$\text{i.e. } \frac{\text{Net Profits}}{\text{Total Assets}} \times \frac{\text{Total Assets}}{\text{Net Worth}} = \frac{\text{Net Profits}}{\text{Net Worth}}$$

Question 21   What margins should we allow to our distributors?   117

Table 4   The operation of two companies at different levels of margin

Ratios		Company A LOW MARGIN	Company B HIGHER MARGIN
Margin management	Net Profits / Net Sales	2%	4%
Capital management	Net Sales / Total Assets	7	5
Rate of return on capital employed	Net Profits / Total Assets	14% (2 x 7)	20% (4 x 5)
Gearing ratio	Total Assets / Net Worth	2	1
Rate of return on net worth	Net Profits / Net Worth	28% (14 x 2)	20% (20 x 1)

However, because company A turns its capital over 7 times in a year compared with B's 5 times and because company A makes use of debt funding whereas B does not, company A is able to produce a superior rate of return on net worth.

In summary, the question of margins (both the margin retained by the firm and thus, by implication, the margin allowed the distributor) cannot be examined without consideration of the wider implications of overall marketing strategy and the financial policy and capital structure of the firm.

Application questions

21.1   What margins are expected by the intermediaries with whom your organisation has to work?   Are these margins justified?   Is there any way in which the margins can be reduced without undermining the efficiency of your channels of distribution?

21.2   Could your organisation replace its intermediaries in any way?   What costs would be incurred and what benefits would be gained?   Should such changes be considered seriously by your organisation?

21.3   Over the last ten years what trends have occurred in margins operating in your industry?   Are these trends acceptable?   What policy does your organisation adopt towards these trends?

Unit VI   Promotion decisions

Question 22   How can we communicate with our customers?

Question 23   How can we persuade our customers to buy our products?

Question 24   How can we measure the effectiveness of our advertising?

Question 25   Do we need a sales force?

Question 26   How should our sales force be organised and managed?

Question 22

How can we communicate with our customers?

Overview

Communication with customers can be undertaken either on a personal or an impersonal basis. The call of a salesman is a clear example of the personal approach; a mass advertising campaign is an example of the impersonal. Within these broad divisions, there is a wide range of communications methods which the marketer can use: this range is known as the COMMUNICATIONS MIX. Organisations also communicate with their customers in a number of less obvious ways. These means of indirect communication include all the ways in which the customer comes into contact with the organisation and its products; the quality of the product or service offered; and the price set on the organisation's offering.

Managers also have available to them a wide range of tactical marketing support activities, generally known as SALES PROMOTIONS. Sales promotions must be used with precisely the same attention to objectives, testing and evaluation as is customary in advertising. The cost-effectiveness of any sales promotion, including price reductions, must be established. It is also important to ensure that sales promotional activity is integrated into the overall marketing plan for the organisation. Carefully developed sales promotional schemes can be just as effective in industrial markets as they are in consumer markets. Sales promotions can be undertaken as a marketing tactic for any of the four 'P's.

Personal and impersonal communication

Organisations communicate with their customers in a wide variety of ways. A German manufacturer of recycling equipment for plastic waste chose to meet his potential customers at a specially convened technical briefing conference in Hamburg. Invitations were sent to public health and sanitation engineers and also to heads of local government committees throughout the EEC. The managing director of the company spent two days with the customers. First, he indicated the general principles of the process; he then went on to show all his guests a nearby installation actually at work; and, finally, he led a discussion on the commercial and social advantages which accrued to the satisfied customer.

He then turned over the leadership role to his economists and technical officers who spent eight hours with the guests in small groups of six, discussing the particular nature of the problems each guest had in his own local government activity. By the time the conference ended, each guest had seen the recycling process at work and had a grasp of the economic implications for his own sphere of operation. The mechanism chosen for communication had been to conduct *person-to-person* exchanges and to explore in detail how the product could meet the needs of each customer.

In contrast, when the British banking system launched its two major credit cards - Barclaycard and Access - a mass advertising campaign was undertaken. Few bank managers invited their customers for tea in order to discuss the merits and demerits of a credit card from the clearing bank compared with American Express.

Instead, the national press was filled with display advertisements which were predominantly concerned with emphasising that credit cards could "take the waiting out of wanting". In fact, strict control of credit limits ensured that each customer could only take advantage of this claim once or twice. But the advertisements did not stress that the amount of credit offered was carefully adjusted to an individual's total financial position: this information might have deterred too many potential card holders. Instead, all holders of existing bank accounts which had been relatively trouble-free were either encouraged to take a card, or sent one automatically. This was an *impersonal* approach to communicating with one's customers.

In both examples, *point-of-sale promotional literature* was also employed. In the case of the German manufacturer of recycling equipment, guests at the conference were provided with technical documentation and costs and benefit data. The British banks ensured that the counters of their branches and the doormats of their customers were amply covered with explanatory leaflets.

Clearly, the above discussion examines communication only in a new launch situation. Activities of this kind may create a high level of awareness of a product or service but, if enough potential customers are to acquire what is on offer, these activities need to be supplemented either by follow-up personal contact or by reminder advertisements. It can never be assumed that one communications impact on a customer is noted, let alone that it will lead, without further support, to a positive action like purchasing a product. Equally, we cannot assume that, once a potential customer has made use of a product or service, the task of communication is complete. Quite the contrary. The characteristics of the product or service in use, the nature of the contacts or service at the point of purchase, the after-sales service if needed - all these will communicate with the customer, either reinforcing his judgement that he was correct in the way he chose or deterring him next time around. In either event, he is apt to talk, to convey impressions by word of mouth, about the organisation to his colleagues and friends; and these impressions will influence them.

The communications mix

We have taken two examples in some detail in order to explore how organisations communicate with their customers and users. In general terms, the recycling equipment was handled by person-to-person technical selling and the credit card service was mass promoted by advertising. There is, of course, a much bigger armoury of techniques of communication available to the marketer. He will seek to deploy these techniques both singly and in combination for the maximum effect within a given budget. The major methods of communication constitute a tool-kit for all marketers, whether they are operating in consumer or industrial goods markets or service markets. Although different types of communication tend to be more widely used in different markets (personal selling, for example, is the major form of communication in industrial markets), there are no hard and fast rules about what methods can and cannot be used in any particular market. Specific marketing situations must be evaluated on their own terms and an appropriate communications strategy devised. Indeed, some of the most successful communications campaigns have resulted from the use of a different method of communication in a market which had become accustomed to receiving messages in one or two particular ways.

In the communications mix, as in the marketing mix as a whole, the marketer will arrange the basic elements so as to achieve the emphasis desirable for his particular market.

The major methods of communication which are widely available in Europe are the following:

National and regional newspapers.

These appear daily or weekly. Typically, they are confined to just one country but in recent years a number of links between the serious or quality dailies have appeared.

Trade and professional magazines. These cover everything from architects' materials, computers, caravans and model railways to the accountancy and professional marketing periodicals.

National, regional and Pan-European radio and television, particularly commercial television and radio.

Exhibitions. These are held either on a national, European or international basis and cover everything from dairy products to offset lithographic printing equipment and machine tools. Many are open to trade members only; others restrict the attendance of the general public to a specific time during the exhibition.

Direct mail. This employs circulars or leaflets conveyed through the post or delivered door-to-door. The main advantage of direct mail as a method of communication is that it can allow the development of a personal relationship between company and customer.

Public relations. This includes the dissemination of information to the press and television for possible news coverage and the general development of an organisation's image with the public. This latter activity can often constitute a major asset in marketing terms.

Back-up/point-of-sale literature. This covers the supporting literature produced by organisations to supplement other communications. It includes catalogues, price lists and technical specifications, as well as special displays at the point-of-sale in consumer goods markets.

Packaging. This is a particularly important influence in consumer markets. Packaging must be viewed not only in terms of how it helps to persuade customers to purchase but also in terms of the extent to which it minimises damaged goods that need to be returned or replaced. The consequences of inadequate packaging upset customers and significantly damage the effectiveness of communications.

Personal selling. We have left this aspect to last but it is by no means the least important. It is given full discussion in Questions 25 and 26. Suffice it to observe here that it embraces the activities of individuals travelling to established and potential customers; the use of telephone selling, increasingly common in consumer and fast moving industrial goods markets; and the activities of any person who sells to customers, such as the managing director of a capital goods industry, or a giant food manufacturer selling to major supermarket chains that control ten to twenty per cent of his total business volume.

Marketing communicates with its customers by employing some or all of these possible methods. The use of one approach on its own will seldom suffice. A pharmaceutical manufacturer who sought to gain widespread sales for his ladies' hair colouring found that the chemist outlets into which he wished to sell his product were unwilling to respond to the blandishment of his sales ladies in a personal selling approach. The chemists required reassurance that a major advertising campaign would be launched both on television and in the fashionable women's magazines. They believed that only in this context would they be able to sell the product.

If we look closely at this example, we can see the importance of the distinction we made in Question 7 between customers and users or consumers. The hair colouring manufacturer had to communicate to two quite different groups - his customer and his customer's customers. The manufacturer's customers, the chemists, were not confident that point-of-sale display and elegant packaging would be adequate as a total communications effort to put the product through the channel of distribution to the women whose hair needed colouring. Accordingly, they were unwilling to stock the product until an additional communications effort was made.

An alternative way of expending an organisation's communications budget would be by direct personal selling on a home-by-home basis. The Avon organisation has pioneered this system in Britain for a wide range of cosmetics. Their system is in fact typical of that used in industrial markets where sales or technical representatives combine their sales activities with advisory services on how best to tackle and solve problems.

The effective marketing organisation is continually experimenting with the mix of communications media it employs to find out either how to make a fixed expenditure more cost-effective or how to reduce its budget in achieving a similar level of effect.

Indirect communications

Organisations also communicate with their customers in a number of less obvious ways, which we can term indirect. We have already referred to the *image* which an organisation has in the mind of potential customers prior to their receiving any new message about it. If it exists at all, that image will have been built up from a range of past experience and hearsay. It will affect not only how customers perceive any particular communications message but will also affect their behaviour or response as a result of receiving a communication. This indirect communication from the image is supplemented or reinforced by the way in which any enquiry or order is handled. In technical markets, where products require installation, or in service industries, where a service relationship takes some time to settle down, the kind of service which customers receive from the employees of the organisation communicates its own definite message. Efficiency and courtesy, for example, promote a positive image of the organisation; inefficiency and rudeness work in the opposite way.

Another major means of communication is, of course, the *product or service itself*. The type of arrangements which KLM, British Airways or SAS make for their customers, both on the ground and in-flight, are vehicles for communication with the customers which will influence their attitudes and perhaps their subsequent behaviour towards the particular carrier. This also holds good for the freight forwarder who uses the air cargo facilities of these organisations. If delays, damages or misdirection occur, these misfortunes communicate to him an impression of the airline which cannot fail to influence him later on.

Pricing is also an extremely meaningful communications cue to customers. In unsophisticated markets, where customers are unsure of the criteria for judgement of a product or service (say, wines, restaurants or hotel accommodation), price will frequently be used as an indication of quality. As the customer becomes more certain of himself, he begins to rely more on his own judgement and does not fear to take a more discriminating view of price. Where the price is known to other colleagues or friends, however, the fact that it has been paid can also act as a communications message to such folk about the customer himself.

Different levels of pricing can convey a good deal about a product. If the price is low, the product may be seen as being too cheap to be satisfactory. If the price is high, the product may be assumed to be of correspondingly high quality. Certain price levels may prompt the customer to believe that the product or service is a bargain not to be missed.

The complexity of customer reaction to price levels can be illustrated by the fortunes of Turtle Wax car polish. When it was launched in America at 59 cents, the polish was considered to be so cheap that its quality was suspect. The manufacturers increased the price to $US1.59 but made no changes in the product itself; the result was that the polish, now the most highly priced car wax on offer, rapidly took a major share of the market.

It is well worth reiterating the benefits of *word-of-mouth* communications.

These are closely allied to the conspicuous visual display of products which have been purchased - be it the latest piece of electronic equipment in a factory or service industry, or new furnishing fabrics or garden furniture for the home. Other customers can both see and discuss the product in use. They can mull it over and receive advice from someone else who has already taken the risk and made a purchase. Such advice is seen as more objective than the salesman's word or the advertising. Any organisation should be delighted to have satisfied customers and users communicating for it in this way.

Word-of-mouth communications are particularly important for industrial purchases. In such transactions, great reliance is placed on the recommendations of "respected peers" both within the company and among colleagues in other organisations. This type of communication is also commonly associated with the purchase of consumer durables when purchase is infrequent and also conspicuous. If, for example, a particular make of dishwasher has acquired a reputation for ineffective performance and high incidence of breakdown, sales are likely to be adversely affected.

Using featured sales promotions

We have just seen that all organisations have at their disposal a very considerable range of communications media, including personal sales activity and the more impersonal advertising. At any one time, an organisation will have adopted a mix of these means of promotion that interacts appropriately with the other three 'P's - price, product and place.

One aspect of communication and promotion, however, is sometimes overlooked. This is short-term or tactical marketing activity which uses some or all of the four 'P's. The tactical requirement may be, for instance, to secure additional product trial, or to increase distribution or display. Tactical marketing activity of this kind is termed *sales promotion*. The essence of sales promotion is that it features an offer to defined customers or consumers within a specific time limit. To be termed a sales promotion, an offer must be made over and above the normal terms of trade, the objective being to increase sales beyond what would normally be expected. The benefit offered must not be inherent in the product or service itself.

Sales promotions are part of tactical marketing and can make use of the communications media or of price, product or place. Insofar as such tactics are an integral element of an organisation's annual marketing plan, they constitute a subset of integrated marketing rather than an element of the promotional 'P'.

Tactical strategy

Because sales promotions are essentially tactical devices, they often amount to little more than a series of spasmodic gimmicks lacking any coherence. Yet the very same managements who organise spasmodic sales promotions usually believe that pricing, distribution or advertising should conform to an overall marketing strategy, enshrined in an annual plan. The reason for this discrepancy may lie in the fact that marketing plans have always been based on a philosophy of building a long-term customer and consumer franchise, whereas the basic rationale of sales promotions is to help the company gain and/or retain tactical marketing initiative.

Sales of Heinz soups during January and February account for 24 per cent of the company's annual sales. The company's "Love Songs" promotion was designed to give the sales force a pre-Christmas selling tool to enable them to reach forecast sales. The promotion was also intended to achieve prominent price displays in stores, thus encouraging increased sales, and to link in with the current major advertising theme, "the one you love". The promotion included an exclusive LP which was offered to the trade as a loader or free gift in return for specific orders for Heinz soups and guaranteed display space. The record was also offered to consumers for £1.99 plus three soup labels as proofs of purchase; this offer helped to pay for the dealer give-away. In addition, consumers were offered top LP records and cassettes at £1.20 off the recommended retail price if they sent in proofs of purchase. The prime objectives of this promotion were to increase consumer sales by "selling in" more soup to retailers and to gain prominent in-store display. The sell-in over the first four weeks of the promotion was 20 per cent over target.

There is no reason why there should not be a strategy for sales promotions, with each promotion increasing the effectiveness of the next. In this way, a bond between seller and buyer can be built up and tactical objectives can be linked in with the overall plan, thus ensuring better deployment of resources.

There are some dangers associated with using price reductions and promotions on a brand. The fruit squash market, for example, had been highly branded. In a period of fierce competition, the manufacturers dropped prices to a level where they were indistinguishable from those of the own label brands. The manufacturers also ran many promotions in the form of competitions and the like. This led to the feeling among purchasers that the branded products were no better than the own label products and that there was no justification for the premium price of branded squashes. Eventually, this spelled the death of branded squashes. In the cooking oil market, competition has led to demands from the sales staff that price cutting and promotions should be used to gain market share. Reflecting on the fate of the fruit squash market and believing that the long-term future of their own market is at stake, the manufacturers have resisted this short-term means of gaining sales.

However, recent years have shown that the intelligent use of sales promotions is both possible and desirable. Successful campaigns have included the Home Pride Flour Graders, who first appeared in the early sixties; the 20 million enamel Golly brooches given out by Robertsons since the nineteen-thirties; Mighty Ajax; Miss Pears; and the Ovalteenies. Many other campaigns have used schemes and devices which have been consistently incorporated into a product's total communications and marketing strategy. More recent schemes, such as the Esso tiger and the Smurfs, have proved that it is possible to establish a style of sales promotion which, if consistently applied, will help to establish for a product objectives which are flexible and have staying power.

In Question 4 we asserted that industrial goods are always sold to other organisations and that this has the effect of changing the emphasis placed on certain elements of the marketing mix, rather than fundamentally affecting the relevance of the marketing concept. It will not be surprising, therefore, to learn that the consumer goods sales promotional techniques described above can also be applied to industrial goods. Yet, in spite of this, sales promotions are comparatively rare in industrial markets. This may be partly because of a belief held in engineering that if a firm has to promote its products that aggressively, there must be something wrong with them.

In recent years, however, industrial goods companies have begun to take note of the enormous success of campaigns such as Yorkshire Imperial Metal's Golden Spanner and schemes in the Herbert Morris Group. They are becoming more aware of sales promotion as a flexible and competitive tactical tool in marketing. Through an advertisement in a Sunday newspaper, 3M recently offered a £50 coupon to prospective buyers of photocopiers. A major European industrial goods company, with divisions spanning a range of products from fast moving industrial to high priced capital goods, has developed a massive range of special promotion schemes. They are offering featured time period trade-in allowances, desk-top give-aways and custom-built guarantees. All these are featured offers outside and above the normal terms of trade.

Making featured sales promotions effective

There is widespread acknowledgement that sales promotions are often badly mismanaged. The main reason for this is that confusion about the exact nature and purpose of a sales promotion often results in expenditures not being properly recorded. Some companies regard sales promotion as part of advertising, some as part of sales force expense, others as a general marketing expense, and yet others as a manufacturing expense (as in the case of giving extra quantity for the standard price or producing special labels to announce a special offer). The loss of unit sales revenue from special price reductions is often not recorded at all.

Few companies can afford not to set objectives for sales promotions or to fail to evaluate results after the event. For example, a £1 case allowance on a product with a contribution rate of £3 per case has to increase sales by 50 per cent just to maintain the same level of contribution. Failure to attain this, or to meet alternative objectives set for the promotion, easily results in loss of control and a consequent reduction in profits.

There are two essential steps to the more effective management of an organisation's sales promotion expenditure. First, current spending must be analysed and categorised by type of activity, such as special packaging, special point-of-sales material or loss of revenue through price reductions. Next, within a total strategy for sales promotions, objectives for each promotion must be clearly stated, such as trial, repeat purchase, distribution, display, a shift in buying peaks or combating competition in a specified manner.

Thereafter, the following procedure must always be followed:

- select the appropriate technique;

- pre-test the ideas;

- mount the promotion;

- evaluate its impact in depth.

A leading manufacturer of self-assembly kitchens embarked on a heavy programme of sales promotion after a dramatic reduction in consumer demand. While the firm managed to maintain turnover, the managers involved were worried that their sales promotional activities had been carried out in such a haphazard and piecemeal fashion that they were unable to evaluate the cost-effectiveness of what they had done. They were also very concerned about the effect of the promotion on the company image and on their long-term franchise with consumers. Accordingly, they made a concentrated study of this area of expenditure which had come to represent over half their total communications budget. Next time round, they had clear objectives, a clear promotional plan fully integrated into their marketing plans and an established, on-going means of assessment. The company took their competitors by surprise and made substantial gains in market share. In one promotion alone, they hired an entire hall in an international exhibition centre. They converted it into a giant showroom with 40 kitchen displays and a 250 seat theatre. For an expenditure of £90,000, the company presented a new range to over 2,500 customers, obtained 900 display orders against a target of 750, and sold to their entire national distribution network in one operation.

At the same time, they convinced the trade of their professional, business-like approach, and of their confidence in the future.

Some of the many types of sales promotions that can be used are listed in Table 5. Each of these different types are appropriate for different circumstances and each has advantages and disadvantages. For example, case bonusing relates cost to volume, is fast and flexible, effective where the customer is profit conscious, can last as long as required, and is simple to set up, administer and sell. On the other hand, it has no cumulative value to the customer, is unimaginative, and can often be seen as a prelude to a permanent price reduction.

Points schemes (where channel members are allocated points according to quantity purchased in a given time, and receive some reward when adequate points are collected) are flexible, have wide appeal, do not involve the company in holding stocks of gifts and are easy to administer. On the other hand, they offer no advantages in bulk buying, are difficult to budget, and lack the immediacy of dealer loaders which encourage bulk buying by channel members.

Table 5 Various types of sales promotion

TYPE OF PROMOTION		CONSUMER	TRADE	SALES FORCE
MONEY	DIRECT	• Price reduction	• Dealer loaders • Loyalty schemes • Incentives • Full-range buying schemes	• Bonus • Commission
	INDIRECT	• Coupons • Vouchers • Money equivalents • Competitions	• Extended credit • Delayed invoicing • Sale or return • Coupons • Vouchers • Money equivalents	• Coupons • Vouchers • Points systems • Money equivalents • Competitions
GOODS	DIRECT	• Free goods • Premium offers (eg: 13 for 12) • Free gifts • Trade-in offers	• Free gifts • Trial offers • Trade-in offers	• Free gifts
	INDIRECT	• Stamps • Coupons • Vouchers • Money equivalents • Competitions	• Coupons • Vouchers • Money equivalents • Competitions	• Coupons • Vouchers • Points systems • Money equivalents
SERVICES	DIRECT	• Guarantees • Group participation events • Special exhibitions & displays	• Guarantees • Group participation events • Free services • Risk reduction schemes • Training • Special exhibitions & displays • Demonstrations • Reciprocal trading schemes	• Free services • Group participation events
	INDIRECT	• Co-operative advertising • Stamps, coupons • Vouchers for services • Events admissions • Competitions	• Stamps, coupons • Vouchers for services • Competitions	• Coupons • Vouchers • Points systems for services • Events admissions • Competitions

Question 22   How can we communicate with our customers?

Clearly, great care is necessary in selecting a scheme appropriate to the objective sought.

Application questions

22.1   What was the last major purchase you made for your household? When you were considering alternatives how did the product manufacturers communicate with you? Which of the communications used influenced your final choice?

22.2   Within your organisation, how do you communicate with your customers? Are there other ways in which you could communicate? What is the purpose of each form of communication which you presently employ? In what ways do they: (a) complement each other; (b) act as reinforcements to each other; (c) fulfil a specific task which could not be undertaken by any other form of communication?

22.3   Are your organisation's communications co-ordinated in any way? Who is responsible for the co-ordination?   Do you encounter any problems when co-ordinating your organisation's communications? How can these problems be solved?

22.4   How is sales promotion used as a form of communication by your organisation? In what ways does it relate to the other forms of communication used? Are there any other ways in which sales promotion could be used more effectively? How would you justify additional sales promotion of this kind?

Question 23

How can we persuade our customers to buy our products?

Overview

A vital element in devising successful persuasive appeals is an understanding of how particular purchase decisions are reached. The process of persuasion can be analysed in many markets through a series of steps up which potential customers climb, covering initial awareness, interest, attitude formation, the emergence of intention and the decision to act. If our product or service has been matched with customer needs, the customer must normally be persuaded to want our particular organisation's offering in preference to any other. This can often be accomplished by developing a psychologically unique appeal for our product or service (possibly through branding), correctly judging the price and making the product available in a convenient way.

Successful persuasion also depends on knowing who will be involved in the many stages of decision making leading up to the decision to purchase. Different information must be fed to the various groups in the most appropriate form at the most appropriate time.

The process of persuasion

The key factor in successfully persuading customers to buy any product is an understanding of how particular purchase decisions are reached (see Figure 27). This requires analysis both of the decision-making process employed by the customer and of the criteria used in arriving at a decision. (Ways of approaching such analysis, it will be remembered, were discussed in Question 9, "Why do customers behave the way they do?"). The sounder the grasp of the customers' decision-making process, the more likely an organisation is to find the right balance of elements in its marketing mix and hence to match customer expectations with company resources.

The process of persuasion cannot begin unless *awareness* exists. Accordingly, it is useful to begin our answer to this Question by emphasising the need to create awareness of the existence of any product or service. As we have seen in Question 22, this can be accomplished in a variety of ways. It should be noted at this point, however, that without a favourable attitude and intention and opportunity to purchase, awareness by itself will not bring about the desired result.

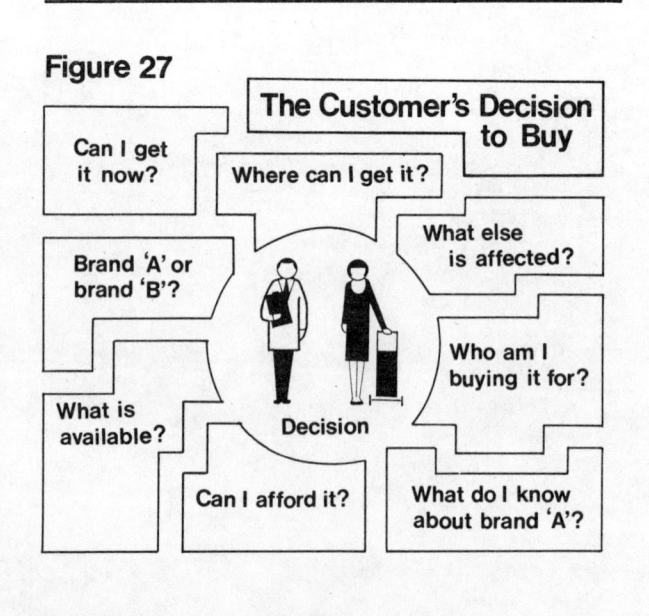

Figure 27

The Customer's Decision to Buy

- Can I get it now?
- Where can I get it?
- What else is affected?
- Brand 'A' or brand 'B'?
- Who am I buying it for?
- What is available?
- Decision
- Can I afford it?
- What do I know about brand 'A'?

Unit VI Promotion decisions

A large brewer in Britain distributed his draught beers through a limited number of public houses. Most of these were in the south, although some were located in other areas of the country. In order to promote his product the brewer initiated a national television advertising campaign. An extremely high recall of the product and the message was achieved but, since the beer was only available in limited areas, much of this investment in awareness was wasted. Similar waste occurs in industrial markets when product advertising creates awareness but no further activity is undertaken to build upon it.

Once awareness has been created in the mind of a potential customer, *interest in learning more* about the product or service will normally follow if the product or service appears relevant to the customer's needs. Frequently, the medium used for arousing awareness will include enough further information to satisfy this interest. Technical details or demonstration of potential benefits that can accrue can be an integral part of the initial communications message. In the context of these first two steps, *attitudes* may begin to form. Potential customers may reject the service offered, not believing that a draught beer brewed in London could possibly slake the thirst of an Anglian farmer. Equally, the emergent attitude could be that an up-and-coming Anglian farmer might well want to drink what the smart young men in London drink to wash down their ploughman's lunch in Fleet Street or on the King's Road.

The significance of *understanding* how the Anglian farmer will react when he becomes aware of the draught beer will not have escaped notice. Successful persuasion requires the most careful attention to how attitudes towards particular products are formed. All the evidence available indicates that only a few generalisations can be made which cover more than a limited group of products or services. However, these generalisations tell us a great deal about how to create successful persuasive appeals. As was discussed in Question 9, customers' attitudes are in part dependent on their purchase or choice criteria (that is, the attributes judged most desirable and important in a product or service) and their belief about the presence or absence of those attributes in any given brand. Appropriate material, it appears, can indeed use the customer's initial interest to stimulate the formation of favourable attitudes and beliefs. Information of itself never seems to change attitudes. If an attitude is well entrenched, it will lead to a distorted perception of any information which is at variance with it, in order to make it fit. Hence, persuasive appeals must either *create fresh attitudes* or *build upon those which are already there*.

Once the relevant attitudes have been located and understood, the appeal can concentrate on offering the arguments which match the attitudes. Favourable attitudes, like unfavourable attitudes, affect the perception of information received. If the audience is well disposed, it will use the advocate's information to confirm and reinforce its own prior attitudes. It is reassuring, after all, to know that one is right - a point, incidentally, which must not be overlooked *after* the purchase when reinforcement of attitudes is vitally important.

We should perhaps pause here for a moment to reflect on the timing of these two stages, interest arousal and attitude development, as far as the potential customer is concerned. Purchasing officers in industrial companies, housewives acting on behalf of their families, service organisations acting on behalf of clients - all may be both aware and interested but in no position to act. There may be no need for the product or service at the time when interest is at its height. Evidence from this field clearly indicates that the investment made in taking customers up these early steps of the persuasion process can be all too easily dissipated. The favourable attitudes, the interest, even the awareness can decay. A good filing system or a conscientious housewife might preserve the information for a time, but persuasion processes are not static. Accordingly, a crucial part of the marketing effort to persuade is to first pinpoint those who are potentially in the market or who can be brought to the market by one's efforts. This point can be summed up in the expression *intention to buy*.

The customer's decision to buy

ICI Paints Division sells non-drip emulsion paint. The paint is available both to tradesmen for use in professional decoration and to amateur do-it-yourself customers in homes across Europe. Television advertising creates an awareness of the brand, and the content of the advertising arouses an interest. Both tradesmen and amateur decorators hold favourable images of ICI as a chemical company and have little doubt that the product will do the job adequately. ICI's problem is to ensure that at the moment of decision making its brand is preferred to others.

The first step the company took in exploring the decision-making process was to identify the criteria used in deciding to buy different brands of paint. It was hoped that the key dimensions of that decision could be used to create a unique appeal - a factor very important in a market which included competitors such as Du Pont, major French and German companies and the firmly established British companies, Crown Paints and Bergers. ICI found that the decision-making process was extremely complex. In almost all cases, the end consumer had been reluctant to make the basic decision to decorate, whether or not a professional tradesman was to be employed. The home would be disrupted and considerable expense would be involved. In any event, paint was unlikely to be the only purchase considered: other items would also have to be purchased. Accessories could well be required, and wallpaper might be used in association with the paint. ICI's research showed that among married couples it was most common for the wife to decide that there was a need for decoration. This underlines the need in all markets to determine the identity of the dominant influencers on the purchase decision. In the case of ICI Paints, on the occasions where a professional decorator was employed, the role of the decorator in influencing decisions as to colour of paint, style of decoration, and so on, was far from clear. Other companies might benefit from considering the investigation of the hierarchy of decision makers in their markets. A simplified statement of the various elements leading up to the paint decision is given in Figure 28.

Clearly, the brand specification for paint is the last stage of the total decision process. ICI's advertising could well trigger awareness, create interest, sway attitudes and crystallise intention, but it could then be unsuccessful if the colour card did not contain a colour which matched or blended with the wallpaper. In any event, a process of this kind inevitably made ICI's position look weak in relation to other manufacturers whose range of products included wallpapers. In the British market, Crown form part of the Wallpaper Manufacturers' Group of companies. They were not slow to specify which of their paint colours would go well with their wallpapers. Taking all these factors into consideration, ICI entered the wallpaper market in the mid-sixties in a massive way.

It was not only the customers' decision-making process which left ICI vulnerable to effective competitive activity by other companies. ICI was also vulnerable because of the limited channels of distribution available to it. Crown again owned a very considerable proportion of the specialist paint and wallpaper retailers, although they were not so strong in the merchants which supplied the trade decorators. To persuade customers to buy ICI's paints, as opposed to any other brand with the appropriate colour, required the development of a brand loyalty or franchise. This applied chiefly to men since they generally specified the brand; women usually chose the colour. Advertising activity could create the franchise, provided that a sufficiently wide range of retail outlets or merchants carried the product. One could hardly expect potential customers to undertake a voyage of discovery around their town to track down the ICI stockist. ICI pursued discount policies to persuade retailers and merchants to carry the product and to sell it in competition with the other brands which would often be carried as well. The company then used point-of-sale promotional material and colour shade cards in order to sway customers in their favour.

Figure 28

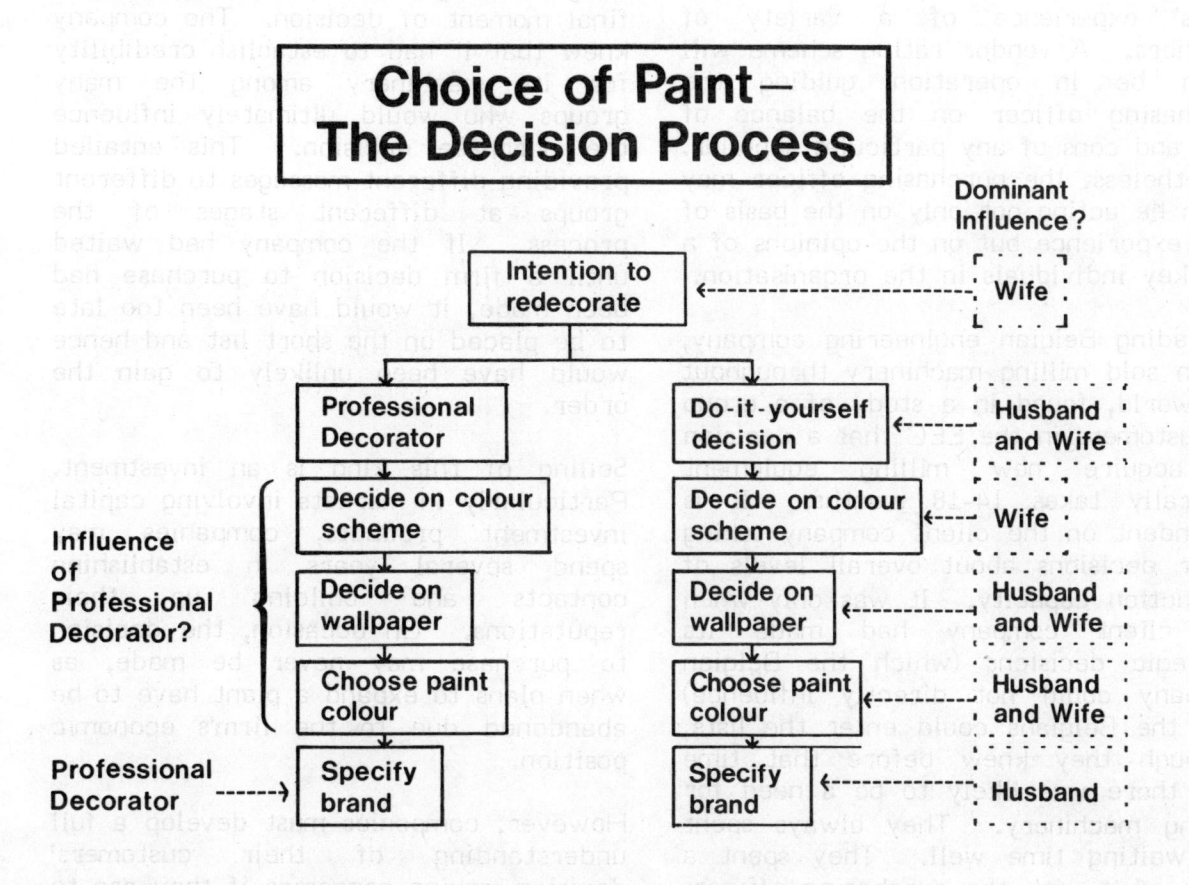

Choice of Paint – The Decision Process

```
                    Intention to
                    redecorate  ←-------------------- Wife

        ┌───────────────────┐           ┌───────────────────┐
        │ Professional      │           │ Do-it-yourself    │  ←----  Husband
        │ Decorator         │           │ decision          │        and Wife
        └───────────────────┘           └───────────────────┘
                │                                │
        ┌───────────────────┐           ┌───────────────────┐
        │ Decide on colour  │           │ Decide on colour  │  ←----  Wife
        │ scheme            │           │ scheme            │
        └───────────────────┘           └───────────────────┘
Influence       │                                │
of        ┌───────────────────┐           ┌───────────────────┐
Professional │ Decide on     │           │ Decide on         │  ←----  Husband
Decorator?   │ wallpaper     │           │ wallpaper         │        and Wife
          └───────────────────┘           └───────────────────┘
                │                                │
          ┌───────────────────┐           ┌───────────────────┐
          │ Choose paint      │           │ Choose paint      │  ←----  Husband
          │ colour            │           │ colour            │        and Wife
          └───────────────────┘           └───────────────────┘
                │                                │
Professional ┌───────────────────┐           ┌───────────────────┐
Decorator ---→│ Specify brand  │           │ Specify brand     │  ←----  Husband
          └───────────────────┘           └───────────────────┘
                                                         Dominant
                                                         Influence?
```

As the ICI example suggests, husbands and wives may have different influences on the purchase decision. One British manufacturer of washing machines found that 73% of purchases were replacements and only 23% were first time buys. Furthermore, in 80% of the couples the wife was the more influential partner; indeed, in 25% of the cases the wife took sole responsibility. Moreover, husbands and wives have different criteria for evaluating washing machines. The wife is predominantly interested in reliability, manufacturer's reputation, service and guarantee, while the husband's greatest concern is price. For specific features, the wife's interest is load capacity, automatic action, hot/cold filling and spin speed, whereas the husband is concerned with features like ease of installation and quiet running. This means that different features for the same washing machine are promoted to the husband and wife respectively; the wife receives the principal emphasis but only on those features which interest her.

Persuasion in repeat custom

Many customers or users of a product or service approach the buying decision with considerable knowledge of the product's performance. In a typical industrial purchasing situation, the organisation will have accumulated many years' experience of a variety of suppliers. A vendor rating scheme will often be in operation guiding the purchasing officer on the balance of pros and cons of any particular supplier. Nonetheless, the purchasing officer may often be acting not only on the basis of past experience but on the opinions of a few key individuals in the organisation.

A leading Belgian engineering company, which sold milling machinery throughout the world, found in a study of a group of customers in the EEC that a decision to acquire new milling equipment generally takes 14-18 months. It is dependent on the client company taking major decisions about overall levels of production capacity. It was only when the client company had made its strategic decisions (which the Belgian company could not directly influence) that the Belgians could enter the lists, although they knew before that time that there was likely to be a need for milling machinery. They always spent the waiting time well. They spent a little of it with the purchasing officers but most of that time was spent with the consulting and operating engineers who were responsible for the design and operational switch-on of the new capacity. They also devoted some of their persuasive effort to reaching senior management of the company concerned, reminding them of their technical strength and tradition of total reliability. They were fully aware that few senior managements would risk spoiling the whole job by errors at the milling machinery level. This was exactly the same attitude, by the way, that ICI found in relation to the quality of paint used in home decorating.

This Belgian company reinforced its image throughout the build-up to the final moment of decision. The company knew that it had to establish credibility for its machinery among the many groups who would ultimately influence the purchase decision. This entailed providing different messages to different groups at different stages of the process. If the company had waited until a firm decision to purchase had been made, it would have been too late to be placed on the short list and hence would have been unlikely to gain the order.

Selling of this kind is an investment. Particularly in markets involving capital investment products, companies may spend several years in establishing contacts and building up their reputations. On occasion, the decision to purchase may never be made, as when plans to expand a plant have to be abandoned due to the firm's economic position.

However, companies must develop a full understanding of their customers' decision-making processes if they are to persuade these customers to buy their products. If that understanding can be matched with a product or service that matches the needs and wants of customers, then success is within an organisation's reach.

Application questions

23.1 How does persuasion work in your markets? What assumptions do you make and on what are they based? How is your "model of persuasion" reflected in your promotional plan?

Question 23 How can we persuade our customers to buy our products?

23.2 How do you identify your customers? Is there a single group that you have to reach, or do you need to make a number of groups aware of your product offering? If you are marketing to a number of groups, how do you approach each of these groups? Is there any opportunity to adapt your approach to meet the needs of the different segments? What would you do if your communications budget were reduced by 50%: (a) concentrate on a limited number of market segments; (b) adopt a single approach to everyone in the market until the budget was used up?

23.3 How do potential customers become aware of your product offering? Are there any other ways in which you could create awareness? Once potential customers have become aware of your product offering, how do you ensure that they gain all the information necessary to decide in favour of buying your product in preference to competitors' products?

23.4 Within your own organisation, who becomes involved with the persuasion process? What monitoring is done to build up knowledge of the way in which the process works in your market? How could this be improved?

Question 24
How can we measure the effectiveness of our advertising?

Overview

The effectiveness of advertising can only be measured against clearly stated objectives. Once clear objectives have been identified, evaluative research techniques can be used to assess the extent to which they are being achieved. Before an expensive campaign is launched, small-scale research can check whether the advertisement is capable of achieving its objectives. After the campaign, post-evaluation procedures can assess how effective it has been and can indicate what the organisation still has to learn in the successful deployment of advertising.

Advertising objectives must always be clearly distinguished from the marketing objectives of the organisation. Where the objective can be achieved by advertising alone, it can be deemed an advertising objective. Where its achievement is dependent on other aspects of the marketing mix, it is a marketing objective. Achieving advertising objectives cannot guarantee sales success unless all other aspects of the marketing mix are also effectively deployed.

The importance of advertising objectives

Contrary to much folklore, the effectiveness of advertising can be measured with some degree of accuracy, provided always that *valid objectives* have been set. It is important to emphasise at the outset the need for the objectives to be valid. Before we can make any decisions on advertising we have to know precisely what role it is expected to play in the overall marketing effort. Is it expected to explain why the product is more expensive than the customer might otherwise expect it to be? Is it to communicate details about a completely new approach to some task which will require the rethinking of habitual practices by an industrial purchasing officer? Is it intended to emphasise that service is widely and speedily available in the event of a breakdown of machinery, thereby reassuring a client organisation that it can expect few major problems if it buys that particular machinery?

Each of these objectives might be achieved effectively by an advertising campaign but the total marketing operation could still be a failure. The expensive product may not be easily available, or may fail to live up to performance expectations. The quality of service provided may not be as high as the buying organisation had anticipated. In such instances, which are not infrequent, there is little point in laying blame at the door of the advertising. The advertising objectives have been achieved effectively; but the customers' hopes have been dashed by the failure of the rest of the marketing activity. The lesson is to ensure that the advertising objectives are appropriate to the marketing effort overall and that the organisation's communications do not over-claim.

Unless a company is using direct response advertising (where all the available information is conveyed by direct communications and the product is only available direct from the manufacturer or agent offering the product), the role of advertising is to help implement marketing objectives. As we have indicated, it is quite possible to communicate effectively but fail to achieve the marketing objectives of sales, market share and so on: the successful achievement of marketing objectives depends also on the satisfactory interaction of the other three 'P's - product, price and place. In addition, the successful achievement of advertising objectives will only lead to the fulfilment of marketing objectives if the marketing manager has been correct in his assumptions of how the achievement of the advertising objectives will affect customers' buying decisions.

An example of successful advertising combined with the failure to achieve marketing objectives can be found in RHM's introduction of a pastry mix. The company advertised this new product nationwide but in one area of the country the product was not well received. Research showed that the advertising objectives had been achieved. However, there was a local product on the market and customers preferred to support this. Although the RHM campaign had encouraged the overall use of pastry mixes, in this area a competing product had benefited from the increased interest. In the circumstances, RHM decided to spend no more money on advertising their brand of pastry mix; instead, they used other forms of promotion in order to achieve the marketing objective of selling their product.

A final point to be borne in mind is that since advertising can seldom make sales on its own, it is almost always appropriate to resist the temptation to relate advertising expenditure to levels of sales achieved.

The nature of advertising objectives

Recent studies at Cranfield with many of the leading British and European commercial organisations have shown that there are four major objectives which organisations traditionally set. They are as follows:

Branding and image building

Whether the organisation is engaged in industrial products (like the National Coal Board, British Petroleum and Dunlop), in consumer goods (like Cadbury Schweppes, Weetabix and Watney Mann) or services (like the British Tourist Authority and the Midland Bank), it always seeks to communicate an overall image of the organisation and its work to actual and potential customers. Since most organisations believe that a favourably perceived image creates a constructive environment in which to market their outputs, they commonly set the building of such an image as an advertising objective. In markets where there is little product differentiation, branding is frequently used to distinguish a product from its direct competitors.

Education and information

Organisations generally know far better than do their customers what exactly they are trying to achieve in the way of product or service performance. In the well organised marketing activity, that performance level will have been set on the basis of a very close analysis of customer and consumer needs and wants. The importance of ensuring that customers are aware of, and comprehend, the organisation's offering along with the benefits it can potentially bestow cannot be understated. It is all too easy to assume prematurely that customers are aware and understand. This objective is especially important in market development strategies, when customers are being encouraged to use the product or service in new and different ways. Education and information are also all-important during the early stages of introducing a new product or service to the market.

Affecting attitudes

The initial campaign of education and

information must be followed by a campaign to affect potential customers' attitudes in a way favourable to the organisation's output. In Question 23, it will be remembered, we discussed the problems involved in seeking to change attitudes and we came to the conclusion that the better course was to build on or develop them.

Influencing potential customers' attitudes was the communications goal set by Plessey when it launched its automatic ignition system for gas installations, especially domestic cookers. Cadbury's faced similar problems when they launched Marvel and Smash. In all three product instances, customers had historical attitudes to products of this type. In the first case, gas ignition systems had a long record of doubtful efficiency. Cadbury's, in their turn, were up against World War II stereotypes of dried milk and powdered potato, as well as being anxious not to damage their image as a manufacturer of chocolate which used real milk. In both cases, the image which the companies had nurtured enabled communications activities to develop attitudes towards the products like, "If a well established firm like that has produced the product it will be well worth trying, even though I would be extremely doubtful if an unknown firm had attempted it".

Many assume that the more favourable the attitude held toward the product or service being promoted, the greater the predisposition to purchase. Large budgets are allocated based on this assumption. In some circumstances this relationship does not hold good. Advertisers need to check that the assumption applies to them before they commit their advertising budgets.

Loyalty reinforcement and reminding

The fourth major objective has two dimensions. The first constitutes the *reinforcement of loyalty*. On the one hand, companies wish continually to reinforce their customers' loyalties to their products or services. On the other hand, customers need to be convinced that their pattern of habitual behaviour (in always going to a particular supplier, for example, or always shopping at a specific department store in Paris, London or Rome) is not shortsighted on their part. The advertising objective in such circumstances will be to reinforce the feeling that the habit is correct and sensible and does not need breaking.

The corollary to loyalty reinforcement is, of course, *reminder communication*. Customers can easily forget to keep adequate stock levels of products, or not avail themselves of services often enough. This is especially true in areas of discretionary purchasing or behaviour, where failure to be reminded may well lead to another more recently communicated message having a greater influence on the customer. This point can be illustrated by the example of domestic or office decorations and furnishings. "Old furniture must go" was a classic campaign by the furniture industry in the mid-sixties, designed to encourage customers to enter a discretionary market. The same style of advertising campaign is used by brewers to remind us to visit their pubs instead of watching television or following other social pursuits.

Finally, the combination of loyalty and reminder communication is intended to ensure that any custom generated does indeed come to the organisation undertaking the campaign rather than to any conveniently available brand. (The case of the RHM pastry mix described earlier in the Question underlines the importance of this form of communication.)

Clearly, the relative importance of these four major objectives varies according to the state of the market and the life cycle of the particular product. At the introductory stage of a product or service, the generation of awareness and the conveying of information are vitally important. Later in a product's life cycle, branding, image, loyalty and reminding take on much greater significance. The effective marketing operation ensures that appropriate communications goals are set for each of its product ranges or groups of services offered.

Pre-exposure testing of advertising

We offer no apology for devoting much of the answer to our present Question to a discussion of advertising objectives.

As was observed at the outset, without valid objectives no real attempt can be made to measure effect. In addition, valid objectives are needed in order to construct appropriate promotional or advertising campaigns to meet these objectives. Different objectives will call for different approaches to communication in the market place. The generation of ideas for campaigns is a specialist task although most managers consider themselves gifted amateurs. The most appropriate promotion may be a sales presentation using a variety of media to communicate the different points, some form of predominantly visual communication such as a brochure, direct mail circulars and press advertisements, an exhibition presentation with supporting materials and samples, or a television commercial. As far as possible, the ability of the chosen promotion to achieve the objective set for it needs to be ascertained. Pre-testing is one means of doing this.

Pre-testing constitutes sensible insurance against errors in the creative development and execution of ideas. It is a means of checking whether material is technically capable of achieving its objectives. It is not a substitute for other research to identify whether particular advertising objectives are the most appropriate for the product or service being promoted. Available as a standard service, it involves presenting the promotional material to a sample of the correct target audience of customers and measuring their reactions to it.

The customers are presented with the communication in as realistic a context as possible. They may have been questioned beforehand to establish a benchmark for their awareness, interest, attitudes, loyalty, and so forth. After exposure to the communication, these characteristics are measured again. In addition, the opportunity can be taken to allow customers to give verbal reactions to the communications message. Negative aspects of the messages can then be screened out. For many advertisers the major concern is to ensure that negative reactions which could damage the product or service do not occur. It is assumed that if the potential customer holds a negative reaction the likelihood of purchase will be diminished. A common occurrence in pre-testing is that the customer is found to be confused by the communication. So much information may have been packed into the message that nothing registers clearly with the customer. The customer may be confused too by the use of star personalities in promotional activities: it is often the case that there are inappropriate associations in the mind of the customer. It is also common for the potential customer to pick up a communication not intended by the advertiser. "You are never alone with a Strand" was interpreted by smokers to mean that people smoking the brand had no friends and therefore had to turn to smoking as a substitute for human company.

Pre-testing procedures can also be used to compare several alternative approaches to, or mixtures of, communications in order to see which gives the best impact. Yardsticks for comparison with previous advertising campaigns or other promotional activity emerge as data begins to build up. Comparisons can be made with the communications activities of competitors to see how well any particular campaign matches up. Furthermore, pre-exposure tests can be undertaken from the very earliest stages of development when rough formats can be used to test ideas and concepts. The advertiser is well advised to take full account of the results of his pre-testing. If the correct message cannot be conveyed in the artificial test situation, the advertisement stands little chance of communicating effectively in the market context amidst surrounding distractions.

In calculating a budget for pre-testing, it is necessary to consider the cost of *not* carrying out such tests. Unless an advertisement is carefully pre-tested, the advertiser runs the risk of conveying an incorrect message about the product and discouraging people from using it. He may also confuse potential customers about the product being advertised. Where a serious mistake of this nature occurs the entire campaign may have no impact or, even worse, create negative reactions.

Post-exposure evaluation

The execution of the full advertising campaign, including any pre-testing needed, is normally seen as a very expensive affair. In consumer goods industries such as cosmetics, budgets for advertising run as high as 30 per cent of total sales income. For a major company this can mean several million pounds each year. The food industries of Europe have similarly massive advertising campaigns. In industrial markets, communications expense tends to be associated more with personal contact of a technical, advisory and after-sales service nature. Nonetheless, total expenditure on communications for industrial goods can reach very substantial levels.

Accordingly, it is normally only sensible to set aside some of the total communications budget to measure how effective the advertising or other promotional activity was in practice. How much should be expended on evaluative research will depend on the benefits which will accrue from knowing how effective the communication has been. Certainly, any organisation which intends to spend further substantial sums in a subsequent year is extremely unwise if it does not seek to learn carefully from its expensively bought experience. Much of the post evaluation work undertaken concentrates on measuring the effectiveness of media advertising. Advertising or commercial television, in particular, will account for the major share of the total communications budget.

As in pre-exposure testing, research methods in post-exposure evaluation involve survey work amongst potential and actual customers. Whatever objectives were adopted for the advertising campaign should be checked to see whether they have been achieved. It will be recalled that different levels of effect may have been accomplished. Most customers may well have been aware of the campaign but failed to receive clearly the information it was intended to communicate; or they may have covered both these stages and failed to develop or evolve their attitudes.

Campaigns often have worthwhile effects, but effects that are somewhat at variance with what an organisation hoped to achieve and what pre-tests may have suggested would be achieved. The cause of slippage could be the media which the organisation employed in its major campaign. Pre-testing methods cannot really simulate adequately a television commercial in mid-evening or a colour advertisement in the Sunday Telegraph, or a page in Waterways World. Any slippage that does occur, however, provides vitally important evidence for the next campaign.

It is both possible and necessary to evaluate the effectiveness of any advertising campaign. How much is spent on evaluating any particular campaign will, of necessity, be determined by what is at stake. What can be at stake is well demonstrated in the instance of a French consumer durable manufacturer based in the electronics industry. The size of the market was some Fr.45-50 million per annum. The manufacturer's was an old established brand with some Fr.1 million spent annually on advertising in the media and a further Fr.300,000 spent on point-of-sale activities. Private brands by retailers held some 10 per cent of the market while the manufacturer held a more considerable share. There were 10 other branded competitors and the market was highly competitive among them all. The main advertising objectives set were to convey the benefits to be derived from using the product, to develop and convey favourable attitudes towards the product, and to maintain loyalty amongst current purchasers who repurchased relatively infrequently. For several years, advertising for the product had tried to emphasise a key attribute of the product's performance but had failed to persuade customers of the credibility of the claim. Research showed that certain changes in market conditions had reduced the perceived relevance of the attribute for purchasers. Guided by the research results, the manufacturer proceeded to emphasise other aspects of the product. Customers found the new claims more credible and showed themselves willing to acquire the product.

Media selection

Clearly, an ineffective message will cause the quality of the communication to deteriorate. However, if media are not properly selected then no one is likely to hear the message, regardless of its effectiveness. Furthermore, media buys that are too diffuse (in other words, have a much larger readership or viewership than is the target market) are not likely to give much return on the pound. The fundamental principle in media buying is to select those media vehicles that are seen, read and viewed by a large percentage of the target audience. The nature of the message is likely to determine the type of media, depending on whether sight or sound or motion are required: those requirements would frequently correspond to print, radio and television. The amount of media purchased also determines the frequency with which individual customers are exposed to the message.

In other words, media selection is the quantity part of the advertising effectiveness equation. Total advertising effectiveness is a function of both the media and the message or of quantity (media) and quality (message).

Other marketing communications

The guidelines contained in this Question are based on research undertaken at Cranfield into the effectiveness of media advertising. The main finding of this research was that valid and measurable objectives are the keystone to the success of any advertising campaign. Associated with this finding were the conclusions that the risks attendant on advertising campaigns can be minimised by the careful construction of a pre-exposure check and by appropriate research into the success or failure of earlier campaigns. Clearly, specific and quantifiable objectives are a pre-requisite of all such research.

This framework can also prove useful in the assessment of the other forms of communication (such as sales promotion and personal selling) outlined in Question 22. Although a different approach to evaluation may have to be adopted, no organisation should exempt its communications activity from justifying the investment made in it.

Application questions

24.1 How do your various communications contribute to the achievement of the marketing objectives for each of the products and services you offer? Does everyone in your marketing department agree with your distinction between communications and marketing objectives?

24.2 What pre-testing of advertising does your organisation do? What are the advantages and disadvantages of the procedures which you employ? What were the occasions when you changed your communications as a result of the pre-testing undertaken? What would have happened if you had not undertaken any pre-testing on these occasions? If you do not undertake advertising pre-testing, what is the justification for this decision? Under what circumstances would the organisation undertake pre-testing?

24.3 How is post-evaluation of your communications carried out in your organisation? How has this contributed to the development of the products monitored? Is there additional post-evaluation research which would help you decide on the allocation of future marketing budgets? On a cost-effective basis, how could such research be justified?

24.4 If you work in an organisation where no pre- or post-evaluation is carried out, how do you gain the confidence to promote your products or services? Are there any occasions where you regret not having access to pre-and post-evaluation research? By what means could you persuade your organisation to undertake such research?

Question 25

Do we need a sales force?

Overview

For a variety of reasons, sales force management and personal selling often suffer from neglect by marketing management. The solution to poor sales force management can only be found in the recognition that personal selling is a crucial part of the marketing process and that it must be managed as carefully as any other aspect. The sales force cannot be managed in isolation from broad corporate and marketing objectives.

Personal selling can be seen most usefully as a component element of the communications mix discussed in Question 22. A decision as to the role of personal selling in this mix can emerge only from the organisation's thorough understanding of the buying process which operates in its markets. Research into buying decisions offers some help to organisations in achieving a suitable match between information required by the customer and given by the company.

Particularly in industrial marketing, personal selling has a number of advantages over other forms of marketing communication; these should be intelligently exploited.

Sales force management: some common problems

Most organisations had an organised sales force long before they introduced a formal marketing activity of the kind described throughout this text. In spite of this fact, sales force management has traditionally been a neglected area of marketing management.

There are several possible reasons for this. One is that not all marketing and product managers have had experience in a personal selling or sales management role; consequently, these managers often underestimate the importance of efficient personal selling.

Another reason for neglect of sales force management is that sales personnel themselves sometimes encourage an unhelpful distinction between sales and marketing by depicting themselves as "the sharp end". After all, isn't there something slightly daring about dealing with real live customers as opposed to sitting in an office surrounded by marketing surveys, charts and plans? That such reasoning is misleading will be obvious from what was said in Question 2 about the difference between selling and marketing. It will be recalled that unless a good deal of careful marketing planning has taken place before the salesman makes his effort to persuade the customer to place an order, the probability of a successful sale is much reduced.

The suggested distinction between marketing "theory" and sales "practice" is further invalidated when we consider that profitable sales depend not just on individual customers and individual products but on groups of customers (that is, market segments) and on the supportive relationship of products to each other (that is, a carefully planned product portfolio). Another factor to be taken into account in this context is the constant need for the organisation to think in terms of where future sales will be coming from rather than to concentrate solely on present products, customers and problems.

The authors of this text have investigated scores of European sales forces over the last decade and have found an alarming lack of planning and professionalism. Salesmen frequently have little idea of which products and which groups of customers to concentrate on, have too little knowledge about competitive activity, do not plan presentations well, rarely talk to customers in terms of *benefits*, make too little effort to close the sale, and make many calls without any clear objectives. Even worse, marketing management is rarely aware that this important and expensive element of the marketing mix is not being managed effectively. The fact that many organisations have separate departments and directors for the marketing and sales activities increases the likelihood of such failures of communication.

A survey was carried out recently to examine the effectiveness with which sales representatives made contact with those responsible for influencing purchase decisions. The survey showed that in companies with over one thousand employees, where there were about seven major influencers of the purchasing decision, on average only two contacts per visit were made. A similar proportion of contacts was made in smaller companies. Another survey showed that advertising in the trade and technical press was the major source of information for large companies, while personal visits from sales people constituted the most important source of information for small companies. In both cases, exhibitions and direct mail were also important sources of information. This survey pointed up the fact that any company which uses personal selling as its sole means of communication with customers is unlikely to be fulfilling its communications objectives.

The solution to the problem of poor sales force management can only be found in the recognition that personal selling is indeed a crucial part of the marketing process but that it must be planned and considered as carefully as any other element. Indeed, it is an excellent idea for any manager responsible for marketing to go out into a territory for a few days each year and himself attempt to persuade customers to place orders. It is a good way of finding out what customers really think of the organisation's marketing policies.

The role of personal selling

Although its importance varies according to circumstances, in many businesses the sales force is the most important element in the marketing mix. In industrial goods companies, for example, it is not unusual to find less than £10,000 being spent on other forms of communication and £150,000 or more being spent on the sales force in the form of salaries, cars and associated costs.

Personal selling is also widely used in many service industries where customers are looking for very specific benefits. Insurance companies, for example, do use media advertising but rely for most of their sales on personal selling. Customers for insurance policies almost invariably need to discuss which policy would best fit their particular needs and circumstances; it is the task of the salesman to explain the choices available and to suggest the most appropriate policy.

Personal selling can most usefully be seen as part of the *communications mix* described in Question 22, itself an aspect of the "promotion" element of the total marketing mix. (Other common elements of the communications mix, it will be remembered, are advertising, public relations, direct mail, exhibitions, and so on.) The surveys described earlier show that organisations cannot safely leave the communications task to the sales force. The question remains, however, as to how the organisation is to define the role of personal selling in its communications mix. The answer lies in a clear understanding of the buying process which operates in the company's markets.

Understanding the buying process

It is perfectly feasible to set specific quantifiable objectives to each marketing communication task. But the company can only determine how much relative effort to devote to personal selling and other forms of communication if it has a very clear idea of the buying process in its markets. Question 23 gave a simple model of the consumer purchase decision in relation to paints. During the past decade, there has been a great deal of similar research into the industrial buying process. This process is clearly very important: after all, comparatively few companies sell their goods direct to the end user. In addition, personal selling is a particularly important element in industrial marketing.

The efficiency of any element of communication depends on achieving a match between information required and information given. To achieve this match, the marketer must be aware of the different requirements of different people at different stages of the buying process. This approach highlights the importance of ensuring that the company's communications reach *all* key points in the buying chain. No company can afford to assume that the actual sale is the only important event.

In order to determine the precise role of personal selling in its communications mix, the company must identify the major influencers in each purchase decision and find out what information they are likely to need at different stages of the buying process. Most institutional buying decisions consist of many separate phases, from the recognition of a problem through to performance evaluation and feedback on the product or service purchased. Furthermore, the importance of each of these phases varies according to whether the buying situation is a first-time purchase or a routine re-purchase. Clearly, the information needs will differ in each case.

Using personal selling effectively

Personal selling has a number of advantages over other elements of the communications mix:

- it is a two-way form of communication, giving the prospective purchaser the opportunity to ask questions of the salesman about the product or service;

- the sales message itself can be made more flexible and therefore can be more closely tailored to the needs of individual customers;

- the salesman can use in-depth product knowledge to relate his message to the perceived needs of the buyer and to deal with objections as they arise;

- most importantly, the salesman can ask for an order and, perhaps, negotiate on price, delivery or special requirements.

Once an order has been obtained from a customer and there is a high probability of a rebuy occurring, the salesman's task changes from persuasion to reinforcement. All communications at this stage should contribute to underlining the wisdom of the purchase. The salesman may also take the opportunity to encourage consideration of other products or services in the company's range.

Clearly, in different markets different weighting is given to the various forms of communication available. In the grocery business, for example, advertising and sales promotion are extremely important elements in the communications process. However, the food processor must maintain an active sales force which keeps in close contact with the retail buyers. This retail contact ensures vigorous promotional activity in the chain. In the wholesale hardware business frequent and regular face-to-face contact with retail outlets through a sales force is the key determinant of success. In industries where there are few customers (such as capital goods and specialised process materials) an in-depth understanding of the customers' production processes has to be built up; here, again, personal contact is of paramount importance. In contrast, many fast moving industrial goods are sold into fragmented markets for diverse uses; in this area forms of communication other than personal selling take on added importance.

Many companies in the electronics business use personal selling to good advantage. Word processors, for example, vary enormously in the range of capabilities which they offer. Technical details can be supplied in brochures and other promotional material but the administrative staff likely to be taking the purchase decision often find it difficult to evaluate the alternatives. A good salesman can quickly ascertain the requirements of a particular client and identify to what extent these will be fulfilled by his equipment. For his part, the customer can quickly identify whether the company understands his requirements, whether it appears credible and whether or not it is able to provide the back-up service necessary to install the equipment and establish its use in the organisation. Such considerations are likely to be far more influential than the comparison of technical data sheets in a decision to purchase.

Sales objectives

In the next Question, we shall be examining the problem of how many salesmen the organisation needs and what they should be asked to do. We shall complete our present discussion of the link between selling and the overall marketing activity by looking at the relationship between corporate objectives and sales objectives.

All companies set themselves overall objectives which in turn imply the development of specific marketing objectives. In this Question we have discussed personal selling in the context of the overall marketing activity. This approach leads us to the following hierarchy of objectives: *corporate objectives - marketing objectives - sales objectives.*

The benefits to sales force management of following this approach can be summarised as follows:

- co-ordination of corporate and marketing objectives with actual sales effort;

- establishment of a circular relationship between corporate objectives and customer wants;

- improvement of sales effectiveness through an understanding of the corporate and marketing implications of sales decisions.

The following example illustrates the main point that a sales force cannot be managed in isolation from broad corporate and marketing objectives. The sales force of a company manufacturing stainless steel containers was selling almost any kind of container to almost anybody who could buy. This caused severe production planning and distribution problems throughout the business, down to the purchase of raw materials. Eventually, the company's profitability was seriously affected. The sales force was finally instructed to concentrate on certain kinds of products and on certain kinds of user industries. This decision eventually led to economies of scale throughout the whole organisation.

Application questions

25.1 What was the most recent purchase made for your own household during which you relied heavily on the information given by a salesman? If you had not had access to a salesman, would you have made the same decision? In retrospect, do you believe that you made the best possible decision?

Question 25 Do we need a sales force?

25.2   When you are buying products for your organisation when do you find salesmen particularly useful? Are there any circumstances when you find visits from salesmen a nuisance? Why is this?

25.3 How is your own organisation's sales force used? Is this the best possible use of the sales force? In what ways do activities of the sales force complement other forms of marketing communications used? Identify any other ways in which you feel the activities of the sales force could enhance the total marketing communications effort.

25.4   Is your sales force effectively integrated into the marketing activities of the organisation? What problems tend to arise? How could they be overcome?

Question 26

How should our sales force be organised and managed?

Overview

This Question raises three basic issues which must be resolved satisfactorily if the organisation's sales force is to operate in an efficient manner. The first issue concerns the number of salesmen needed. The organisation should first establish the present pattern of work, then consider alternative ways of undertaking tasks. The next step is to analyse the desired workload for each salesman and determine how the work, once measured, can best be allocated in terms of territory and time.

The second issue is concerned with the objectives of the job of the salesman. Sales objectives can be either quantitative or qualitative. Quantitative objectives are concerned with what the salesman sells, to whom he sells it, and at what cost. Qualitative objectives are related to the salesman's performance on the job.

The third issue is the overall management of the sales force. Guidelines are given as to how to increase sales force motivation by increasing incentives and decreasing disincentives.

How many salesmen do we need?

In Question 25 we discussed the strategic role of personal selling in the marketing mix. We now turn to the basic questions which the organisation must ask, and answer, about the management of its sales force.

- how many salesmen do we need?

- what do we want them to do?

- how should they be managed?

The organisation should begin its consideration of how many salesmen it needs by finding out exactly how work is allocated at the present time. Start by listing all the things the current sales force actually does. These might include opening new accounts; servicing existing accounts; demonstrating new products; taking repeat orders; and collecting debts. This listing should be followed by investigation of alternative ways of carrying out these responsibilities. For example, telephone selling has been shown to be a perfectly acceptable alternative to personal visits, particularly in respect of repeat business. The sales force can thus be freed for missionary work, which is not so susceptible to the telephone approach. Can debts be collected by mail? Can products be demonstrated at exhibitions or showrooms? It is only by asking these kinds of question that we can be certain that we have not fallen into the common trap of committing the company to a decision and then seeking data and reasons to justify the decision. At this stage, the manager should concentrate on collecting relevant, quantified data and then use judgement and experience to help him come to a decision.

Basically, all sales force activities can be categorised under three headings. A salesman:

- makes calls

- travels

- performs administrative functions.

Unit VI Promotion decisions

These tasks constitute what can be called his *workload*. If we first decide what constitutes a reasonable workload for a salesmen, in hours per month, then we can begin to measure how long his current activities take, hence the exact extent of his current workload.

This measurement can be performed either by some independent third party or, preferably, by the salesmen themselves. All they have to do for one simple method of measurement is to record distance travelled, time in and out of calls, and the outlet type. This data can then easily be analysed to indicate the average duration of a call by outlet type, the average distance travelled in a month, and the average speed according to the nature of the territory (that is, city, suburbs or country). With the aid of a map, existing customers can be allocated on a trial and error basis, together with the concomitant time values for clerical activities and travel. In this way, equitable workloads can be calculated for the sales force, building in, if necessary, spare capacity for sometimes investigating potential new sales outlets.

This kind of analysis sometimes produces surprising results as when the company's "star" salesman is found to have a smaller workload than the one with the worst results, who may be having to work much longer hours to achieve his sales because of the nature of his territory.

There are, of course, other ways of measuring workloads. One major consumer goods company used its Work Study Department to measure sales force effectiveness. The results of this study are summarised in the following table (Table 6).

Table 6 Breakdown of a salesman's total daily activity

		Per cent of day		Minutes per day	
Outside Call Time	Drive to and from route	15.9		81	
	Drive on route	16.1		83	
	Walk	4.6		24	
	Rest and breaks	6.3		32	
	Pre-call administration	1.4		7	
	Post-call administration	5.3		27	
			49.6		254
Inside Call Time	Business talks	11.5		60	
	Sell	5.9		30	
	Chat	3.4		17	
	Receipts	1.2		6	
	Miscellaneous	1.1		6	
	Drink	1.7		8	
	Waiting	7.1		36	
			31.9		163
Evening Work	Depot work	9.8		50	
	Entering pinks	3.9		20	
	Pre-plan route	4.8		25	
			18.5		95
			100.0		8hrs 32min

This table showed the company how a salesman's time was spent and approximately how much of his time was actually available for selling. One immediate action taken by the company was to initiate a training programme which enabled more time to be spent on selling as a result of better planning.

What do we want our salesmen to do?

Whatever the method used to organise the salesman's day, there is always comparatively little time available for selling. In these circumstances, it is vital that a company should know as precisely as possible what it wants its sales force to do. Sales force objectives can be either *quantitative* or *qualitative*.

Quantitative objectives

Principal quantitative objectives are concerned with the following measures:

- how much to sell (the value of unit sales volume)

- what to sell (the mix of product lines to sell)

- where to sell (the markets and the individual customers that will take the company towards its marketing objectives)

- the desired profit contribution (where relevant and where the company is organised to compute this)

- selling costs (in compensation, expenses, supervision, and so on).

The first three types of objectives are derived directly from the marketing objectives, which are discussed in detail in Question 30.

There are, of course, many other kinds of quantitative objectives which can be set for the sales force, including tasks to do with point-of-sale literature, reports, trade meetings and customer complaints. Salesmen may also be required to fulfil a co-ordinating role between a team of specialists and the client organisation. A company selling mining machinery, for example, employs a number of "good general salesmen" who establish contacts and identify which contacts are likely to lead to sales. Before entering into negotiations with any client organisation, the company selling the machinery may feel that it needs to call in a team of highly specialised engineers and financial experts for consultation and advice. It is the task of the salesman in this company to identify when specialist help is needed and to co-ordinate the people who become involved in the negotiation. However, most objectives are subservient to the major objectives outlined above which are associated directly with what is sold and to whom.

Qualitative objectives

Qualitative objectives can be a potential source of problems if sales managers try to assess the performance of the sales force along dimensions which include abstract terms such as "loyalty", "enthusiasm", "co-operation", and so on, since such terms are difficult to measure objectively. In seeking qualitative measurements of performance, managers often resort to highly subjective interpretations which cause resentment and frustration amongst those being assessed.

However, managers can set and measure qualitative objectives which actually relate to the performance of the sales force on the job. It is possible, for example, to assess the skill with which a person applies his product knowledge on the job, or the skill with which he plans his work, or the skill with which he overcomes objections during a sales interview. While still qualitative in nature, these measures relate to standards of performance understood and accepted by the sales force.

Given such standards, it is not too difficult for a competent field sales manager to identify deficiencies, to get agreement on them, to coach in skills and techniques, to build attitudes of professionalism, to show how to self train, to determine which training requirements cannot be tackled in the field, and to evaluate improvements in performance and the effect of any past training.

One consumer goods company with thirty field sales managers discovered that most of them were spending much of the day in their offices engaged in administrative work, most of it self made. The company proceeded to take the offices away and insisted that the sales managers spend most of their time in the field training their salesmen. To assist them in this task they trained them how to appraise and improve salesmen's performance in the field. There was a dramatic increase in sales and consequently in the sales managers' own earnings. This rapidly overcame their resentment at losing their offices.

How should we manage our sales force?

Sales force motivation has received a great deal of attention in recent times, largely as a result of the work done by psychologists in other fields of management. There is now widespread appreciation of the fact that it is not sufficient merely to give someone a title and an office and expect to get good results. Effective leadership, it is acknowledged, is as much "follower-determined" as it is determined by management. Whilst for the purposes of this discussion it is not necessary to enter into a detailed discussion of sales force motivation, it is worth mentioning briefly some important factors that contribute to effective sales force management.

If a sales manager's job is to improve the performance of his sales force, and if performance is a function of incentives minus disincentives, then the more he can increase incentives and reduce disincentives, the better will be performance.

Research has shown that an important element of sales force motivation is a sense of doing a worthwhile job. In other words, desire for praise and recognition, the avoidance of boredom and monotony, the enhancement of self image, freedom from fear and worry, and the desire to belong to something believed to be worthwhile, all contribute to enhanced performance. One well known piece of research carried out in the USA examined the reasons for the results of the twenty highest producing sales units in one company compared with the twenty lowest producing sales units. The research showed all the above factors to be major determinants of success.

However, remuneration will always be a most important determinant of motivation. This does not necessarily mean paying the most money, although clearly unless there are significant financial motivations within a company, it is unlikely that people will stay. In drawing up a remuneration plan, which would normally include a basic salary plus some element for special effort, such as bonus or commission, the following objectives should be considered.

- to attract and keep effective salesmen.

- to remain competitive.

- to reward salesmen in accordance with their individual performance.

- to provide a guaranteed income plus an orderly individual growth rate.

- to generate individual sales initiative.

- to encourage teamwork.

- to encourage the performance of essential non-selling tasks.

- to ensure that management can fairly administer and adjust compensation levels as a means of achieving sales objectives.

A central concept of sales force motivation is that the individual salesman will exert more effort if he is led to concentrate on:

1. his expectations of accomplishing his sales objectives, and

2. the personal benefits derived from accomplishing those objectives.

This theory of sales force motivation is known as the path-goal approach because it is based on the particular path the salesman follows to a particular sales objective and the particular goals associated with successfully travelling down that path. The salesman estimates the probability of success of travelling down various paths or sales approaches and estimates the probability that his superiors will recognise his goal accomplishments and will reward him accordingly. Stated less formally, the motivational functions of the sales manager consist of increasing personal pay-offs to salesmen for work goal attainment, making the path to these pay-offs easier to travel by clarifying it, reducing road blocks and pitfalls and increasing the opportunities for personal satisfaction en route.

To summarise, the sales force is a vital but very expensive element of the marketing mix and as much care should be devoted to its management as to any other area of marketing management. This is most likely to be achieved if intuitive sense, which is associated with experience, can be combined with the kind of logical framework of thinking outlined here.

Application questions

26.1 What are the key functions of salesmen in your organisation? How is their work co-ordinated?

26.2 How is the sales force deployed: by geographical territory; by product range; by type of customer? Is this deployment optimal? What other patterns of deployment should be considered by your organisation?

26.3 Who is responsible for the sales force in your organisation? What is the relationship between this post of responsibility and other marketing responsibilities in the organisation? Does this cause any problems? Where problems arise, how could they be solved?

26.4 Can you make a case to justify the present size and type of sales force used? Could you defend your position if you were requested to cut back the sales force by 30%? How would you make your case? What do you believe would be the consequences of a 30% cutback in the sales force?

Unit VII   Planning and control

Question 27   What is marketing research?

Question 28   What role does marketing research play in effective marketing?

Question 29   How can we audit our environment and operations?

Question 30   How can we prepare our marketing plan?

Question 31   How can we organise a marketing department?

Question 32   How can we set the marketing budget?

Question 27

What is marketing research?

Overview

Marketing research is an integral part of the marketing task. It provides the manager with the means of identifying market opportunities, it aids his understanding of marketing processes and it can provide data for control of marketing programmes. Recent years have seen rapid growth in the use of marketing research by companies in all sectors and also in the range of techniques available to the researcher. While marketing research must always be less than precise in that it deals with notoriously unstable behavioural phenomena, it nevertheless provides an invaluable means of contact with the market place.

This Question examines the various approaches to the marketing research task that are commonly encountered today and considers their application to marketing problems. It is emphasised that much valuable marketing information can be gained from an examination of existing data which may be to hand within the company or may be available from published sources.

The role of marketing research

Many of the Questions that we have addressed so far in this text have raised the need for gathering information from the market place. We have asked, for example, "Who are our customers?", "Are all our customers the same?" and "How can we measure the effectiveness of our advertising?". Questions such as these can only be accurately answered in the light of detailed knowledge about our customers, their behaviour, their beliefs and their reactions to our marketing effort.

As we have noted frequently in this text, the marketing concept is grounded in the notion that the profitable development of the organisation can only be ensured through a constant attempt to match the resources of the organisation with the needs of its customers. Before they can be met, these needs must be identified. And after the needs have been identified, a careful assessment must be made of the suitability of the organisation's marketing offering. These activities can only take place if some type of information flow has been instituted between customers and organisation. It is the role of marketing research to provide a flow of information which will allow the organisation to make a suitable match between its own resources and the needs of its customers.

A distinction is sometimes drawn between marketing research and market research. The former, it is suggested, is concerned with research into marketing processes whilst the latter is more specifically research about markets. However, for the purposes of this Question we shall use the term "marketing research" to embrace both aspects of the task.

The use of marketing research by European companies has grown considerably in the last ten years or so. Its use is not confined, as is sometimes thought, to companies selling into consumer markets. Some of the most interesting work to have been conducted in recent years has been on behalf of industrial marketing organisations, service organisations (such as banks) and social organisations (such as voluntary and government agencies).

With this growth of marketing research has come an increasing sophistication in the use and range of the techniques available to the researcher. Developments in the handling and analysis of multivariate data have been particularly significant in this respect. Use of computers now enables the researcher to map potential customers' reactions along several dimensions simultaneously. Thus, customers' perceptions of motor cars, for example, can be assessed in regard to various attributes of the products, such as pricing, performance, economy factors and styling. It then becomes possible to identify which cars are most competitive with each other and to make detailed investigation of customer preferences among the different vehicles.

The marketing researcher is now a professional whose advice is sought more and more in marketing decision making. The number of companies which provide specialist marketing research services has multiplied until marketing research is a major industry in its own right. The marketing manager now has available to him the facility both to monitor the effectiveness of his marketing performance and also to gain a better feel for what opportunities exist in the market place. How this information can be integrated into the marketing planning and control task will be discussed in the next Question. Our immediate concern is to consider what tools the marketing researcher has at his disposal and how and where these may be used.

Forms of marketing research

Marketing research can be classified as being either ad-hoc or on-going. *Ad hoc* marketing research refers to situations where the identification of a research problem leads to a specific information requirement. An example was a French manufacturer of proprietary pharmaceuticals who found that sales of his long-established cough remedy were falling. The company conducted a study of consumer attitudes and beliefs about cough remedies and used the information gained to relaunch the brand. On the other hand, *on-going* research, as the title implies, provides more of a monitoring function, giving a flow of information about the market place and the organisation's performance in it. The Confederation of British Industries, for example, maintains a regular monitor, based on surveys, of business confidence and investment intentions in the UK.

A further distinction can be made between external marketing research and in-company marketing research. *External* research is conducted within the market or competitive environment in which the firm exists. It normally uses primary data: that is, the researcher seeks out and collects data specifically for the purpose of his research. A road transport company, for example, decided that it would be useful for it to know how its different customers took the decision whether to buy or to hire a commercial vehicle. In these circumstances, where this information was nowhere else available, the researcher went direct to the customers in order to acquire the necessary information.

In-company research, on the other hand, is based on an analysis of performance gained from data such as sales trends, changes in the marketing mix involving price, advertising levels and so on. In this case, the researcher is using secondary data: that is, data which is accessible to him but which has been collected for another purpose. (Secondary data, of course, also includes all published sources which are relevant to the research; this form of secondary data is described later in the Question when desk research is discussed.) Much valuable intelligence can be gained from internal marketing analysis; external information gathering should always be seen as a complement to internal information.

The kind of data which might be useful in this context can be illustrated in relation to the same road transport company mentioned earlier. The company offered a range of transport services, including car and truck hire. However, management had no clear overall picture of who their customers were or of the frequency with which they bought or hired vehicles. In addition, they knew little about patterns of repeat custom or how many of their customers for one service also used other services offered by the company. This lack of knowledge meant that the company was unable to manipulate its marketing mix to the best advantage. However, the company did in fact have available in its own files a great deal of the information which it needed.

Copies of the invoices sent out to customers could have told the company much of what it wanted to know about the identity and purchasing patterns of its clients. An in-company research project could have collated this material and presented it in a form suitable for marketing action.

The basic split between *reactive* and *non-reactive* marketing research is important in any discussion as to methods. The reactive approach is based on the assumption that information about the market place and the customers who inhabit it can be gained by "poking a stick at it and seeing if and how it moves". Non-reactive methods are based not on reaction but on interpretation of observed phenomena or extant data.

Reactive research

Reactive marketing research can involve either asking questions or performing experiments, or both (see Figure 29). Let us examine first the role of question asking. This is perhaps the main activity which most people associate with marketing research. The ubiquitous survey is a tried and trusted research device and the questionnaire is a favoured means of data gathering.

The *questionnaire* This is a particularly flexible instrument. It can be administered by an interviewer or by the interviewee himself; it can yield information on the respondent's doorstep, by telephone or through the mail. The format of the questionnaire can also vary a great deal. Depending on the requirements of the particular research, the questionnaire can provide either very detailed information or basic facts about customers and their behaviour. The researcher who is concerned to know only what products are being bought in a particular store, for example, is likely to use a simple checklist. On the other hand, the researcher who wishes to probe deeply into customer motivation will use a full-length questionnaire which gives respondents the opportunity to answer questions in their own words.

There are, however, a number of problems that can arise when a questionnaire is used without very careful pre-planning or checking. Everyone knows about the "loaded" question or the dangers of ambiguity, yet such dangers are not always easily detected. Even the order of the questions can have a distorting effect on the answers. The errors in the final population estimates from a questionnaire administered to a sample are termed the bias (or systematic error) of the estimates. In other words, the true characteristics of the population (for example, relative customer preferences amongst several types of industrial compressor) may be different from the estimate produced by the sample survey. This bias may result either from the way in which the sample was chosen or from the means by which the survey data were collected. Problems of this kind can be reduced by a careful approach to the design of the questionnaire. The probability of bias occurring can also be reduced by pilot testing the questionnaire; in other words, by giving it a trial run on a sub-group of the intended sample in order to identify any problems that may arise. If systematic bias does manifest itself, the researcher will be forced to qualify the results obtained.

Group discussions and extended inter-

views Sometimes it may be more appropriate to attempt to draw insights for marketing action from smaller scale, more detailed studies. Such studies are intended to provide qualitative cues rather than quantitative conclusions. Frequently, they precede the use of quantitative studies and are used to find out what dimensions are most important to the population involved. For example, the Meat and Livestock Commission asked faculty at Cranfield to conduct a series of group discussions amongst housewives in order to gain an understanding of their attitudes towards the purchase of frozen meat rather than fresh meat. A group discussion is a loosely structured interview-type situation where the leader - often a trained psychologist - attempts to draw from the group their feelings about the subject under discussion. The group is chosen to be representative of the population in which the researcher is interested; any conclusions emerging from the discussions may lead to qualitative generalisations about that population. Such interviews need not be conducted in groups but can be used to derive information from individuals. This technique is called an extended or depth interview and will often be used when information on specialised markets is required in industrial marketing research.

Figure 29

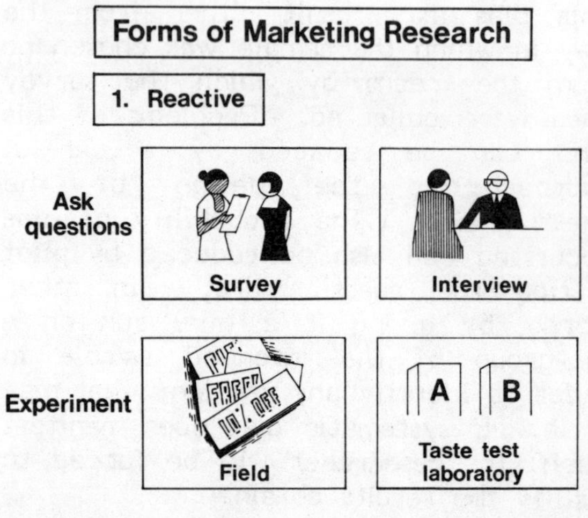

Forms of Marketing Research

1. Reactive

Ask questions: Survey, Interview

Experiment: Field, Taste test laboratory

Experimentation This is the other main type of reactive marketing research. The marketing experiment can help us gain a better understanding of how marketing processes work. As in all experimental work, the condition for success in marketing experimentation is that the researcher should be able to control the variables in his experiment. For example, a Swedish manufacturer of confectionery wanted to know if a "money-off" offer had a greater effect on sales than spending a similar sum on in-store merchandising improvements. The information he needed in order to answer this question could really only come from an experiment whereby a number of stores were selected in different areas of the country and used as the testing ground for these alternative promotional approaches. The stores chosen for the experiment were as near alike as possible in terms of turnover on the brand in question and served similar types of customers. One third of the stores ran the "money-off" promotion, one-third used the improved in-store merchandising, and the remaining one-third carried on selling the product without any changes. After a period of two months, the manufacturer felt able to draw conclusions about the relative effectiveness of the two promotional methods.

Market experimentation need not involve setting up large-scale experimental designs of the type just discussed. Sometimes laboratory-type situations can be used to test marketing stimuli. In taste-test laboratories, for example, researchers test the ability of customers to distinguish between products. Advertisements also are often pre-tested in laboratory conditions. Respondents from the target audience for the advertisement are exposed to the advertisement and their reactions obtained. In some cases, more than the verbal reactions of the sample are sought. Eye cameras and tachistoscopes are just some of the devices that have been used to record physical reactions to marketing stimuli. The use of eye cameras enables the researcher to make a detailed analysis of how people view a particular communication in terms of what holds their attention and what is ignored. The tachistoscope is designed to test the rapidity with which people can respond to a visual cue. Use of this device is particularly helpful in assessing the effectiveness of posters and billboards which are often seen only momentarily.

While the theory of market experimentation is sound enough, there are a number of drawbacks to its operation in practice. It is often difficult, for example, to set up experimental situations that are microcosms of the total market. Furthermore, there is always the problem of controlling all the variables in the experiment, such as the actions of competitors. And, finally, of course, the cost of setting up and maintaining experiments can be prohibitive.

Non-reactive research

In contrast with this type of research are those methods that are classified as non-reactive, indicating that they do not rely on data derived from respondents. (See Figure 30.)

Observation is one technique of this kind which can be very effective in appropriate situations. How people behave in real-life situations and how they react to stimuli can often best be discovered through watching and interpreting their reactions. Some observational methods, such as a camera in a supermarket, do not involve the direct participation of the researcher. This can be a limiting factor because the facets of activity in which we are particularly interested may only occur infrequently so that the observation may have to be sustained over a considerable period of time in order to capture a single activity. On the other hand, *participant observation*, a phrase borrowed from anthropology, involves the observer in attempting to become a part of the activity that is under observation. This form of marketing research is very limited in its scope, although one British research organisation, Mass Observation, did some early pioneering work in a number of studies, a famous example being a major study of consumer behaviour in public houses.

The *retail audit* is one widely used secondary source of observational data. The retail audit has been developed and perfected as a technique over a period of time and, properly controlled, it can be a highly accurate source of marketing information on brand shares, market size, distribution coverage and sales trends. The audits conducted by A C Neilsen Limited are perhaps the most widely known and work on a simple basis. Within a particular product field, a representative sample of stockists is chosen and their co-operation obtained. At regular intervals the investigator visits the stockists and notes two things: the current level of stocks of the product group being audited and the invoices or delivery notes for any goods in that group delivered since the investigator's last visit. With the information on stock levels obtained on his last visit, it is a simple matter for the auditor to determine sales of each item being audited during the period between visits. The calculation can be expressed in the following way: opening stock + deliveries between visits - closing stock = sales during period.

Figure 30

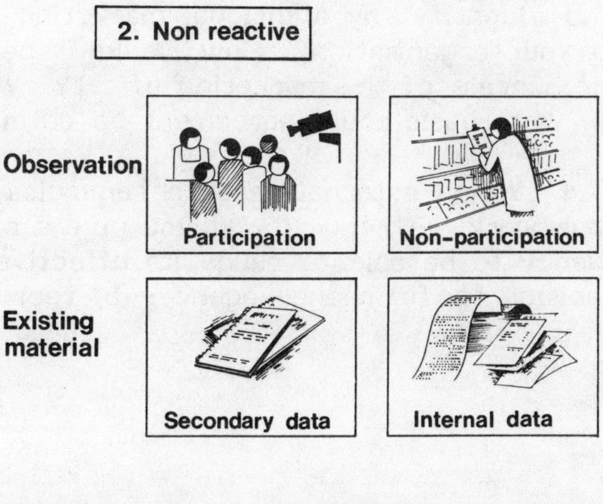

Forms of Marketing Research

2. Non reactive

Observation
- Participation
- Non-participation

Existing material
- Secondary data
- Internal data

The *customer panel* constitutes a similar source of data. This is a sample group of customers in a particular product field who, over a period of time, record their purchases and consumption in a diary. This technique has been used in industrial as well as consumer markets and can provide continuous data on patterns of usage as well as other data, such as media habits.

The *desk research* study is the last but certainly not the least in our survey of marketing research methods. The use of existing information should in fact be the starting point of any marketing research programme. Desk research involves the use of existing information to determine the extent of prior knowledge about the subject under study. It also involves the use of in-company data of the kind described in this Question. Information obtained from the great wealth of material in both published and unpublished sources can reduce the need to "rediscover the wheel". Official statistics, such as those published by governments, OECD, the EEC, the United Nations, and so on, can provide detailed data on markets and patterns within those markets. Other sources such as newspapers, technical journals, trade association publications and published market studies will provide a supplement to any later field work that might be needed. Similarly, internal data derived from sales figures and salesmen's reports can also be a guide to the direction that later studies might need to take.

This brief survey of research methods in marketing indicates the considerable scope of marketing research. It must always be borne in mind that even the most carefully designed and conducted studies can at best provide only imperfect descriptions of market phenomena. Nevertheless, marketing research remains the link between the identification of market opportunities and the successful exploitation of these by the organisation.

Application questions

27.1 What kinds of marketing research are commissioned by your organisation? Which are found to be cost-beneficial? Explain how they contribute to the effectiveness of the marketing effort. Which are not a good investment of time and money? How could the waste be avoided?

27.2 What decisions are taken in your organisation which involve the use of marketing research as an input? Are there any marketing decisions which have been taken without reference to research where you feel that research would have led to a different decision? Why is such research not done?

27.3 Identify any additional marketing research which you feel would be of benefit to your organisation. How would it be used? What contribution would it make to the success of the marketing effort? What prevents the adoption of such research? On what basis could agreement be obtained to introduce the suggested research?

27.4 Which external research agencies do you work with? What problems arise in your work with them? Do you give a sufficiently well defined research brief to the agency to be able to gauge its effectiveness? What would be the criteria used in a decision to: (a) change agency; (b) recruit an agency?

Question 28

What role does marketing research play in effective marketing?

Overview

Marketing research is the basic source of information on the markets we serve and on the performance that we achieve within those markets. The successful marketing organisations are those who have learned how to convert marketing information into marketing action; in other words, those organisations who successfully use marketing information as a management resource. One of the problems that faces many companies is that they have no shortage of marketing "data", but marketing "information" and "intelligence" are in short supply. There are crucial differences between these three commodities.

One of the key questions posed must always be, "how can we place a value on marketing information?". All information must be assessed in cost/benefit terms against previously defined needs. The organisation can then go on to explore the nature of its management information needs and develop a marketing intelligence system for the application of marketing information to marketing decisions.

Marketing information as a management resource

It is sometimes said that the prime management concern in marketing is "the conversion of uncertainty into risk". Uncertainty implies an inability to state the likelihood of any possible outcome occurring. By implication, all outcomes must be treated as equally likely. Under uncertainty, the manager must consider, say, the chance of failure in a new product launch to equal the chance of success. Risk, on the other hand, suggests that the likelihood of outcomes can be assessed more precisely. The marketing manager might calculate, for example, that a particular new service launch has only a five per cent chance of failure. Our ability to make successful decisions is clearly enhanced if we are operating under conditions of known risk rather than uncertainty.

If the conversion of uncertainty into risk is the prime marketing management task, the second is undoubtedly the reduction or minimisation of that risk. If the marketing manager is to convert uncertainty into risk and then go on to minimise the risk, he must be assured of a steady supply of relevant information. Good information facilitates successful marketing action; indeed, marketing management can be seen as first and foremost an information processing activity (see Figure 31). Looked at in this way, marketing research is

Figure 31

The Role of Marketing Research

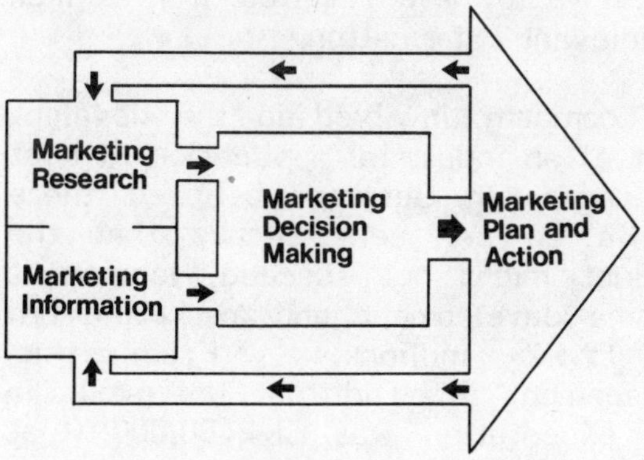

161

concerned with much more than simply telling us something about the market place. Rather, it is a *systematic and objective search for, and analysis of, information relevant to the identification and solution of any problem in the field of marketing.*

How should marketing managers approach the integration of marketing research with marketing action?

In the first place, it is necessary to view marketing information as a resource. This means that we must be concerned with the problems of producing, storing and distributing it. Marketing information has a limited shelf life - it is perishable. Like other resources, information has a value in use: the less the manager knows about a marketing problem, and the greater the risk attached to a wrong decision, the more valuable the information becomes.

This latter point is an important consideration in assessing marketing research budgets. It implies the need for a cost/benefit appraisal of all sources of marketing information. There is no point in investing more in such information than the return on it would justify. Naturally, it is easier to determine the cost than the benefits. The managerial benefits of marketing research are difficult to pin down. They can be expressed in terms of the additional sales or profits that might be achieved through the spotlighting of marketing opportunities. The benefits can also be calculated in terms of the avoidance of those marketing failures which would have resulted from a lack of relevant information.

One company involved in the development of an industrial application of heat exchangers in Germany believed there was a 20 per cent chance that the product might not succeed, leaving it with a development and marketing bill of DMk2 millions. From this, management inferred that the maximum loss expectation was DMk400,000 (that is, DMk2,000,000 x 20%) and that it was worth paying up to this sum to acquire information that would help them avoid such a loss. However, the company realised that its cost-benefit calculation did not reflect the fact that the information obtained would not be totally reliable; in other words, it would not all form the basis for effective marketing action. The company therefore drew up a reduced budget for research which reflected more accurately the degree of confidence which it had in the results of the research. This example illustrates the need for a careful use of managerial judgement in association with cost-benefit analysis of marketing research.

Data, information and intelligence

Reference is frequently made to the information explosion, a phenomenon wherein the manager is confronted with a mass of data, often produced in an indigestible form with the aid of computer-based processing systems. More properly, this should perhaps be referred to as the *data* explosion. Data are facts presented in some specific format; by themselves, however, they do not represent *information*. Information is data combined with direction; it is "active" while data are purely "passive". The messages which information contains and which can be revealed by analysis should be the ultimate service sought from marketing research - a service that can be referred to as *intelligence.*

The differences between data, information and intelligence are more than semantic. They are crucial to a proper integration between research and marketing management. The problems of how data can be organised and analysed to provide information which will in turn lead to marketing intelligence is an issue to which the marketer must continually address himself.

Management decision and marketing research

Given that the appropriate analysis of marketing information can provide the basis of marketing action, what sort of decisions require what sort of information? This approach to management information needs is central to the successful construction of *marketing intelligence systems* (MIS) for the application of marketing information to marketing decisions. We can identify three basic levels of marketing decisions where an input of information is essential. The first is marketing information for strategic, long-term decisions; the second is marketing information for tactical, short-term decisions; and the third is marketing information for one-off marketing problems. The first two situations require a continuous, on-going input of marketing information, whereas the last needs an ad hoc but speedy response from the marketing research function.

Until the late 1960s, marketing research was largely limited in application to the ad hoc and static analysis of marketing problems. Use of techniques such as the retail sales audit and the customer panel (described in the previous Question) would have been of great value to the short- and long-term performance of many organisations, particularly in the field of fast-moving consumer goods, such as breakfast cereals. However, during the 1950s and 1960s, few organisations employed such methods: generally speaking, marketing research was not used to monitor the marketing environment on a continuous basis. In the late 1960s, a major shift in orientation by hitherto largely ad hoc users of marketing research, along with the conversion of new organisations and service industries to the use of marketing research, led to substantial interest in the setting up and deployment of integrated marketing intelligence systems.

Today, sophisticated marketing intelligence systems are widely used. International oil companies and airlines with headquarters in Europe, for example, have marketing intelligence systems which enable their executives to know on a weekly basis sales levels for all products in all market areas, levels of inventory at all intermediate stations, current production levels and capacity utilisation. In addition, their systems can provide trend data, market share estimates, cost information, and data on the comparative profitability of all products or services on a market to market basis. The organisations held all this information previously but, before an MIS was introduced, the information was in a fragmented and unco-ordinated form. The adoption of a "systems" approach to information requirements and the use of existing computer facilities meant that these companies were able to provide management with a *data bank* oriented to well defined information needs.

Organisations need not limit their MIS to the analysis of current and historical data such as sales statistics and other commonly collected market data. Information on consumer attitudes, advertising levels and changes in competitive marketing activity now also forms an input to such systems in many areas of marketing endeavour.

The benefits of an integration of marketing information from all sources, internal to the company and external to it, lie chiefly in the "direction" that is given to otherwise unco-ordinated data. An integration of this kind does not necessarily imply the use of a computer, although the power and flexibility of any MIS can potentially be increased many-fold through such means. What is implied, however, is that management must define clearly its information needs. That is, managers must examine the marketing decisions that they need to make and specify the information, both on-going and ad hoc, that they require in order to make those decisions effectively.

Developing a marketing intelligence system

Any organisation wishing to build an MIS faces a number of basic questions. How should we organise? How sophisticated should the system be? Do we build a total system or do we adopt a piecemeal approach? What should be the split between macro-level data and micro-level data? How much should we spend?

Organisation Most companies will have to accommodate existing organisation structures in the construction of the MIS. One team of experts in this field has suggested the appointment of a top-level "information Czar", or co-ordinator, who is capable of understanding both management information needs and systems problems. They suggest that this person should be the prime contractor who develops MIS plans and specifications and co-ordinates and reviews the work of the various sub-contractors or suppliers contributing to the programme.

Sophistication The question of sophistication of the system is crucial. Naive companies may attempt to introduce systems which do not reflect the level of sophistication actually required by managers in making decisions. Recent research in the marketing sphere has shown that many marketing managers, particularly those at the operating level, do not use explicit planning and control systems. The aim of building the MIS should be to strike a balance between the sophistication of the system and that of its users.

Total or piecemeal? It is always tempting when thinking in terms of systems to wish to build a totally integrated MIS from first principles - a system that brings together financial, logistical and marketing information. Experience suggests that such attempts are rarely successful. As a general rule, it is better to think "total" but to build "piecemeal". One company in the UK construction supply industry reports that it is adopting such an approach. It is building an MIS on the basis of putting together a number of building-blocks each of which represents a sub-system for meeting a discrete information need. Together these building-blocks will eventually form a total system. The development of the total system will be governed by experience and the growing sophistication of users.

How much micro, how much macro? One of the most frequently encountered problems in marketing management is that data tend to be aggregated: that is to say, the figures relate to total markets rather than to segments, to countries rather than to regions, and so on. On the other hand, the manager can easily be overwhelmed if he is flooded with data. A key requirement of the MIS, therefore, is that, while the system is based on a micro-data bank, the system should be capable of providing output at any requested level of aggregation.

How much to spend? This problem has already been addressed earlier when the notion of information cost/benefit was raised. Building and developing the MIS is normally an expensive task. One major French company has so far spent well over Fr.7 million in developing an integrated, real-time system. While this is an extreme example, even the simplest MIS does not come cheaply. Management must specify the benefits that it expects to derive from the MIS and be prepared to put a value on them. In this way, by concentrating on the outputs required from the MIS, a surer basis for setting the information budget is provided.

As a high-level information processor, the marketing manager occupies a vital position in any organisation. He is positioned between a wealth of data and feedback flows from the market place on the one hand, and internal information flows on corporate capabilities and performance on the other. Marketing research has thus the essential role within the organisation of providing an organised means of maintaining and utilising these disparate information flows and ensuring their effective conversion into marketing

Question 28   What role does marketing research play in effective marketing?

intelligence.

Application questions

28.1 If you were asked to establish a marketing information system within your organisation, what would it contain? How would the information be co-ordinated? Who would be responsible for providing input to, and output from, the system? What use would you expect to be made of information provided? Who would you expect to make most use of the information?

28.2 What would be the benefits to your organisation of running a marketing information system? Can you identify opportunities which were exploited or failures which were avoided by using an MIS?

28.3 If your organisation does not have an MIS, on what grounds is this justified? Is the decision one which you support? Under what circumstances would an MIS be justified for your organisation?

Question 29

How can we audit our environment and operations?

Overview

A marketing audit is a systematic, critical review and appraisal of the marketing environment (including external market opportunities and competitive threats) and the organisation's internal marketing operations. It is a powerful tool in ascertaining whether a company is in phase with its dynamic and rapidly changing marketing environment. It also helps the organisation to ensure that advantage is taken of opportunities, that preparations are made to overcome threats, that strengths are developed and that weaknesses are overcome.

Organisations are likely to find marketing audits most beneficial if the following points are borne in mind: (1) audits should be carried out on a regular basis; (2) audit procedures should be institutionalised and defined in detail; (3) management should be trained to use these procedures effectively; and (4) top management should be committed to the audit and closely involved in its implementation.

What is a marketing audit?

In Question 3 we looked at the need for marketing planning and outlined a series of steps that have to be gone through in order to arrive at a marketing plan. In the next Question we shall be taking a detailed look at the preparation of a marketing plan. The purpose here is to go into more detail about one of the most important steps in the marketing planning process - the marketing audit. The marketing audit does not itself appear in the marketing plan but it provides much of the information on which the plan is based. Any plan will only be as good as the information on which it is based, and the marketing audit is the means by which information for planning is organised.

The process of auditing is usually associated with the financial side of the business and is conducted according to a defined set of accounting standards which are well documented and easily understood. The total business, however, can also be audited, though the auditing process in this case is more complicated and demands considerable powers of judgement and ability to innovate rather than simple adherence to a set of rules. Basically, an audit is the means by which an organisation can understand how it relates to the environment in which it operates. It is thus a way of helping management to make an informed decision on what position it wishes to hold in that environment.

The purpose of a corporate plan may be simply expressed as the attempt to answer three basic questions: where is the company now? where does the company want to go? how should the company organise its resources to get there? The audit is the means by which the first of these questions is answered. A *management audit* is a systematic, critical and unbiased appraisal of the environment and of the company's operations. A *marketing audit* is part of the larger management audit and is concerned with the marketing environment and marketing operations.

The information gathered during a marketing audit is likely to help an organisation identify many different areas in which business performance could be improved. One company, for

Unit VII Planning and control

example, found that many of its customers would prefer to buy a product range rather than individual products from one manufacturer. Accordingly, the company increased the range of products which its salesmen were offering to include both cut-price and luxury brands in addition to the medium range brand already carried. The salesmen went on to sell many more products to the same number of customers.

Another manufacturer made use of information gained during its audit to establish exactly how the 80/20 rule or Pareto effect applied to its operations. (The Pareto effect, it will be remembered, was discussed in Question 7, "Who are our customers?") The manufacturer found that it had a good many customers who contributed comparatively little to the total volume of sales. These customers, it was decided, should in future be encouraged to buy from wholesalers rather than direct from the manufacturer.

Often the need for an audit does not manifest itself until things start going wrong for a company, in the form of declining sales, falling margins, lost market share, underutilised production capacity, and so on. At times like these, management is often driven by a sense of urgency to take immediate action, such as introducing new products, reorganising the sales force or reducing prices. However, such measures are unlikely to be effective if there are more fundamental problems which have not been identified. Essentially, the argument is that problems have to be properly defined, and the audit is a means of helping to define them before they offer a serious threat to the company's profitability. To summarise, the audit is a structured approach to the collection and analysis of information and data essential to effective problem solving.

How should an audit be structured?

Any company carrying out an audit will be faced with two kinds of variables. First, there are variables over which the company has no direct control. These usually take the form of *environmental* and *market* variables. Secondly, there are variables over which the company has complete control. These we can call *operational* variables.

This division indicates that an audit can most usefully be structured in two parts: *external* and *internal*. The external audit is concerned with uncontrollable variables, while the internal audit is concerned with the controllable variables. The external audit starts with an examination of information on the general economy and then moves on to the outlook for the health and growth of the markets served by the particular organisation. The internal audit sets out to assess the organisation's resources as they relate to the environment and to the resources of competitors.

Figure 32 shows a checklist of areas which should be investigated during the marketing audit. Each one of these

Figure 32

The Marketing Audit

What are the
Opportunities and Threats, Strengths and Weaknesses
for the

Business and Economic Environment
Economic
Political/fiscal
Religious
Social
Cultural
Business
Legal
Technological
International

The Market Environment
Size and trends
Supply and demand

Competitive Environment
Market shares and trends
Product range
Pricing
Place
Promotion
Operations and resources

Own Company
Market shares and trends
Product range
Pricing
Place
Promotion
Operations and resources

headings should be examined with a view to isolating those factors which are considered critical to the company's performance. Initially, the auditor's task is to screen an enormous amount of information and data for validity and relevance. Some data and information will then have to be reorganised into a more easily usable form, and the auditor will go on to judge what further data and information is needed to complete the picture.

The auditing process consists of two basic stages:

- the identification, collection, analysis and measurement of all the relevant facts and opinions which impinge on a company's problems;

- the application of judgement to areas which remain unclear after this analysis.

When and how should the marketing audit be carried out?

As we have already mentioned, many people hold the mistaken belief that the marketing audit should be a last-ditch attempt to define an organisation's marketing problem. Other people believe that the correct approach is for an independent body to carry out a marketing audit from time to time in order to ensure that an organisation is on the right lines. However, since marketing is such a complex function, it seems ill-advised not to carry out a thorough audit at least once a year prior to the beginning of the planning cycle.

There is much evidence to show that many highly successful companies, as well as using normal information and control procedures throughout the year, start their planning cycle each year with a formal review of everything which has had an important influence on marketing activities. Certainly, in many leading consumer goods companies, the annual self-audit approach is a well tried and tested procedure built into an integrated management process.

Certain circumstances may justify the hiring of outside consultants to carry out a marketing audit as a check that a company is getting the most out of its resources. However, it seems an unnecessary expense to have this done every year. The answer is to have an audit carried out annually by the company's own line managers on their own areas of responsibility.

Reluctance to undertake this normally stems from concern about time and objectivity. In practice, these problems are usually overcome, first, by institutionalising procedures in as much detail as possible so that all managers have to conform to a disciplined approach and, secondly, by thorough training in the use of the procedures. However, even these measures will not result in the successful completion of an audit unless the need for rigorous analysis is understood and accepted from the highest down to the lowest levels of management involved in the audit. In drawing up an audit, managers must constantly guard against taking a narrow view of their environment and making easy extrapolations from past trends. One of the great values of the exercise is that it challenges managers to consider in what ways their environment is changing and the implications of such changes for their marketing strategies.

What happens to the result of the audit?

The final, all-important issue, of course, is what happens to the result of the audit. Some companies consume valuable resources carrying out audits that bring very little by way of actionable results. Indeed, there is always the danger that, at the audit stage, insufficient attention is paid to the need to concentrate on analysis that determines which trends and developments will actually affect the company. While the checklist provided earlier in the Question demonstrates the most complete analysis possible, the people carrying out the audit should discipline themselves to omit from their plans all information that is not central to the company's marketing problems. Thus, inclusion of research reports which lead to no action whatever only serves to rob the audit of focus and reduce its relevance. Since the objective of the audit is to indicate what an organisation's marketing objectives and strategies should be, it is clearly desirable that a relevant format should be found for organising the major findings.

One useful way of doing this is in the form of a SWOT analysis (discussed in Question 14) which involves a summary of the audit under the headings *strengths* and *weaknesses* as they relate to *opportunities* and *threats*. This analysis is then incorporated into the marketing plan itself.

To summarise, carrying out a regular and thorough marketing audit in a structured way helps to give the organisation a detailed knowledge of the business, including trends in the market and competitive activity. The marketing audit provides the basis for setting realistic marketing objectives and strategies.

One company in the Spanish footwear business was suffering a sudden decline in profitability. The marketing audit which the company undertook revealed fundamental weaknesses in almost every area of marketing, the most serious of which was that the company's sales were completely out of step with the trends in the market. The company was quickly able to rectify many of the faults indicated by the audit and this led to a gradual recovery of their market position and profitability. Since then, the company has been sure to carry out a thorough marketing audit at the beginning of every planning cycle.

Application questions

29.1 Who has responsibility for carrying out the annual marketing audit within your organisation? How is the information gained from the audit used? Is there any way in which greater use could be made of the information?

29.2 How has the product portfolio of your organisation been affected by the use of information gained from a marketing audit? If the audit had not occurred, how would the product portfolio have been developed?

29.3 If you belong to an organisation which does not undertake an annual marketing audit, what prevents your organisation from doing so? In the absence of an audit, how do you decide how to manage and develop your product portfolio? Have any problems arisen which could have been overcome by conducting an annual audit?

Question 30

How can we prepare our marketing plan?

Overview

It is not possible to plan a company's marketing activities in isolation from other business functions. Consequently, the marketing planning process should be firmly based on a corporate planning system.

As outlined in Question 3, the marketing planning process consists of a series of steps: the marketing audit and SWOT analysis; the formulation of planning assumptions; the setting of objectives and strategies; and the development of detailed programmes for action. The key steps in the process are the setting of marketing objectives and the development of marketing strategies. Marketing objectives always express the match between products and markets; marketing strategies are the means by which the marketing objectives will be achieved.

The corporate planning process

We discussed the total marketing planning process in Question 3, and in Question 29 we looked at one of the most important steps in this planning process - the marketing audit. Before we turn our attention to the other important steps in the marketing planning process, it would be useful to examine how marketing planning relates to the corporate planning process. It will be remembered from the previous Question that the corporate plan aims to answer three questions: where is the company now? Where does the company want to go? How should the company organise its resources to get there? The marketing plan is constructed so as to answer these same questions with regard to the marketing function. In doing this, it makes a major contribution to the overall shape and content of the corporate plan. Table 7 will help us to see the marketing plan in relation to the overall planning task.

The table shows six steps in the corporate planning process. As can be seen, the starting point is usually a statement of *corporate objectives* for the long-range planning period of the company. These are often expressed in terms of turnover, profit before tax and return on investment, but may also express intention with regard to growth, market share, and so on. More often than not, this long-range planning horizon is five years, but the precise period should be determined by the nature of the markets in which the organisation operates. For example, five years would not be a sufficiently long period for a glass manufacturer, since it takes that period of time to commission a new furnace. In some fashion industries, on the other hand, five years would be too long a period. A useful guideline in determining the planning horizon is that it should allow a period at least long enough to ensure that sufficient products or services are sold to cancel out the capital investment associated with their introduction.

The next step is the *management audit*, which was discussed briefly in Question 29. A thorough situation review of this kind, particularly in the area of marketing, should enable the company to determine whether it will be able to meet its long-range targets with its current range of products in its current markets. At this stage, the technique of gap analysis (discussed in Question 14) can, if necessary, help the

Unit VII Planning and control

Table 7 Marketing planning and its place in the corporate planning cycle

Step 1	Corporate objectives, including financial objectives, stock market image, corporate image and social responsibility objectives				
Step 2 Management audit	*Marketing* product; price; promotion; place; business & economic environment; market environment; competitive environment	*Distribution* e.g., stocks and control; transportation; warehousing	*Production* e.g., value analysis; engineering development; work study; quality control; labour; materials; plant and space utilisation	*Finance* e.g., credit; debt; cash flow & budgetary control; resource allocation; long-term finance	*Personnel* e.g., management, technical & administrative ability
Step 3 Setting of functional objectives	Marketing	Distribution	Production	Finance	Personnel
Step 4 Setting of functional strategies	Marketing	Distribution	Production	Finance	Personnel
Step 5 Development of functional implementation plans	Marketing	Distribution	Production	Finance	Personnel
Step 6	Issue of corporate plan to include corporate objectives and strategies, production objectives and strategies, long-range P & L accounts and balance sheets				
Measurement, review and amendment (if necessary) of operating plans continuous					

organisation to identify appropriate strategies which will ensure that targets are met.

The most important, and the most difficult, stage in the corporate planning process involves the third and fourth steps, *objective* and *strategy setting*. A clear distinction can be made between these two processes. A company might, for example, agree on a marketing objective of broadening its market by product diversification. It will still find it necessary, however, to decide on the most appropriate means of achieving this objective. A number of choices will immediately present themselves, principal amongst which is likely to be the choice either to acquire an on-going business or to invest in additional capacity to broaden the company's own range. The choice here is between two strategies; the criteria by which one strategy will be chosen in preference to another will relate to the company's overall objectives, resources and position in the market.

If these two steps are not carried out properly, everything that follows will be of little value. Later in this Question, we shall discuss marketing objectives and strategies in detail. The essential point to be made in the present context is that the setting of objectives and strategies marks the time in the planning cycle when the organisation has to decide how the individual objectives of the different functional areas are to be reconciled into practicable targets. It is often the case that individual functional objectives have to be modified at this stage. A marketing objective of penetrating a new market, for example, is of little use if the organisation does not have the production capacity to cope with the new business and if capital is not available for investment in additional capacity. At this stage, objectives and strategies will be set for the length of the long-term planning period.

The fifth step of the corporate planning process involves producing *detailed plans for one year*, containing the timing and costs of carrying out the first year's objectives, together with a full description of how responsibilities for the various activities are allocated within the organisation. *Broad plans for the following years* should also be provided at this stage. These plans can then be incorporated into the final corporate plan, which will contain long-range corporate objectives, strategies, plans, profit and loss accounts and balance sheets.

One of the main purposes of a corporate plan is to provide a long-term vision of the organisation's future, taking account of shareholder expectations, environmental trends, market trends, and the distinctive competence of the company as revealed by the management audit. What this means in practice is that the corporate plan will contain the following elements:

- A statement of the desired level of profitability.

- An indication of future developments in each of the functional areas. Guidance will be given, for example, as to the kinds of products to be sold to different markets (marketing); the kinds of facilities to be developed (production and distribution); the size and character of the labour force (personnel); and the sources of funding (finance).

- Other corporate objectives, such as social responsibility, corporate image, stock market image, employee image, etcetera.

A corporate plan of this kind, which contains projected profit and loss accounts and balance sheets, is likely to provide greater long-term stability than would plans which are based on a more intuitive process and which contain forecasts that are little more than extrapolations from previous business trends. One major multinational company had a planning process of this latter type. The company's headquarters had a sophisticated budgeting system which received "plans" from all over the world and co-ordinated them in quan-

Question 30 How can we prepare our marketing plan?

titative and cross-functional terms, such as numbers of employees, units of sale, items of plant, square feet of production area, and so on. The financial implications of all this data were carefully calculated. However, this whole complicated edifice was built on initial sales forecasts, which were little more than trend extrapolations. The result was that the whole corporate planning process developed into little more than a time-consuming numbers game and the really key strategic issues relating to products and markets were lost in all the financial activity. This organisation eventually ran into grave operational difficulties.

Planning assumptions

Having described the context in which the marketing plan must be drawn up, let us return to the preparation of the plan itself.

Figure 33

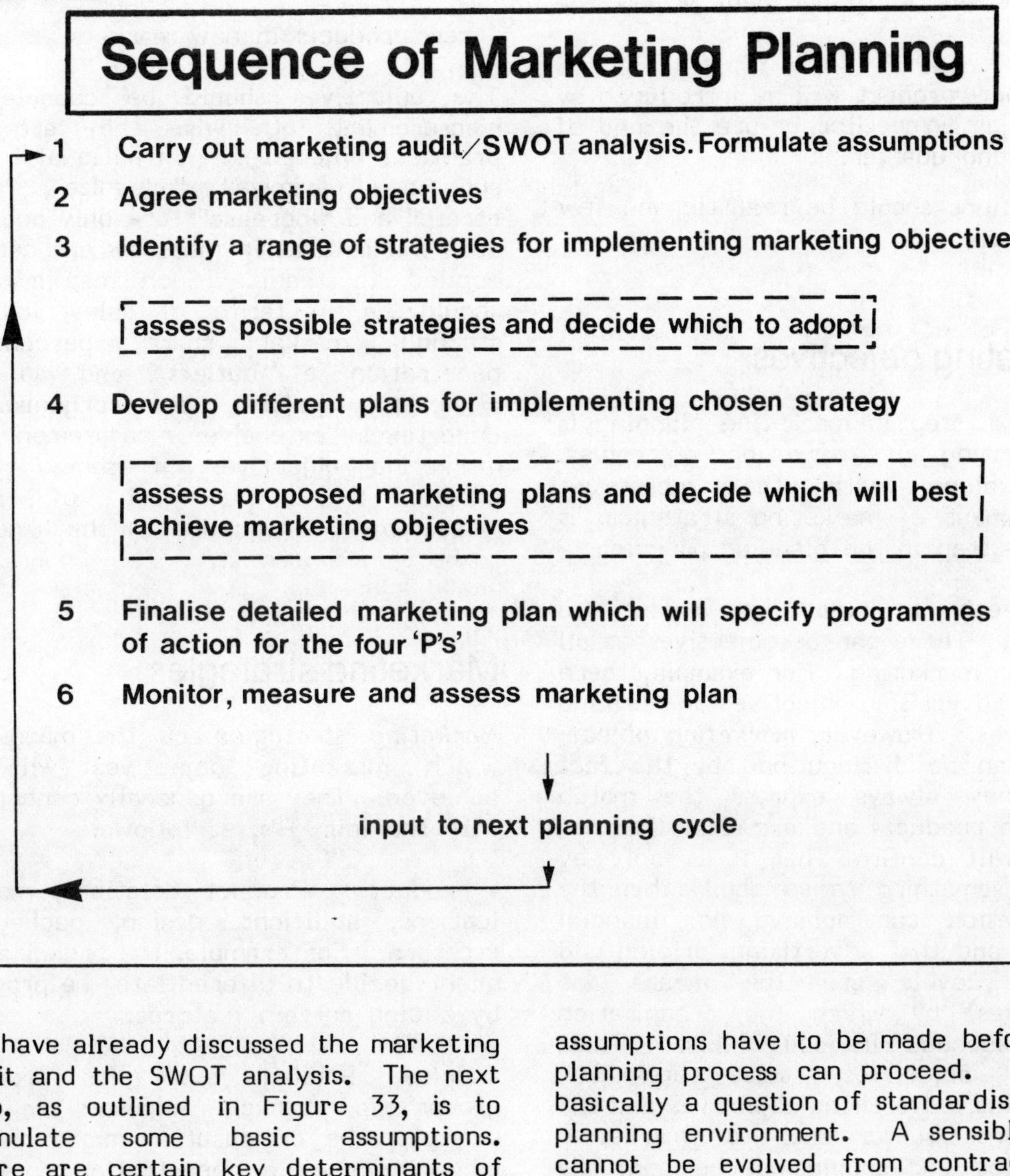

Sequence of Marketing Planning

1. Carry out marketing audit/SWOT analysis. Formulate assumptions
2. Agree marketing objectives
3. Identify a range of strategies for implementing marketing objectives

   assess possible strategies and decide which to adopt

4. Develop different plans for implementing chosen strategy

   assess proposed marketing plans and decide which will best achieve marketing objectives

5. Finalise detailed marketing plan which will specify programmes of action for the four 'P's'
6. Monitor, measure and assess marketing plan

   ↓

   input to next planning cycle

We have already discussed the marketing audit and the SWOT analysis. The next step, as outlined in Figure 33, is to formulate some basic assumptions. There are certain key determinants of success in all companies about which assumptions have to be made before the planning process can proceed. This is basically a question of standardising the planning environment. A sensible plan cannot be evolved from contradictory assumptions, as would be the case, for example, if one product manager asserted that the market was going to decline by ten per cent, whilst another believed the market was going to increase by ten per cent.

Examples of assumptions might be :

"With respect to the company's industrial climate, it is assumed that:

1. Industrial overcapacity will increase from 105 per cent to 115 per cent as new industrial plants come into operation.

2. Price competition will force price levels down by 10 per cent across the board.

3. A new product will be introduced by our major competitor before the end of the second quarter."

Assumptions should be realistic and few in number.

Marketing objectives

The next step in marketing planning is the writing of marketing objectives. This, along with the subsequent development of marketing strategies, is the key step in the planning process.

An *objective* is what you want to achieve. There can be objectives at all levels in marketing. For example, there can be advertising objectives and pricing objectives. However, *marketing objectives* can be distinguished by the fact that they always express the match between *products* and *markets*. Common sense will confirm that it is only by selling something to somebody that the organisation can achieve its financial goals; and that advertising, pricing and service levels are the means (or strategies) by which the organisation might succeed in doing this. Thus, pricing objectives, sales promotion objectives, advertising objectives and the like are subservient to marketing objectives and should not be confused with them. An example of a marketing objective might be "to enter x market with y product and obtain a ten per cent market share within one year".

The simple matrix in Question 12, "What products should we market?", indicates the matching process which is central to all marketing objectives. Marketing objectives are always concerned with one or more of the following combinations:

- existing products in existing markets

- new products in existing markets

- existing products in new markets

- new products in new markets.

The objectives should be capable of measurement, otherwise they are not practical objectives. Directional terms such as "maximise", "minimise", "penetrate" and "increase" are only acceptable if quantitative measurement can be applied to them. Such measurement should be in terms of sales volume, sterling, market share, percentage penetration of outlets, and so on. However, before an organisation undertakes extensive measurement of marketing objectives, it should first ensure that the cost of such measurement is equalled by the benefits to be gained from it.

Marketing strategies

Marketing strategies are the means by which marketing objectives will be achieved. They are generally concerned with the four 'P's, as follows:

- *Product* Product deletions, modifications, additions, design, packaging, etcetera. For example, the organisation might decide to diferentiate the product by adding certain features.

- *Price* Pricing levels for product groups in market segments. For example, the organisation might choose to introduce a penetration pricing policy.

- *Place* Types of channels and customer service levels. In this area, the organisation might think it best to sell only through certain kinds of retailer.

- *Promotion* Means of communicating with customers in the different ways available such as advertising, sales force, sales promotion, public relations, exhibitions, direct mail, etcetera. For example, the organisation might decide to employ heavy advertising to create widespread awareness.

Usually, an organisation will identify a range of strategies for achieving marketing objectives. The final choice of strategy will follow a process of assessment and analysis of the firm's particular circumstances, both internal and external. At this juncture, as throughout the marketing planning process, the information gleaned through the SWOT analysis is likely to prove helpful.

The marketing plan

The next stage of the marketing planning process involves the development of different plans for implementing the chosen strategy. Those plans contain detailed sub-objectives, strategies and programmes of action for each of the four 'P's. Thus, an organisation might set as a *sub-objective* for its promotional activities the creation of a ten per cent awareness level amongst its target audience. The *strategy* chosen to meet this goal might be heavy advertising on television to explain the benefits to be gained from the product. The *programme* devised to implement this strategy might be 20 or 30 second bursts of advertising on television.

The final plan chosen from the range of possible plans identified will be the one which will most effectively achieve marketing objectives.

Measuring progress

The final step in preparing an effective marketing plan is to establish some standards against which actual performance can be measured. These standards should relate to performance in the different activities associated with the four 'P's: product development, pricing, promotion and distribution. The decision as to whether or not to undertake measurement depends, as mentioned earlier, on the results of a cost-benefit analysis.

Actual performance in each area should be monitored. Whenever performance deviates from the standard set, some control action may be necessary. It is clear that if, say, customer service levels were to drop significantly below standard, some action would be taken before demand was damaged seriously. However, control action might also be necessary if customer service levels were to *exceed* by a significant degree the standards set for performance. As we have seen in Question 19 ("What level of availability does our customer want?") there is always a danger of incurring unnecessary additional costs by providing service levels which are well above the level required to meet the market demand.

The identification of deviations between standards and performance allows management to institute effective controls. In this way, progress towards the achievement of the marketing objectives set in the plan can be measured and, if necessary, regulated.

Use of marketing plans

A written marketing plan is the backcloth against which operational decisions are taken on an on-going basis. Consequently, all the different steps of the planning process should relate directly to the organisation's operating needs. The major function of the marketing plan is to determine where the company is now, where it wants to go, and how it is to get there. The plan lies at the heart of a company's revenue-generating activities and from it flow all other corporate activities, such as the timing of the cash flow, the size and character of the labour force, and so on. As such, it is a key element in the corporate plan.

The marketing plan should be distributed only to those managers who will make use of it. It must be made clear that the marketing plan should be used as an aid to effective management. It cannot be a substitute for it.

Application questions

30.1 Identify the marketing planning process adopted in your organisation. Who contributes to the plan and what does each individual contribute? What is the sequence of the planning process? What problems arise during this process? How can they be minimised or eradicated?

30.2 What are the marketing objectives set for your organisation's major products or services? Is the achievement of these objectives adequately monitored? Are there additional monitoring procedures which ought to be employed? What prevents their adoption?

30.3 How are the sub-objectives for each of the four 'P's related to the major marketing objectives? How is the achievement of these sub-objectives monitored? Does the organisation have sufficient feedback from the market place to enable it to identify where a marketing policy is failing and to help it develop a more effective marketing effort?

30.4 For the product or service with which you are most familiar, distinguish between marketing objectives, overall strategy and implementation plans as they relate to the four 'P's. What alternatives could have been adopted and why were they rejected?

Question 31

How can we organise a marketing department?

Overview

The main objective of the marketing department in any organisation is to acquire a sufficient understanding of customer needs, present and future, to be able to contribute to the development of overall corporate objectives. The marketing department seeks to achieve this objective by generating the right mix of products, at the right time, in the right place, and with the right promotion. The structure of the marketing department accordingly must be based on the allocation of responsibilities both for achieving successful management of the four 'P's and for co-ordinating the strategies which are employed in the management of this marketing mix.

The marketing department can usefully be seen as just one part of an integrated pattern of activities which is designed to achieve corporate goals. Marketing management must work alongside its colleagues to ensure that the organisation's offering meets present and future customer needs.

The co-ordination of marketing responsibilities

In Question 1, we identified marketing's role in any organisation as ensuring that the four 'P's - product, price, promotion and place of sale - are successfully managed. Success in this context means both that the customer is satisfied and that the organisation makes effective use of its human, physical and financial resources. We can therefore expect any marketing department to be organised in such a way that these goals are accomplished.

In practice, this is easier said than done. The types of situations and problems which organisations face vary so widely that marketing departments operate in very different ways. However, certain basic marketing tasks are common to all organisations and are neglected at the organisation's peril. Marketing's main endeavour is to generate the right mix of sales with customers, at the right prices, in the right place and with the right promotion. This means that the organisation's structure must be based on the allocation of responsibilities both for achieving each of these objectives *and* for co-ordinating the strategies which are pursued in order to achieve these various goals. In classical organisation chart terms, this gives rise to a pattern of responsibilities as shown in Figure 34.

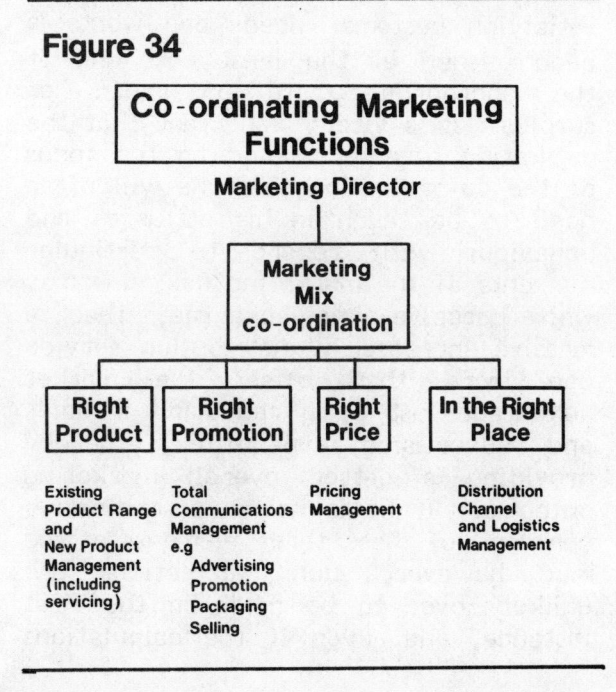

Figure 34

```
        Co-ordinating Marketing
              Functions
           Marketing Director
                  |
            Marketing
               Mix
          co-ordination
    _____|_____
   |         |         |          |
 Right     Right     Right    In the Right
Product  Promotion   Price       Place
```

Existing Product Range and New Product Management (including servicing)

Total Communications Management e.g
Advertising
Promotion
Packaging
Selling

Pricing Management

Distribution Channel and Logistics Management

177

Getting the product right involves activities which we discussed in detail in Questions 12, 13, 14 and 15. If a company has a great many products, it may well wish to group them. If it has a number of important brands, it will often ask a member of the marketing department to take particular care of them. Such a person is frequently known as the Brand or Product Manager. Getting the promotional activity right was discussed in answer to Questions 22, 23 and 24. First of all, we saw the need to co-ordinate all the communications activities. Later, in answer to Questions 25 and 26, we examined in detail how personal selling, often a very important element in marketing, can be successfully developed.

The product or service must also be in the right place at the right time. Strategic decisions have to be made on distribution networks and on levels of availability and customer service. These issues were discussed in Questions 17, 18 and 19. Finally, as described in Questions 20 and 21, the product must be sold at a price which is both attractive to the customer and acceptable to the organisation.

The marketing director must manage these operational responsibilities in such a way that the marketing objective of satisfying customer needs and wants is accomplished at the least cost and at the appropriate rate of profit or surplus. It is vitally important that the marketing director should be the focus of the co-ordination since he will often need to be tough in his attitudes and behaviour with regard to particular elements of the marketing mix. He may well perceive, for example, that a massive increase in distribution service can more than offset the market advantage lost by a reduction in sales and advertising expenditure, thereby providing a better overall marketing outcome. If he is not in co-ordinative command of those three elements of the mix, however, such calculations are unlikely ever to be made in the first instance, and, even if the calculations are made, their implementation may well be effectively opposed by the sales and advertising managers. The organisation of the marketing department must ensure that all management of individual mix elements is subordinate to marketing direction.

This goal may seem an obvious and straightforward one. However, organisations tend to find that several factors can mediate against effective marketing direction. In some cases, the traditional structure of the company may work against co-ordination as when, for example, the marketing and sales departments have their own parallel hierarchies. In other cases, companies may appoint fairly senior executives to control advertising or sales budgets; these executives are then likely to rebel against co-ordinative authority.

The difficulties involved in effective marketing co-ordination can be illustrated by the case of an oil company which, during a period of price cutting among petrol dealers, launched a competition to attract petrol sales. The competition was so successful that additional volumes had to be imported from the Continent in order to satisfy demand. However, the company subsequently realised that it had lost money on the venture: the high price that it had had to pay for the additional supply had more than cancelled out the profit from increased sales. Effective marketing direction would have prevented such a situation from occurring.

Marketing posts

We have been careful so far in this text to talk about responsibilities rather than particular posts. We have also failed to introduce into our discussion the need for marketing management to have available to it supporting services, such as those provided by the marketing training officer. Figure 35 shows how a Swiss textile fabric manufacturer

Question 31   How can we organise a marketing department?   179

assigned roles within its marketing department.

Figure 35

One Marketing Department's Operational Structure

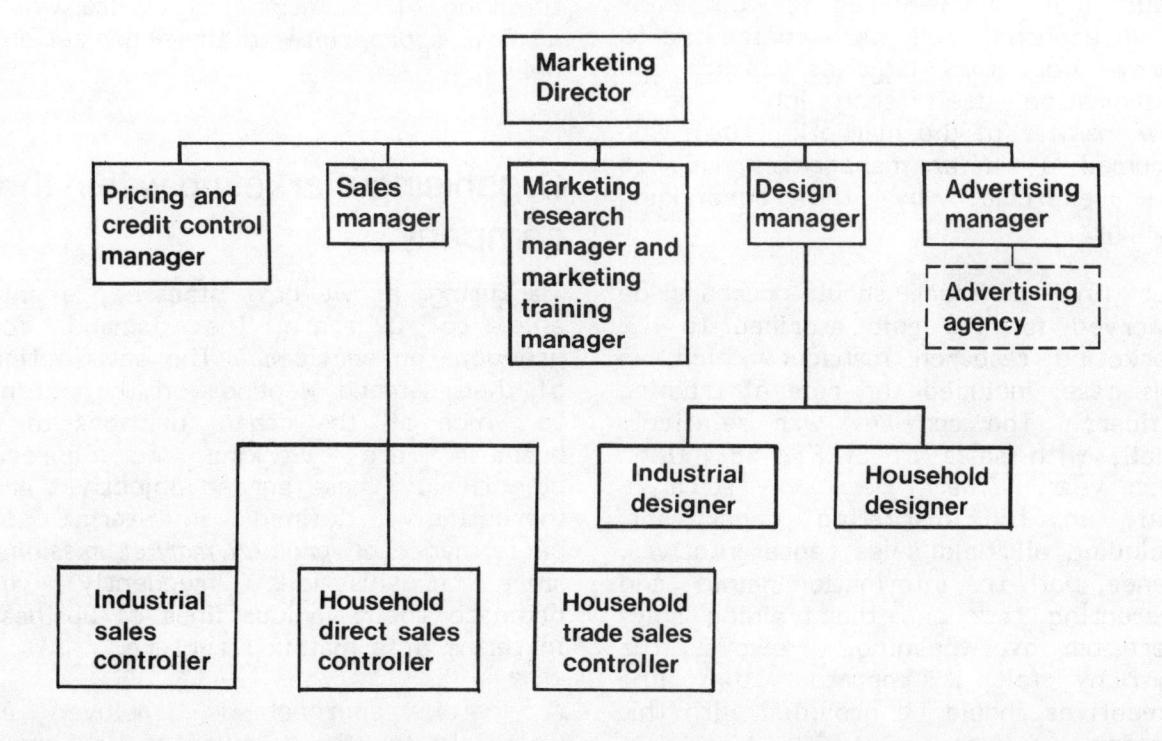

```
                          Marketing
                          Director
    ┌──────────┬──────────┼──────────┬──────────┐
Pricing and   Sales    Marketing   Design    Advertising
credit control manager research    manager   manager
manager                manager and             │
                       marketing          Advertising
                       training           agency
                       manager
                 │                     │
         ┌───────┼───────┐        ┌────┴────┐
   Industrial Household Household Industrial Household
   sales     direct sales trade sales designer designer
   controller controller  controller
```

The roles allocated can be seen to be related to the specific nature of the organisation. Its markets include both industrial purchasers and households. The sales manager has three controllers who report to him, two of them dividing household sales between them according to whether the sales are sought direct from customers via direct mail response to advertising or occur through trade sales to wholesalers and retailers. The distinction between household and industrial markets also affects the activities of the design manager, who has overall responsibility for the product. The advertising manager works through an agency which is accustomed to handling industrial, trade and direct response advertising work. Similarly, the pricing and credit control manager handles all areas of activity.

The element missing in the co-ordination undertaken by the marketing director is distribution, the management function that determines which channels to use for reaching the end customer and, in particular, takes care to ensure that the correct level of logistical support is given. This was a serious bone of contention within the organisation. Because the company was part of a wider grouping of companies in the man-made fibre industry, it was expected to employ the logistics support system used by the other members of the group. There was common warehousing and a common scheduling of deliveries. Direct response sales was the only area where the company had a logistics system tailored to its specific needs.

Compromises of this kind are sometimes necessary even if they appear counter-productive for the particular part of the group concerned. In this case, after careful studies to establish the correct service levels, a change was made in the allocation of responsibility for logistics. Sub-contractors who would meet the required service levels at an economic cost were contracted to carry out the logistics task. The organisation itself then introduced a new member of the marketing team who assumed a similar management role to that exercised by the advertising manager.

Our final comment should perhaps be reserved for the role ascribed to the marketing research manager which, in this case, included the role of training officer. The company was relatively small, with sales of Sw.Fr. 48 million each year. There were only some 26 staff in the marketing department, including all field sales representatives. Hence, both the information gaining and presenting task and the training roles were not overwhelming. However, the company felt it important that line executives should be provided with this service.

Our illustration of a marketing department's operational structure has deliberately been kept simple. We have emphasised the need, first, to define the responsibilities involved and, secondly, to identify the posts which the organisation needs to establish. We have seen that the responsibility for several tasks can be assigned to one individual; and that, on occasion, the performance of the tasks can be sub-contracted. What cannot be sacrificed is the marketing director's overriding need to be in a position to co-ordinate all the posts.

The decision as to whether or not to sub-contract the performance of tasks and, if so, how extensively to use external services, is one which many organisations find difficult. Should the company have a research department or employ a research agency? Should the company rely on a full service advertising agency to provide continuity on a brand or should it undertake this task itself? Should the company with many branded products employ its own media manager to monitor the buying efficiency of the advertising agencies used? The answers to vital questions of this kind will provide another pointer to the kind of operational structure which is most appropriate to the organisation's needs.

Organising marketing within the company

Marketing, as we have stressed, is only able to generate the demand for products or services. The satisfaction of that demand depends on the extent to which all the other functions of a business are working to agreed objectives. These agreed objectives are increasingly defined in terms of performance on *product/market missions*, since organisations frequently co-ordinate their various lines of business in terms of a matrix structure.

A matrix approach is employed at Cranfield for the conduct of its School of Management. The vertical inputs to the organisation are teaching inputs and the horizontal outputs are trained students. (Education is, of course, an example of a non-profit service of the type discussed in Question 5.) Cranfield has three major teaching product/market missions, each of which is co-ordinated by a director. Thus, there are separate directors for the MBA Programme, Doctoral Studies and Continuing Studies. Various professors head the subject groups which work together to make each mission a success. Success comes when all the groups work effectively together to achieve the output; in Cranfield's case, this is a well educated or trained manager.

The matrix approach to organisational structure has also proved successful in a

Question 31   How can we organise a marketing department?

commercial context. A specialist book publisher, for example, has established an operational structure which effectively matches products to markets. The vertical inputs to this organisation are the company's finance, marketing, production and management information functions. The horizontal outputs are publishing missions in marketing and logistics, human resources, social economics and managerial law, and information transfer. Each of these missions is responsible for the publication of books and journals in its particular subject area; it is also responsible for developing a pattern of activity which fits in with the overall resources and requirements of the organisation.

In Figure 36 the matrix-based approach is applied to a major Italian concern selling its products into catering establishments, grocery supermarkets and wholesalers.

Figure 36

The Matrix Structure

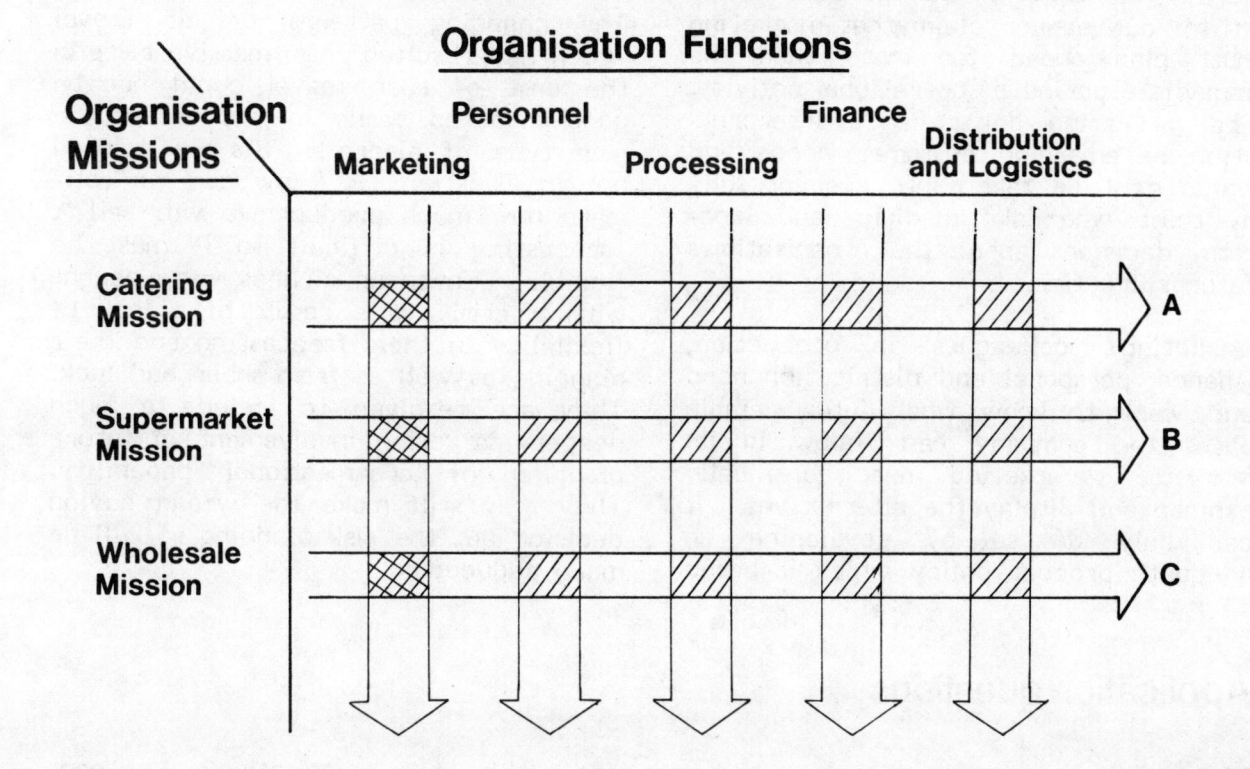

Organisation Functions

Organisation Missions — Marketing, Personnel, Processing, Finance, Distribution and Logistics

- Catering Mission → A
- Supermarket Mission → B
- Wholesale Mission → C

It will be seen that the marketing effort in this company is just one part of an integrated pattern of activity which is designed to take the right processed food products to catering establishments, to national supermarket chains and to wholesalers who supply the smaller retail grocery outlets. At each of the interstices in the matrix shown in darker blocks, marketing will need to co-ordinate its activities in a different fashion in order to relate effectively with all other company activities. With its existing plant, the processing function may not be able to make the product mix which is ideally suited to the market. The development engineers may not be able to raise or allocate the desired level of funds to support customer credit policies. Each product/market mission must balance out such competing claims within its total perspective. This allocation of responsibility for achieving an appropriate balance between company resources and customer needs ensures that skills and functions are co-ordinated in order to have the greatest impact on the market.

The marketing department's role in developing the future

The discussion which has taken place during this Question can be seen to re-affirm our earlier claim that marketing must plan ahead for more than the immediate period of operational activity. The marketing department's interpretation of emerging customer needs and wants must be taken into account fully by those who take medium- and long-term decisions about the organisation's future direction.

Marketing's colleagues in production, finance, personnel and distribution need and want to know what future viable paths the company can follow in its markets. Marketing must continually explore and display the alternatives. It can only do so by developing an adequate product policy which is based on understanding what customers will need and what they can be persuaded to want. Marketing must give its colleagues their bearings on the market place as they seek to invest in new manufacturing capacity, locate new facilities, develop the skills of the workforce, or analyse cash requirements to fund the business in the years ahead.

We can conclude by demonstrating this role in sharp yet realistic relief with the situation which affected the European airlines in 1975. In 1975, the airlines took delivery of fleets of TriStars in order to meet the levels of business activity forecast three years previously. However, market demand for medium-range air travel dropped drastically in 1975; in fact, it eventually fell by 25 per cent. The fleets were not needed but the product had arrived. The changing patterns of air travel which had resulted from massive rises in the cost of such travel could not be accommodated easily by the use of the new type of aircraft. As we pointed out in Question 16, "How can we estimate how much product we will sell?", forecasting is difficult so it must be flexible. European airlines were caught with a crisis as a result of a lack of flexibility in their forecasting and their planning as well as from sheer bad luck. They are resolved to include a much deeper marketing involvement in future planning of organisational capability. They may still make the wrong buying decision but the risk of doing so will be much reduced.

Application questions

31.1 Who comprises the marketing department within your organisation? For each job title identified, what are the major responsibilities allocated? Are all aspects of marketing allocated somewhere within the department?

31.2 Identify any aspects of marketing management not under the control of members of the marketing department. Where are these responsibilities located if anyone within the organisation assumes them? Is this situation satisfactory, or does it undermine the effectiveness of the marketing department in some way?

Question 31 How can we organise a marketing department?

31.3 How are the many aspects of marketing co-ordinated? Is logistics and distribution adequately co-ordinated with the marketing effort? Identify any major problems you believe to exist because of inadequate co-ordination of the four 'P's. How could these problems be solved?

31.4 If you were responsible for your organisation's marketing department, how would you use external resources? How does this recommendation differ from your organisation's present use of such resources? Why would you make the change?

Question 32
How can we set the marketing budget?

Overview

Marketing budgets can only be imaginatively created if an organisation has a clear understanding of how sales and profitability respond to differing levels of marketing effort. Such understanding arises when sustained research and analysis of marketing activities is undertaken on a collaborative basis between financial and marketing managers. The identification of a realistic inventory of marketing expense and its appropriate allocation to tasks over time is the important starting point. Thereafter, determined management must seek to measure and isolate the time-related effects of such expenditures on demand.

While organisations are never able to understand completely how sales respond to different marketing activities, such analyses give rise to greatly reduced risks and a clearer appreciation of just how much marketing expense can be beneficially incurred. It also meets financial management's crucial need to assess the total cash and cash flow implications of marketing action.

Developing a dynamic approach to budgeting

In Questions 3, 29 and 30, we discussed in detail the preparation of an organisation's marketing plan. Once this plan has been completed and specific strategies and programmes have been developed, management will have a clearer view of both *revenue expectations* and *estimated costs of implementation*. These are the two key ingredients in the preparation of any marketing budget. Both should be monitored carefully as the year progresses and, if necessary, corrective action should be taken to ensure a satisfactory outcome. Management control of this kind depends on a thorough understanding of the nature of the revenue flow and of cash incidence. Most organisations find particular difficulty in assessing the additional revenue likely to accrue from any additional spending on the four 'P's. If an organisation decided to employ an extra salesman, for example, it would find itself faced with such questions as "What additional revenue will he generate? Would the money spent on employing him in fact be better spent on media advertising or on reducing the price of the product? How can we make the calculations necessary to answer these questions?".

Since revenue is not directly under the control of the marketing manager, revenue forecasting poses a major problem in the preparation of the budget. In consumer markets, the best laid plans can be thrown off course by a competitive development that catches the imagination of customers. In industrial markets, fluctuating confidence in the economic future can have major effects on the sales of capital equipment as well as stockholding policies. In a service industry such as tourism, a movement in the exchange rate can result in changes in popularity among countries. For reasons such as these, sales forecasting (as described in Question 16, "How can we estimate how much product we will sell?") must be conducted carefully both for unit volumes and for gross monetary values. At budget preparation time, it is also foolhardy in most circumstances to base

Unit VII Planning and control

all plans on a single point forecast of sales. Anticipated sales outcomes are inevitably imprecise because of factors that are external to the company. In addition, factors within the company may sometimes prevent fulfilment of orders even if the sales have been made. Production or distribution delays, for example, may lead to substantial losses in sales revenue.

Such uncertainty frequently leads companies to adopt a safe approach to sales revenue forecasting: that is, they forecast only what they are *very* confident they can achieve. This approach has the merit of limiting the scope for unpleasant surprises but it can have disadvantages. In their zeal for reliable budgets, organisations adopting this approach will often ignore good opportunities within the market place, simply because they have a high level of risk.

Let us examine more closely the kinds of sales pattern which are commonly encountered in the market place and which are likely to lead organisations to form conclusions about how they should allocate future expenditure. The response curves in Figure 37 illustrate the fortunes of three different products. The point of interest in each case is the interpretation of the relationship of marketing expenditure to sales level.

In the case of Product 'C', sales have increased in direct proportion to marketing expenditure and show no signs of falling off. The conclusion likely to be drawn here is that further expenditure will continue to lead to increased sales. With Product 'A', the curve marks the point at which sales have started to stabilise rather than grow. The likely conclusion to be drawn here is that marketing expenditure is resulting in replacement sales rather than in the attraction of new custom. Accordingly, a re-assessment of the marketing budget is called for. It may also prove worthwhile to reconsider the nature of the marketing mix for this product: a different mix may result in a new growth in sales.

Product 'B' has followed the pattern described for Product 'A' but has moved beyond this to the point where sales have started to decline. In these circumstances, the likely conclusion would be that all potential customers have been reached and that further marketing expenditure on this product is not worthwhile. Product 'B' is likely to be a very specialised product or service within a very limited market. It could also be one in which the product is in decline, perhaps due to a better alternative becoming available to the market.

The construction of response curves of this kind for the different products or services within an organisation's portfolio can prove very helpful in the allocation of the marketing budget. The organisation can draw on data and feedback on different products to identify the optimum point of return on expenditure and to ascertain the weight which should be accorded to the different elements of the marketing mix.

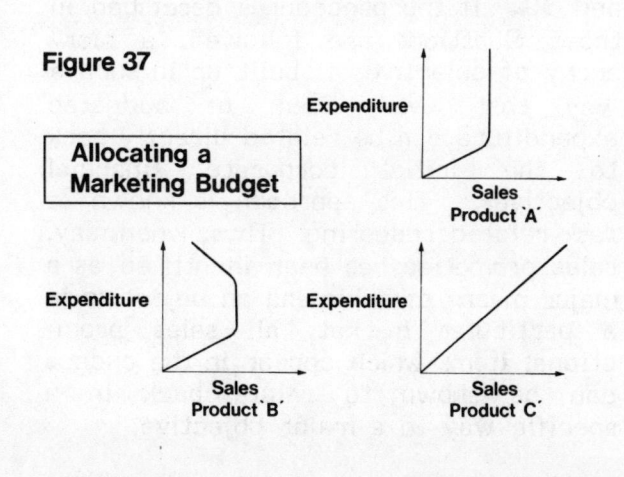

Figure 37

Allocating a Marketing Budget

Designing a system which takes a truly dynamic approach towards marketing budgets, as opposed to a static annual view, is a major challenge to the marketing and financial directors of all organisations. Whenever the response to a valid marketing opportunity is that "the budget has been spent already this year", it is clear that something is coming between the company and its effective prosperity. It is equally the case that matters are none too satisfactory when uneconomic expenditure is continued in an organisation simply "in order to spend the budget". This all too frequently occurs when organisations base subsequent years' budgets on previous levels.

The most satisfactory situation for a marketing director is typically that where he is required:

1. To justify each year from a zero base all his marketing expenditure against the tasks he wishes to accomplish and for which he has clearly identified his gross revenue expectations;

2. To review progress continually to ensure that no lapses in interdepartmental communications can hinder good marketing.

This approach is the logical result of tackling the problem of planning the company's marketing activities through the process described in Questions 3, 29 and 30. If the procedures described in those Questions are followed, a hierarchy of objectives is built up in such a way that every item of budgeted expenditure can be related directly back to the initial corporate financial objectives. This approach is known as task-related budgeting. Thus, when, say, sales promotion has been identified as a major means of achieving an objective in a particular market, all sales promotional items which appear in the budget can be shown to relate back in a specific way to a major objective.

The essential feature of this system of budgeting is that budgets are set against both the overall marketing objectives and the sub-objectives for each element of the marketing mix. One main advantage of the system is that it allows the organisation to build up an increasingly clear picture of its markets. Whenever the marketing director allocates budgets, he is making assumptions about buyer behaviour in his organisation's markets. By identifying these assumptions and subsequently monitoring market behaviour, he can go on to allocate future budgets with more confidence. Even if his assumptions are proved false, and the budget has been inappropriately allocated, the marketing director can discover exactly where he has gone wrong and can take the necessary corrective steps in the future. Let us take as an example of this approach to budgeting the following entry which appeared in the marketing plan of a major British consumer goods company (Table 8):

This extract is then combined with all other promotions for Product 1 to form the entries under PROMOTIONS in the consolidated promotional budget shown in Table 9.

Thus, items A-D in Table 8, totalling £16,500, are part of the entry, "National and regional multiple tailormade promotions" (£44,000) in the consolidated budget. Similarly, item E (£2,000) is part of "Discretionary spend - regional managers") (£15,000) and item F (£5,000) is part of "Major national promotions" (£26,750).

This method of budgeting allows every item of expenditure to be fully accounted for as part of a rational and objective approach. It also ensures that when changes have to be made during the period to which the plan relates, such changes can be made in such a way that the least damage is caused to the company's long-term objectives.

However, the organisation must be careful to ensure that any changes in resources allocated to the marketing function are accompanied by appropriate changes in the marketing objectives. One travel company, for example, put together a task-related budget of this kind. The budget was subsequently reduced to 60 per cent of that requested but the marketing objectives were not scaled down accordingly. The result was that the now quite unrealistic marketing objectives were not met and the company's corporate objectives were also adversely affected.

Question 32 How can we set the marketing budget?

Table 8 Sales promotions – product 1 (extract)

Item	Cost	Timing	Promotion	Anticipated results
A	£5,000	Continuous with effect from Period 1	S.E. distribution and placement drive	To remedy major regional distribution weaknesses
B	£5,000	Periods 1-3	Selected multiple tailor-made promotions	To develop fully distribution and volume through the major multiple chains
C	£5,000	Continuous from Period 6	Selected multiple tailor-made promotions	To develop fully distribution and volume through the major multiple chains
D	£1,500	Period 6	National grocery retail distribution and placement drive	To improve in-stock situation prior to Easter
E	£2,000	Continuous with effect from Period 1	Sales manager's discretionary spend	For fast response to local and tactical promotions
F	£5,000	Periods 2 and 3	National, all grocery trade sectors (case bonus 13 for 12)	To hold seasonal volume forecast and distribution during period of intensive competitive activity. Also to extend distribution and placements wherever possible

Table 9 Consolidated promotional budget – product 1

SPACE & TIME:	Consumer	– Press	97,000	
		TV	177,200	
	Trade		48,700	
	Miscellaneous		1,000	
	TOTAL SPACE			323,900
PRODUCTION:	Consumer	– Press	24,000	
		TV	30,000	
	Trade		18,600	
	Miscellaneous		1,000	
	TOTAL PRODUCTION			73,600
				£397,500
PROMOTIONS:	Major national promotions		26,750	
	National & regional multiple tailor-made promotions		44,000	
	Scotland promotions		12,300	
	Group promotions		5,300	
	Discretionary spend:			
	– Regional managers		15,000	
	– National a/cs manager		2,750	
	– Trade sales manager		2,000	
	– Grocery sales manager		2,000	
	TOTAL PROMOTIONS			£110,100
DISPLAY:	Posters		50,902	
	TOTAL DISPLAY			£ 50,902
PUBLIC RELATIONS:	PR fees		6,000	
	PR activities		17,050	
	Factory visits		1,000	
	TOTAL PUBLIC RELATIONS			£ 24,050
EXHIBITIONS:			2,250	
				£ 2,250
PACKAGING:			5,000	
				£ 5,000
CONTINGENCY:			21,460	
				£ 21,460
	AGGREGATE TOTAL			£611,262

What is the marketing expense?

With one notable exception, the marketing expense is made up of all additional costs that are incurred after a product is made available in the factory or after definite resource provision is made to offer a service. Expenses involved in the physical movement of the product or service facility are excluded from this calculation. This latter group of costs are typically called the distribution expense and, while distribution may sensibly be regarded as an integral part of marketing, its costs represent a discrete sub-set.

It is always a difficult matter to draw the line between marketing and distribution costs. The division between production and marketing costs is also sometimes unclear. When, for instance, is packaging a marketing cost, when a distribution and when a production cost? While there can be no universal answer, careful analysis, tempered by the wisdom that continually seeks for simplicity, can normally yield an acceptable solution. Organisations that use all or some of their packaging simply to reduce damage normally call it a distribution cost, whereas those who use their packaging to communicate and to sell (as in most consumer markets) typically regard much or all of it as a marketing cost. In the situation where a free sample is given away with the intention of generating future purchase of the product, the cost of providing the additional amount of product needed to provide the samples would normally be put down as a marketing rather than a production cost.

The major areas of marketing cost incurred by any organisation are related to the four 'P's. We shall examine each of these areas in turn.

Product The most typical marketing cost associated with product is its packaging (although the considerations mentioned above should be borne in mind here). On occasion, however, there will also be a wastage or obsolescence expense, as in the case of perishable products and services. British Rail recently reported that it has several million unsold seats on its trains each day; these perish as a saleable service the moment the train leaves a station. Many factories also have spare capacity available that could be producing product to sell. The extent to which marketing fails to make use of such capacity, over a medium-term period, is the cost of marketing failure. It constitutes lost opportunities. Few companies look at product or service costs in this way. When they begin to do so, marketing's attention can be constructively focussed on the considerable challenges implicit in taking on marginal contribution business or in specific markets or market segments.

However, it should be borne in mind that in certain circumstances it may be more profitable for a company not to operate at full capacity. For example, a sweet manufacturer sold gift presentation tins of the product into Japan in very small volume. The product was sold through exclusive outlets and was seen as a luxury/gift product. An opportunity arose to sell in much larger quantities by introducing the product into the supermarket chains. The manufacturer decided not to take this opportunity. The premium price could not have been charged. The product would have ceased to be exclusive and would have competed with local products. With the additional distribution charges, little would have been gained and an assured market would have been lost.

A further area of product cost that is all too frequently overlooked is related to decisions taken by marketing on the different sizes or capability levels of a product to be offered. The different sizes of product offered are of considerable significance to the retailer in terms of his stockholding capabilities and costs. The manufacturer should consider the benefits to be derived by his customers from different sizes of a brand as carefully as he considers the benefits of different product lines.

Price Three major elements of marketing cost under this heading often escape careful attention. The first is any form of discounting that the organisation may engage in which results in a reduction in its otherwise-to-be-expected gross income yield for each unit sold. Discounting may take the form of quantity discounts, promotional discounts, loyalty rebates, etcetera. The second element is the amount of customer credit allowed. Unpaid invoices cost money and customer credit is a standard device for gaining business. Its terms will often vary but it will have the effect for a customer of transforming the total real price of the product or service. The third price-related cost is commission, typically paid to salesmen or agents in such a way that it increases in relation to the number of sales made. Such commissions whittle directly away at the gross revenue of the organisation.

Place The present authors include among place-related costs both the direct costs of marketing channel members to the company and the discrete physical movement or distribution costs that create availability. The marketing tasks associated with distribution have been discussed in detail in Questions 17, 18 and 19, the Unit which dealt with place decisions. The channel member's cost is primarily termed the "margin" or "mark-up". The level at which these costs should be set was discussed in Question 21, "What margins should we allow to our distributors?". Suffice it to note at this point that the margin or mark-up allowed to or taken by a channel member at one or more levels within a distribution system should be included as a marketing cost. Many companies in fact fail to analyse such margins or mark-ups in the context of their marketing budget. This is a mistake. Without such information, a full view of the marketing activities for a company's products or services cannot be gained.

Distribution costs incurred in the physical movement of goods or in making services available to customers are often a very substantial part of the total expenditure of many organisations; accordingly, they are frequently a dominant element in marketing expense. The main determinant of distribution cost is the level of availability that is deemed appropriate for the organisation's success in the market place. High levels of customer service or availability normally involve substantial investment in inventories and/or rapid transportation and delivery back-up. Distribution cost analysis is a major area of investigation in its own right; it is sufficient in this context to observe that the level of distribution cost is determined by a marketing judgement on the profitable responsiveness of sales to different levels of availability.

Promotion Table 10 illustrates clearly the main differences which are typically found between the expenditures of consumer goods and industrial companies. It is in the area of promotion that these differences are most marked. Industrial concerns spend little on advertising on television or in the national or international press, whereas most consumer advertising appears in those media. The industrial concern is more likely to incur costs on exhibitions; on sales and technical literature for the professional buyer or user of his product or service; on technical representatives making personal calls at clients; and on advisory services on applications in diverse situations.

Organisations offering their products or services through distributors are frequently involved in back-up promotion support. The cost of the major supermarket retailers' weekly press advertising is frequently shared with the manufacturers whose products are featured. In insurance and building society agencies, point-of-sale leaflets are always made available. Distributors of industrial items such as engineering equipment are also kept constantly supplied with sales literature.

Sales force costs have already been mentioned. These are often a substantial expense and are on occasion treated

Question 32   How can we set the marketing budget?   191

separately. While there can be no objection to a discrete sub-set of sales force costs, it is necessary that they be brought firmly into the total marketing budget of the organisation. At the

margin, sales force effort and customer service are marketing costs that can perhaps be better spent elsewhere on the marketing field of action.

Table 10   Examples of marketing budgets

	Consumer Product £	%	Industrial Product £	%
GROSS SALES REVENUE FORECAST FOR YEAR	3,000,000	100.00	2,000,000	100.00
less				
Cost of product ex factory	1,000,000	33.33	1,000,000	50.00
	2,000,000	66.67	1,000,000	50.00
less				
Incremental marketing expenses as follows:				
Packaging for display	50,000	1.67	0	0.00
Returns perished/damaged	5,000	0.17	12,000	0.60
Special discounts	160,000	5.30	0	0.00
Customer credit cost	30,000	1.00	100,000	5.00
Sales commissions	0	0.00	20,000	1.00
Distributors' margins	500,000	16.67	0	0.00
Distribution expense for customer service	348,000	11.60	85,000	4.25
Promotion - TV.	100,000	3.33	0	0.00
Press	50,000	1.67	12,000	0.60
Technical	0	0.00	12,000	0.60
Catalogues, etcetera	1,000	0.03	8,000	0.40
Sales force expense	50,000	1.67	108,000	5.40
Information costs	45,000	1.50	30,000	1.50
TOTAL INCREMENTAL MARKETING EXPENSE	1,339,000	44.64	387,000	19.35
Net contribution to Company General Expense	£ 661,000	22.03	£ 613,000	30.65

The place of information costs

We have already described in Question 28 how the collection of marketing information can enhance the effectiveness of marketing activity. We discussed there how the company can organise its activities so that the benefit derived from use of the information justifies the costs incurred in collecting the information. This gives rise to the obvious inclusion in any marketing budget of an information cost. What usually happens is that the information cost is budgeted as a fixed item for a twelve-month period and is associated with a long-term forecast of the level of expenditure required. Typically, this gives rise to mistaken levels of information usage. Information is sensibly collected by any organisation at that juncture dictated by the size of the perceived risk it wishes to take and by which it is confronted. New product or service launches, or moves into new international markets, are the situations most likely to give rise to the need for heavy expenditure on information. Its benefit will, however, be spread over a much longer period than that in which the cost is incurred. Information is an investment in understanding a market situation which could be relevant for one, two, five or even ten years. It is not necessarily a current expense like discounting or sales force commission. It may well deserve a separate treatment in budgetary terms. Once again, the healthiest manner of treatment has been found to be a zero-based dynamic budgeting approach.

Application questions

32.1 How is the marketing budget determined in your organisation? How closely related are the various budgets and marketing tasks to be achieved? If a budget is reduced, are the tasks to be achieved similarly reduced?

32.2 If you were introducing a budgetary system into your organisation for the first time, what procedures would you introduce? What advantages would you see in your chosen system? How would it differ from existing procedures? Where differences do occur, what prevents the new system from being introduced?

32.3 How is the cost-effectiveness of each aspect of the marketing budget monitored? Is this information adequate for you to determine the responsiveness of your budgetary system to the needs of each of your products and services? What additional information do you need to help you set the budgets? How could such information be obtained? How could the cost of collection of the additional information be justified?